Daily
Guideposts,
1988

GUIDEPOSTS®
Carmel, New York 10512

ACKNOWLEDGMENTS

All Scripture references herein and for the Scripture top for the October, "Family Time" devotional are from the King James Version of the Bible unless otherwise noted with the exception of the remainder "Family Time" devotionals which are herewith noted below.

Scripture top for the September, "Family Time" devotional is from THE HEART OF PAUL, A RELATIONAL PARAPHRASE OF THE NEW TESTAMENT by Ben Campbell Johnson. Copyright © 1976 by Ben Campbell Johnson. Used by permission of Word Books, Publisher, Waco, TX.

Scripture verses marked (LB) are taken from THE LIVING BIBLE, copyright 1971 by Tyndale House Publishers, Wheaton, IL. Used by permission.

Scripture top for the February, "Family Time" devotional is taken from THE MODERN LANGUAGE BIBLE: THE BERKELEY VERSION IN MODERN ENGLISH. Copyright 1945, 1959, 1969 by Zondervan Publishing House. Used by permission.

Scripture verses marked (NASB) are taken from THE NEW AMERICAN STANDARD BIBLE, © The Lockman Foundation 1960, 1962, 1963, 1968, 1971, 1972, 1973, 1975, 1977.

Scripture verses marked (NEB) and the Scripture top for the July, "Family Time" devotional is from THE NEW ENGLISH BIBLE; NEW TESTAMENT. Copyright © 1961 by the Delegates of the Oxford University Press and The Syndics of the Cambridge University Press. Reprinted by permission.

Scripture verses marked (NIV) and Scripture tops for the April, May, June, November and December, "Family Time" devotionals are taken from THE HOLY BIBLE: NEW INTERNATIONAL VERSION. Copyright © 1973, 1978, 1984 by the International Bible Society. Used by permission of Zondervan Bible Publishers.

Scripture verses marked (JBP) and partial Scripture top for the August, "Family Time" devotional is reprinted with permission of the Macmillan Publishing Company from THE NEW TESTAMENT IN MODERN ENGLISH. Revised edition by J. B. Phillips. Copyright © 1958, 1960, 1972 by J. B. Phillips.

Scripture verses marked (RSV) and partial Scripture top for the August, "Family Time" devotional are from the REVISED STANDARD VERSION BIBLE, copyright 1946, 1952, 1975 by the Division of Christian Education of the National Council of Churches of Christ in the U.S.A., and are used by permission.

Scripture tops for the January and March, "Family Time" devotionals are taken from THE SIMPLIFIED NEW TESTAMENT by Olaf M. Norlie. Copyright © 1961 by Zondervan Publishing House. Used with permission.

The quotation within text for May 2 is from p. 5, THE ART OF LOVING by Erich Fromm. Copyright © 1956 by Erich Fromm. Reprinted by permission of Harper & Row Publishers, Inc.

The quotation within text for November 16 is from THE COUNTRYMAN'S YEAR by David Grayson. Copyright © 1936. Doubleday, Doran & Co., Inc. Reissued 1985 by: Renaissance House Publishers, A Division of Jende–Hagan, Inc., 541 Oak Street, P.O. Box 177, Frederick, CO 80530.

Reference for John McCormack within the August, "Family Time" devotional is from THE DANIEL DILEMMA by Peggy Stanton. Copyright © 1978 by Peggy Stanton. Used by permission of Word Books, Publisher, Waco, TX.

Spirit Lifter for January, "The New Year—the Road" by Mildred N. Hoyer. Copyright © 1978 by Mildred N. Hoyer. Used by permission.

Designed by Elizabeth Woll
Calendar-Page Artwork by Gail Rodney
Indexed by Mary F. Tomaselli

Printed in the United States of America

Table of Contents

Introduction

"Now you are no longer strangers to God and foreigners to heaven, but you are members of God's very own family."
—EPHESIANS 2:19 (LB)

Surely God's own family includes all those who love and serve Him. And inside this vast number are many smaller groups bound together by ties of love and mutual concern. In the last twelve years there has come into being a very special family—those who write for and those who read the book you are holding in your hands: *Daily Guideposts.*

We know this is true because so many of you have written to tell us of your feeling of kinship with one or another of the writers—their personalities, their experiences, their attempts to expand and develop their faith. They have become not just acquaintances, but friends. We are grateful to God for His guidance in helping us—with you—create this sense of a loving, caring family.

For this twelfth edition of *Daily Guideposts,* the theme we have chosen is the family. In these pages, our writers will often offer ideas, suggestions and insights to enable you as family members—either your immediate family or "family" made up of caring friends or fellow Christians—to grow closer to God, closer to your neighbors, closer to one another. You'll meet a grandson who teaches his grandfather the meaning of "thanks." A mother who learns that loving her teenage son means relaxing her tight parental grip and letting him go, trusting in God. A neighbor, who by her simple offering of food, makes a newcomer feel at home in her new community-family. And many more.

There are special features for 1988, too. On the calendar pages that open each month you will find little "guideposts" for *Your Spir-*

itual Pilgrimage. Watch, too, for *Spirit Lifters* scattered throughout the book, uplifting poems and encouraging quotations that will give you an extra boost for the day.

Many favorite authors are back. On the first of each month, *Carol Kuykendall* will teach you how to maintain a partnership with God that allows "tandem power" to flow into your life. At Easter, *Linda Ching Sledge* shows how ordinary objects that surround our lives can take on a powerful significance during Holy Week. In the spring, *Marilyn Moore Jensen* tackles the difficult topic of loneliness and offers specific remedies for this universal problem. In the summer, *Scott Harrison* shares the lessons of learning to depend on God when he brought his physician's skills to the suffering people of Malawi, Africa. *Marilyn Morgan Helleberg* spends three days showing you how to apply the wisdom of the Psalms to your everyday problems. Then for Advent, *Elizabeth Sherrill* writes with moving reverence about the season that each year prepares us for Christ's coming.

Each mid-month, Family Time, by *Floyd* and *Harriett Thatcher*, will focus on family growth and development with strong emphasis on Bible teachings. And this year, in addition to our regular monthly authors, we welcome a sprinkling of new authors—nineteen *Fireside Friends*. They will visit throughout the year to share their personal experiences with you.

Another popular feature returning under a new name is the *Thank-You-Notes-to-God* section at the end of each month. This mini-diary gives you the opportunity each day to make brief responses or prayers of praise and thanksgiving to our Creator. Once again, *Hospitality House* will be the meeting place for our family of writers to share their pictures and talk about themselves. And finally, there is the useful *Readers' Guide*, a comprehensive index to help you find your favorite devotionals, quotations, topical subjects, authors and Scripture used throughout the year.

In the days and months ahead, we want each of you to know, as St. Paul said, that you are "members of God's very own family." And at the same time, know that you are in loving communion and fellowship with members of the *Daily Guideposts* family. In every way, may you grow closer and closer to Him, the Father of us all.

—THE EDITORS

S	M	T	W	T	F	S
					1	2
3	4	5	6	7	8	9
10	11	12	13	14	15	16
17	18	19	20	21	22	23
24	25	26	27	28	29	30
31						

JANUARY

BE A SELF-STARTER
Your Spiritual Pilgrimage

In the beginning God created the heaven and the earth.
—GENESIS 1:1

What's more exhilarating than a cold, crisp day in January? Now is the time for new plans, new challenges, fresh starts. So here's a real challenge for you. Ask yourself, "How can I grow spiritually in 1988? How can I make this year a pilgrimage away from self-centeredness, toward love and concern for others?"

At the beginning of each month, this book will suggest an area for self-improvement. Practicing these suggestions faithfully will help make 1988 a tremendous year. But remember, every journey begins with a single step. So turn the page and take that first step. Right now!

Tandem Power for January

1 A LIFELONG PARTNERSHIP WITH GOD
And as the Spirit of the Lord works within us, we become more and more like him.
—II CORINTHIANS 3:18 (LB)

Today we stand at the gate of a fresh new year. Stretching before us are 366 (it's Leap Year!) unlived days, bursting with potential. Traditionally, we pause to consider the ways we'd like to change in the coming months.

Usually, I keep lists of such personal promises—commonly called New Year's resolutions. Yet today, as I look back over my lists, I make a discouraging discovery. For the past several years, they look all too similar:

> I will be more disciplined.
> I will get up earlier each morning.
> I will lose ten pounds (fifteen?).
> I will always be on time.
> I will be more patient.

Obviously, I've never been able to cross any of these goals off my list once and for all. Why? I wonder, and then I see an answer. The goals ignore the greatest resource of power for change in my life: God's presence. They focus on me instead of my response to Him; they dwell on external results rather than drawing from internal strength. No wonder I'm not making much progress.

So in 1988, I'm going to try something different. Instead of listing a bunch of desirable external results, I'm going to focus on a single internal goal—cooperating with God by listening to Him and responding; choosing His way over my way. To help I've even made up a visual image—*Tandem Power.* Just as a tandem bicycle is designed to function efficiently when two people cooperate and pedal together, Tandem Power is the idea of combining our human efforts with God's strength and guidance.

Will you join me in a year-long effort to practice cooperating with God? Together we will examine the kinds of daily choices we face: our way or His way; drag our feet or pedal together; resist or cooperate.

Our first choice is before us. We stand at the gate of a New Year. God opens the gate; we choose to walk through. He shows us the way;

we choose to follow. Together, we take the first step into the New Year. That's Tandem Power!

Heavenly Father, as we begin the year of 1988, may we grow increasingly aware of Your presence in our lives, and cooperate with You, choice-by-choice, day-by-day, month-by-month.

—CAROL KUYKENDALL

2 SATURDAY
And Jesus said...Neither do I condemn thee: go, and sin no more. —JOHN 8:11

Recently I heard a speaker relate a classic moment in college sports that occurred back in 1929, when Georgia Tech played the University of California in the Rose Bowl. Late in the second quarter Tech fumbled the ball on its own thirty-three yard line. The California center, Roy Riegels, scooped up the ball, spun around and raced toward the goal line. Just before he reached the end zone, however, one of his own teammates tackled him. You see, Roy Riegels had run sixty-seven yards *in the wrong direction.*

In the locker room at halftime, the big center buried his face in his hands and cried, devastated by his costly mistake. But the coach didn't say a word of condemnation. When halftime was over, he simply announced, "The same team that started the first half will begin the second." The players filed out, but Roy didn't move. "Didn't you hear me, Roy?" the coach asked.

"Please, Coach, don't ask me to go back out there after what I've done," he said.

The coach touched his shoulder. "Get up, Roy. The game is only half over."

Roy went back on the field. And he played with more determination that second half than anyone out there.

We have all made humiliating mistakes and raced off in the wrong direction at times. And in their aftermath, it can be tempting to bury your head and give up. Yet God is always there with a second chance. He wants us to know that no matter how you and I have failed Him, the game isn't over.

Give me the courage to go back on the field, Lord, and give my best. —SUE MONK KIDD

9

| 3 | SUNDAY |

Come into his presence with singing!

—PSALM 100:2 (RSV)

The first hymn I ever sang was "Jesus Loves the Little Children." Along with every child in the rainbow-colored family of God, I knew that I belonged.

The passing of each season was marked in holy song. Living in Hawaii, I had never seen a snowflake or a stalk of wheat; yet how I loved God for sending "the snow in winter, the warmth to swell the grain." In a sun-drenched Hawaiian December, I blessed "the little Lord Jesus asleep on the hay." "Morning has broken," I sang to greet the spring. When summer decked the trees bordering my church with a riot of red plumeria blossoms, I knew indeed that "this is my Father's world."

In my twenties, the hymn-singing stopped. Instead, I sang along with the Beatles on the radio. I scoured their lyrics for their meaning, committing whole phrases to memory as I had done with the hymns of my youth.

But I can barely sing a Beatles song by heart now. What I can remember is "Jesus Loves the Little Children," which I sing to my two kids. Again, the seasons move in time to Christ's music. Again, I belong to Him. Now when I praise God for sending snow, I look out the lead-glass window of my church in New York and see it fall from the sky. The familiar songs are tinged with a deeper meaning, because embracing my old faith, after having lost it for a time, has made me hear poignant notes in the old music, like rich bass tones of an ancient organ.

If you have fallen away from God, music, like prayer, can put your life in tune again. In church today, come back to Him on the wings of song.

Holy, holy, holy, Lord God Almighty!
Early in the morning, our song shall rise to Thee.

—LINDA CHING SLEDGE

MONDAY
The Lord will strengthen him upon…his bed in his sickness. —PSALM 41:3

My son Chris was standing beside our bed at two in the morning. "What's wrong?" I asked groggily. "Why aren't you in bed?" His lips quivered. "My ear hurts a lot, Dad, and I can't sleep." Only five years old, he looked even younger standing in the darkness. He had never chanced the dark hallway between our bedrooms before, so this must have been serious.

That afternoon, his pediatrician had started him on antibiotics for an ear infection. As I tucked Chris back in bed, I knew we'd just have to wait until the medication took effect. Feeling helpless, I bowed my head and prayed that the Lord would relieve my brave young son of his pain.

His small voice interrupted me. "It's okay, Dad. I know how tired you are. You don't have to stay with me." I looked up to protest that I wasn't falling asleep, that I was just praying. Chris stared at me earnestly while he said, "Besides, it doesn't hurt quite as much now."

By focusing on me, not on that throbbing ear, his pain already seemed less. A few minutes later Chris was sleeping peacefully.

When something in my life hurts me—a misunderstanding with a friend, a promotion that doesn't materialize, the loss of a beloved pet—I'm going to remember what Chris taught me and focus my attention on the problems of others until my own hurt lessens.

Christ Jesus, let me focus on concern for others and give You time to heal my own hurts. —SCOTT HARRISON

5 TUESDAY
In all thy ways acknowledge him, and he shall direct thy paths. —PROVERBS 3:6

The other day a friend told me a little story about Paderewski, the great Polish pianist. I have no proof that it's true, but I hope it is because I like it.

It seems a mother took her young son, eight or nine years old, to a concert by Paderewski because she thought the child had some musical talent and might benefit from hearing a genius play. They sat

11

close to the stage, where the curtain was up, revealing the grand piano. Paderewski was in the wings; it wasn't quite time to start.

The mother turned to speak to an acquaintance behind her. As she did, the little boy wriggled out of his seat, ran up the steps to the stage, sat down and began to play "Chopsticks" with all his might. The mother was appalled. The audience gasped as Paderewski himself strode onto the stage.

But instead of being angry the *maestro* smiled, sat down on the piano bench with the little boy, whispered to him to continue and then, putting both arms around the little figure began to improvise a soft but brilliant accompaniment to the childish music. He kept it up until the audience, charmed and fascinated, burst into applause.

I like to think that perhaps when we finally come into God's presence and try to explain our lives with all the faults and flaws, He will put His loving arms around us and turn our faltering notes into a triumphant song of redemption and fulfillment.

Father, bring Your harmony into my life both here and hereafter.   —RUTH STAFFORD PEALE

| 6 | WEDNESDAY |

...They departed into their own country another way.
—MATTHEW 2:12

After Christmas is over, and New Year's has come and gone, I often get a satiated, bloated feeling, as though I've eaten too much divinity fudge. I look at the dry Christmas tree that needs to be thrown out and the thank-you notes that need to be written and wonder, *What was the fuss about?*

Maybe that's why I'm grateful for the reminder of Epiphany, celebrated twelve days after Christmas, commemorating Christ's visit from the wise men. There are many traditions associated with these men from the East: that there were three, Gaspar, Melchior and Balthazar; that they represent the three continents, Asia, Europe and Africa; that they were kings, rich and powerful. The Bible is more circumspect. It tells us wise men (no number) followed the star and met King Herod who asked them to find the Child and then tell him where He was. Led to Christ, they worshiped Him with gifts of gold, frankincense and myrrh. But then instead of going back to Herod, the wise men returned home another way.

That's the part of the story I like best. Of course, they were trying to avoid Herod who was already plotting to destroy the King he feared would usurp his crown. But I think there's another message to the story. Didn't the wise men go another way because they were somehow different? Could they go back the same way after seeing Christ? Could they trudge the old weary road after following the star?

No, I think not. Nor can I. Nor can you.

God, with changed heart and renewed spirit, lead me in new paths in the New Year. —RICK HAMLIN

Spirit Lifter
THY YEAR

God bless thy year,   *The rough, the smooth,*
Thy coming in, thy going out,   *The bright, the drear:*
Thy rest, thy traveling about.   *God bless thy year.*

—AUTHOR UNKNOWN

---

7 | **THURSDAY**
And God saw every thing that he had made, and, behold, it was very good. —GENESIS 1:31

When I was a skinny eighteen-year-old fresh in the service during World War II, I made an impetuous trip to see a boyhood hero of mine. With a precious pass in my uniform pocket, I thumbed my way on empty Georgia roads, sat up all night on an unheated Southern Railway coach, but finally pulled into Lexington, Kentucky. At the USO, a motherly-looking volunteer was just opening up. "Please, ma'am," I said, "can you tell me how I can find Man O'War?"

Would you believe that nice woman couldn't believe I'd made the long trip just to see him? Only the greatest thoroughbred that ever lived, that's all! He was old, twenty-seven, and I had to see him before either he or I died. That's the way we were in wartime.

13

Well, there were all kinds of phone calls with talk about gas coupons, but soon I was being driven out to Faraway Farm where an old black man, Will Harbut, was actually waiting for me. Will was Man O'War's friend and groom—they were never apart. In a large green-painted shed, we crossed to a stall where Will rolled back the door.

"Okay, soldier boy, here he is, 'Big Red,' de mostest hoss."

I stared, mouth open.

Will talked at length about "Red's" speed, his stamina, his courage. I stared at the hero I'd come so far to see. And heroic he was, a massive animal with a coat of polished copper, a head held high, eyes looking beyond me with an imperial gaze. And ancient he was (a human would have been in his nineties) but the fire was still there.

"Come on," Will said, "it's okay," and I reached out and placed my hand on the head of Man O'War.

It's a good thing to have heroes. Seeing that great thoroughbred gave my life romance, ardor. It even deepened my faith in the Almighty, for no one could look at Man O'War without knowing that only God could create an animal so powerful, and yet so noble.

Lord, teach us to know Your masterpieces, and feel reverence in their presence. —VAN VARNER

| 8 | FRIDAY |

Do not withhold good from those to whom it is due, when it is in your power to do it. —PROVERBS 3:27 (RSV)

One drab January day I brought home a perky black-and-white kitten who quickly batted away our mid-winter blahs. We named her Sneakers for her white paws and her habit of pouncing on us from out of nowhere.

By September Sneakers had a boyfriend serenading her nightly beneath our window. He was a muscular fellow whose nasal croon would cause heartburn in Nashville! A few weeks later Sneakers' bulging sides gave her away. She was expecting kittens. We hit upon the idea of guessing how many she would have and on which day.

Thanksgiving weekend Sneakers walked into the kitchen looking...thin. The hunt was on for the kittens. We found them, four clusters of black fluff, hidden under the covers in our daughter's bed.

Several dips into the guessing jar revealed the winners (cheers) and losers (groans). I set the date for our "Kitten Celebration." We began with Garfield the cat's favorite dinner, lasagne by candlelight. For dessert everyone unwrapped a chocolate wafer candy bar. The winners (and losers—I'm a softie!) opened small gifts relating to cats. What fun we shared around the table that evening celebrating our kittens...and ourselves.

It really doesn't take much to etch a joyful scene on a family's "memory pane." Just a trace of creativity, a dot of time, a stroke of love—and that scene will sparkle for years to come!

Why don't we do it more often?

Dear Father, show us how to create beautiful swirly memory-designs from life's ordinary happenings.   —CAROL KNAPP

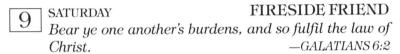

| 9 | SATURDAY | FIRESIDE FRIEND |

Bear ye one another's burdens, and so fulfil the law of Christ.   —GALATIANS 6:2

Before our family acquired the old Farmall tractor, my father always plowed our garden with a team of horses. I remember the first time he harnessed Juniper to that one-bottom plow. Young and inexperienced, she twitched and pranced in the traces. Her partner Flighty stood quietly as Dad adjusted the final buckles. I sat on top of the garden gate and watched them make the rounds, the black ground breaking open with each pass. Juniper pulled and tugged; sweat soaked her coat. Flighty walked with a measured, methodical pace. By the end of the morning, Juniper was exhausted.

As Dad unhitched them, I commented on the difference in the two. Dad smiled. "Juniper's just new to this," he said. "When a young horse is first hooked to a team, he tries to pull the whole load. He wears himself out in no time. Soon Juniper'll learn to lay back and share the load."

Often I find myself, like that inexperienced horse, trying to pull the load alone. I fail to reach out for the support of fellow Christians. I pretend not to need the very assistance I am eager to offer others. By feigning self-sufficiency, I thwart God's ordained system of support and encouragement. So I've hung a reminder on my refrigerator door:

Burdens Are For Sharing. I'm trying harder now not only to share the burdens of others, but also to let them share my burdens.

Keep me, Father, from the pride of private suffering.
—MARY LOU CARNEY

| 10 | SUNDAY
Love is patient and kind...
—*I CORINTHIANS 13:4 (RSV)*

What should you do when someone's behavior or personality exasperates you? St. Paul summed up Christianity's solution in just a few words. Love them and have patience with them.

Often simply being kind has remarkable results. I remember one young man who complained to me bitterly about his wife's mother. The woman had come to live with them, and it wasn't working out well at all. She came down to breakfast in her bathrobe with curlers in her hair and slippers, which she scuffed at every step. Furthermore, her son-in-law said, she slurped her coffee. One more scuff or one more slurp, the young man said, and he would be driven insane.

"I can offer you some advice," I said, "but you must agree in advance to follow it."

He swore that he would.

"All right," I said. "When you get to your office tomorrow, call up your mother-in-law and ask her to lunch. Just the two of you. In the best restaurant downtown."

The young man was aghast. But he had promised and so, with extreme reluctance, he did it. Imagine his astonishment when his mother-in-law appeared: well-dressed, well-groomed, alert and lively, a first-class luncheon companion. Why? Because, like all of us, she reflected the evaluation other people put on her. She responded to kindness, just as she had responded to hostility.

Is there someone who has a tendency to rub you the wrong way? Why not make a special effort to be kind to them? It may change their attitude a lot. It may also change yours!

Father, help us to make that special effort of kindness... knowing that everyone needs love—no matter how unlovable they may appear.
—NORMAN VINCENT PEALE

11 MONDAY
Wherefore let him that thinketh he standeth take heed lest he fall. —I CORINTHIANS 10:12

I went over the directions to the airport one more time as my friend climbed into her rented car. It had been Elsa's first trip east since her husband's death. Now she was returning home to Illinois, half a dozen visits behind her.

"And I haven't gotten lost even once!" she marvelled as she started the engine. On the seat beside her was one reason: detailed directions to each destination carefully written out ahead of time.

But there was a more important reason. "I've prayed over every mile of this trip," she confided. "I've asked God to help me find every route number, every street sign."

I breathed a prayer too as she set off: Getting to Kennedy Airport from our home fifty miles north of New York City is confusing even when you do it often. Sure enough, that night Elsa phoned to say that she'd lost her way.

"And missed your flight!"

"Oh, no," she said. Praying like mad, she'd gotten to the airport just fine. Then she told me where the trouble had come. It was after picking up her own car at the airport in Chicago and heading out on a highway she'd driven all her life. She'd missed a crucial turn and gone fifteen miles out of her way.

"I was sure of myself," she said. "So I stopped praying."

I need You, Father, today. —ELIZABETH SHERRILL

12 TUESDAY
This is the day which the Lord hath made; we will rejoice and be glad in it. —PSALM 118:24

"Have a nice day." What a shopworn phrase this has become. It has been worked to death.

The other day, however, I saw an interesting variation on a card in a local restaurant. It said: "Have a nice day—unless you've made other plans."

Do some people really go around clutching a set of "other plans" that can ruin a good day? Well, yes, as a matter of fact they do. Some are programmed to continue holding a grudge. Some are loaded down with fears and worries. Some have such a low opinion of themselves that they project an aura of hesitancy and depression wherever they go. Some expect misfortune to pounce or disaster to strike, which puts them in the same category with Job, who said, "The thing which I greatly feared has come upon me."

What's the remedy? Well, why not start each day by examining yourself for attitudes that may prevent your day from being a good one. Make a little list. Then make some determined resolutions: "In the next twenty-four hours I *will not* worry about my health." "I *won't* fret about finances." "I *will* set aside the resentment I've been feeling about so-and-so."

That way, chances are that you'll have a splendid day—because you're not planning to have anything else.

Lord, You have given us so many bright and shining days. Give us, too, the wisdom not to spoil any of them.

—ARTHUR GORDON

13	WEDNESDAY

...Joy shall be in heaven over one sinner that repenteth, more than over ninety and nine just persons, which need no repentance. —LUKE 15:7

"Void if detached," I read on my airline ticket. I had stepped into a doorway for shelter one rainy Wednesday evening, and to pass the time I was idly examining the ticket for my flight to a meeting in a distant city the next day.

Suddenly, behind me, I heard voices singing a familiar hymn. I was in the entrance to a small church I'd never noticed before. The door was open and something compelled me to enter. A man in one of the rear seats motioned to me to join him and held out his hymnal to share. In that instant the words on my airline ticket, "Void if detached," took on a new meaning for me.

I had been a churchgoer for years. But my visits had gradually become fewer, and often when I did go my mind wandered. My body was present, but my spirit was detached. And this had produced a void in me: less sharing of love with others, less concern for Him Who had given me life. Gradually I had separated myself from the true Source of happiness and peace.

Why had I let this happen? Was it too late to make amends?

The man in the pew was still offering to share his hymnal. I stepped in beside him with an almost overpowering feeling of joy. For no one has to stay *detached*. It's never too late to *attach*...to come home again.

Father, I will attach *myself to continuous joy through regular church attendance and fellowship.* —WALTER HARTER

14 THURSDAY
The eternal God is thy refuge, and underneath are the everlasting arms... —DEUTERONOMY 33:27

My daughter's call from the hospital emergency room reached me at the convalescent home where I was visiting my ninety-three-year-old mother. My granddaughter Robin, just turned six, had fallen from the high bar at school, injuring her mouth severely. I picked up her sisters, aged two and four, and spent a hectic, tense afternoon supervising the little ones while awaiting Kris's return with Robin.

The doctor had taken eight stitches inside her mouth, six on the outside, and, as the littler ones swarmed over their mother, Robin sat squarely in the biggest chair in the living room. Her face puffed almost beyond recognition, her long hair still ropey with dried blood, she looked tiny and forlorn. Still, I approached her cautiously, for Robin is the least demonstrative, the most private of children.

"Is there anything you want, darling?" I asked.

She looked me firmly in the eye and said, "I want a hug."

Me, too! I thought, as I cuddled her on my lap. *But how and whom does an exhausted grandmother ask?* As we rocked gently the words came: "I will pray the Father, and he shall give you another Comforter, that he may abide with you for ever" (John 14:16).

So I asked, just as simply as Robin had done—and just as simply felt the everlasting arms enfold us.

Holy Spirit, thank You for Your role as Advocate, as Intercessor, as Counsellor; but thank You most especially for Your tender warmth as Comforter when I need a hug.
—ELAINE ST. JOHNS

Family Time

| 15 | MAKING ALL THINGS NEW |

And that you and all your fellow-Christians may receive power to grasp the dimensions and to understand Christ's love, which is really beyond human understanding. —*EPHESIANS 3:18–19*

The sun rode low in the western sky as I stepped to the rail at Hopi Point on the south rim of the Grand Canyon. Stretched out before me was a panorama of copper-colored buttes rising above the shadows cast by the descending sun along the canyon depths. And staring down through two billion years of history I caught sight of the river over a mile below.

Overwhelmed by what I'd seen and felt, I turned away—anxious to share the experience with my wife Harriett. But words weren't enough. "You'll have to see it yourself to believe it," was all I could say.

Late the next afternoon we made our way to a jutting viewpoint on the canyon rim. There in silence with hands clasped we drank in the magnificent picture. In front of us loomed the craggy grandeur of Isis' Temple. And in the distance Buddha's Temple shimmered like fire in the glare of the setting sun.

As we stood there, the splendor of this scene became a part of us and spoke to us of the wonders of God's world, of His love and of the vast dimensions of opportunity that are ours as two people who want to live for Him. Each of us experienced our still small voice, "The God Who carved out this canyon will continue to shape your life if you let Him."

In the days that followed we experienced God's creative handiwork in the canyon from many different perspectives—at sunrise and midmorning, at noon and at twilight. And in descending the switchbacks of the narrow trail on muleback, the changing canyon's dimensions became larger than we had imagined from the rim. Each turn of the trail opened before us a new vision of the canyon's beauty, an exploding awareness of God's creative power.

For us, this experience illustrates the way God wants us as persons and as families to "grasp the dimensions" of what we can *be* and *become* in the months ahead. In a practical way we will explore new dimensions and expressions of our dreams, our goals, and our attitudes and rituals as a family. At each "switchback" in our journey of days we will catch a new view of patterns for talking, listening and loving each other. And more and more, our understanding of the adventure of growth and change as a family will be enlarged.

Among our Lord's last words to us in our Bible is this marvelous statement, "I am making all things new" (Revelation 21:5, LB). This will be our year of discovery, with God's help, of imaginative new dimensions of family living and loving; it is our year of new beginnings!

Give us, Lord, a new vision of what You want us to become.
—FLOYD AND HARRIETT THATCHER

| 16 | SATURDAY |

I know you well—you are neither hot nor cold; I wish you were one or the other! —REVELATION 3:15 (LB)

The heaviest snow in Pawling, New York, since 1963 fell in the winter of '86. While it was great for schoolchildren, it was miserable for homeowners. Everyone I spoke with had trouble with ice in their gutters. Since we had had little snow our first winter here, I wasn't ready for what happens when several inches of snow pile on a roof. The heat from the house melts the bottom layer, and water runs down to the gutters. At night the water refreezes, filling the gutters with ice. Eventually, the backed-up ice can cause leaky ceilings.

When drips started to fall on our living room carpet, my wife Joy sent me scurrying up the ladder to see what could be done. I tried rock salt, a propane torch and a chisel, with scant results. Finally, I tried one last remedy. Hooking the garden hose directly to the hot water heater, I flooded the gutters with scalding water. In just a few minutes the hot water had cut through several inches of ice.

I was struck by the effectiveness of water against water. Tepid water would have done no good, but the contrast of hot and cold made the difference. I think that's what Jesus meant in the verse above. If I am "hot" and anxious to be used by Him, then He can use me to change people who are "cold" and resistant to God's Word.

I'm going to keep that image in mind today as I head off to my office. Perhaps that grumpy gas station owner will be more receptive if I allow a spirit of love and caring to flow through me. It's worth a try.

Lord, build a fire in me today, using me to warm cold hearts wherever I find them. —ERIC FELLMAN

17 SUNDAY

...By one Spirit are we all baptized into one body....For the body is not one member, but many.

—*I CORINTHIANS 12:13-14*

I was feeling a little resentful about not being recognized at church. At coffee hour sometimes people would approach me and ask if I were a visitor. When I replied that I'd been a member for over six months, we'd both be embarrassed and then I'd feel badly. When would they know my name? Would I ever belong?

Last Sunday an usher greeted me with, "Hello, Marilyn." When we passed The Peace a woman behind me said, "Peace be with you, Marilyn." And later the person serving coffee asked, "Marilyn, would you like cream and sugar?" Well, I was tongue-tied—because I didn't know any of *their* names.

As I was leaving coffee hour I spied a bulletin board in a corner with a sign: Our Church Family. The board was covered with photos—evidently snapped without my noticing—of all the church members. And there was my grinning face among all the others, captioned "Marilyn Jensen." I realized then that the people who had spoken to me that morning had taken the time to study that board so that they could call me by name. I'd made no such effort to know them....

This morning I'm going early to church to study that bulletin board. And I'm reading the Church Directory, too. When *I* can say, "Hello, Louise"... "It's nice to see you, Bunny," I will really belong to the church family. It's a two-way effort, isn't it?

Jesus, You are the Shepherd Who knows each of Your sheep by name. Teach me. —MARILYN MOORE JENSEN

18 | MONDAY
...Your young men shall see visions, and your old men shall dream dreams. —ACTS 2:17

March 6, 1965. Selma, Alabama. In living rooms all over America, families watch as men, women and children, marching to end racial segregation, are clubbed and kicked and teargassed.

March 7, 1965. Men and women from all over the country fly in to Selma in response to the violence. They are joining a young black minister, who has continued to proclaim, his voice thick with the emotion of a stricken, trampled people, "I have a dream!" It is a dream they all share. As they prepare to march, white hands clasping black, an elderly woman begins to sing. "Mine eyes have seen the glory of the coming of the Lord...." Waves and waves of marchers add their voices, as a people, long oppressed, take their first great strides into a world of hope.

A moving moment. A great and worthy cause. A country that will never recover its old indifference. And all because one man dared to trust his dream.

I will never be a Martin Luther King, Jr. But I *can* be a dreamer of dreams. I can risk sharing those dreams and pray that, in some small way, God will use them to help heal our wounded world. What are your dreams?

Thank You, Lord, for dreams and visions. Show me how to make them work for You. —MARILYN MORGAN HELLEBERG

19 | TUESDAY
And be ye kind one to another... —EPHESIANS 4:32

In New York City, 5:30 P.M. is known as dog-walking time, especially on weekdays when most business people who own dogs rush home from work in order to feed and exercise their pets.

One evening along Third Avenue, a woman walking a black-and-tan dachshund noticed a "bag lady" standing in front of a drugstore. Unkempt and surrounded by four dirty shopping bags, the woman wasn't begging or making a nuisance of herself. She just stood there, smiling. She seemed to be waiting for someone to smile back. But no one did. In fact, many people dropped their eyes as they hurried past.

23

The woman with the black-and-tan dachshund felt sorry for the bag lady. Yet she, too, was repelled. She reined in her dog's leash so there would be no chance for contact.

At that moment from the opposite direction came a good-looking young man in a three-piece business suit walking a magnificent collie. As the man and the dog drew near, the bag lady pointed. "Nice doggie," she said. The man stopped. "Her name is Amber." He smiled as he spoke. "Would you like to pet her?"

Ever so gently the bag lady reached out to stroke the collie's golden ruff. Amber responded by licking the woman's cheek. The bag lady beamed. "Bless you," she said to the young man. "Bless you, too," he answered. Then he and the dog went on their way.

The woman with the black-and-tan dachshund watched them go. She wished—oh, how she wished—that she'd been the one to give "the little nameless, unremembered act of kindness...." Well, not exactly "unremembered." Because, you see, now whenever I'm out walking my black-and-tan dachshund Heidi, I've learned to watch for bag ladies who look as if they might enjoy a smile. Or perhaps a chance to pet my dog.

Lord, help me to always look for little ways of showing Your love.   —ELEANOR SASS

 WEDNESDAY
...I have showed you kindness, that ye will also show kindness...   —JOSHUA 2:12

My son John is working toward a graduate degree in Boston and his wife Wendy needed a job to provide family income. She landed one with an agency seeking to collect delinquent charge accounts. The job provided a modest salary plus commissions, with the bulk of the work done by telephone.

The first day Wendy noticed the collector working near her shouting on the phone. Then he hung up and snorted, "Deadbeat!" Wendy noted that other collectors used similar harsh language.

There's got to be a better way, she mused as she got ready to make her first call. She breathed a short prayer, then picked up the phone. Speaking in a calm, friendly manner, she established a bond with the woman she was calling. The woman was so startled by a courteous approach that after she found her voice, she volunteered to send in a double payment.

Wendy tried the same approach on her second, third and fourth calls and they all reacted in a similarly cooperative manner. By the end of her first week, over a dozen delinquent payments had been received, resulting in a commendation by her superior.

Are you locked in a stalemate with someone over something that's causing hard feelings, anger or grief? Maybe you should try the courteous approach—using a calm, friendly, reconciling manner, try to reach out in kindness this time. See if you don't get the reward you seek—understanding and restored relationship.

Lord, let our communications be filled with love and good will in dealing with loved ones, neighbors or strangers.

—SAM JUSTICE

 THURSDAY   **FIRESIDE FRIEND**
For he shall give his angels charge over thee…
—*PSALM 91:11*

I remember an old cowboy and mountain man named Ed Jones. For some reason we called him Phonograph Jones—I forget why. He was a camp cook, a round-up cook and a very tough *hombre*. I knew him well and liked him a lot.

One hunting trip found us high up in the Absaroka mountains of northwestern Wyoming. It was cold up there. Jones always got up at daylight and walked over to the Shoshone River carrying a bar of soap and a towel. The river had ice near the banks and the air temperature was somewhere in the twenties. Jones was eighty years old, but every morning he'd strip off his clothes and walk out into that icy water for a bath. He'd keep his hat on and his pipe between his teeth and the water would be up to his neck and the pipe smoke would mingle with the morning mist. He was a tough old bird, all right. I used to ride by and wonder why he didn't freeze.

On this old-timer's shoulders were deep scars that went all down his back, scars made by the claws of a grizzly bear. He told me once how this grizzly jumped him while he was asleep in his bedroll and dragged him fifty yards. Jones said he could not get out of the bedroll. He thought he was done for.

25

I asked him how he finally did get free. He said the only weapon he had to fight the bear was his pillow. But then he added, "You know, God looks after cowboys and mountain men. I prayed, and that bear just dropped me and walked off!"

When you can beat off a grizzly bear using nothing but a pillow, you know Somebody has got to be helping you. Ed Jones knew Who that Somebody was. I knew, too.

God, You are indeed my very present help in time of trouble (Psalm 46:1). —DON BELL

| 22 | FRIDAY |

...By love serve one another. —GALATIANS 5:13

Retired six years, I am now a "house husband." Five mornings each week, I drive Ruby to her tax office in Boston. Then I return home to wash, iron, sew, clean house, run errands and prepare meals. Others watch and tease. "Does Ruby know you're out? Got your housework done?" One friend even presented me with an apron.

But household chores fill me with the satisfaction of a job well done. I feel I'm being paid every day. Sometimes every hour! When I'm cooking, spices and herbs can turn most menus into a delight. Rearranging table lamps can shower a room with soft light, warmth and comfort. The evening meal can bring refreshment, renewal and relaxation to Ruby and our supper guests.

Just as God releases healing breezes following a storm, home can be a haven from the storms of overwork, ridicule, weariness and tension. Perhaps I, too, can bring healing with gentle words, a generous spirit, faithfulness and humor. These can flavor the home and are a reflection of love.

Serving can be most rewarding. Can you think of a more ideal place to serve God and loved ones than in your own home?

O Lord, it is a joy serving You in such a simple way—here with my loved ones. —OSCAR GREENE

23 SATURDAY
Rejoice always. —*I THESSALONIANS 5:16 (RSV)*

Last January a few friends and I had a lighthearted conversation about what it would take to make us happy in the coming year. We talked about exotic trips, new jobs, prestigious honors, big raises. Finally a woman said, "If we wait for these things to happen, we may never be happy!"

We laughed. But the next morning I thought seriously about her words. What was it that created happiness in my life? Looking up at a new wall calendar, I decided to pencil in things during the coming year that brought me a measure of joy.

By year's end, the calendar was sprinkled with serendipitous discoveries like these:

January 28—reading by candlelight during a blackout.
February 2—rubbing noses with a puppy.
March 13—first daffodil in the garden.
April 29—making "milk moustaches" with my children.
May 11—Mother's Day card left on my pillow.
June 30—my son's face when he made the all-star baseball team.
July 17—finding a nest of sea turtle eggs.
August 8—jogging in the rain.
September 7—singing "How Great Thou Art" in church.
October 16—holding hands in the movies with my husband.
November 10—red leaves shimmering in the sun.
December 22—my daughter singing "Jingle Bells" in the shower.

To my surprise I found that the majority of my happy feelings evolved out of small, ordinary moments, from plain, everyday life. Maybe you'd like to start a "serendipity calendar" too, and discover anew that happiness is right here, right now, just waiting to be seized.

Lord, help me grow aware of the abundance of Your blessings that lie in my own backyard. —SUE MONK KIDD

24 SUNDAY

So be careful how you act; these are difficult days. Don't be fools; be wise: make the most of every opportunity you have for doing good. —EPHESIANS 5:15–16 (LB)

A few years ago I complained to an old high-school friend that with four children at home I couldn't find the time to write letters in my Christmas cards. (I'm one of those people who hates to get Christmas cards with nothing but the sender's signature inside.)

My friend looked me straight in the eye and said, "Why, the best thing that ever motivated me was *having* four children at home! I learned to make time for those things that were important to me. I learned to do personal projects—like writing, sewing, painting, cooking—in twenty-minute time blocks."

From that day on I stopped using my children and the hectic hustle-bustle of the season as an excuse. I started writing those Christmas letters to my faraway friends and relatives. I'd take an hour while Andrew, a pre-schooler at the time, watched *Sesame Street*. I wrote letters to Aunt Bernadine and cousin Mary Beth in the car while waiting to pick up Michael from basketball practice and drum lessons. Sometimes I used the kitchen counter while the roast was cooking and daughter Julie was practicing cheerleading in the living room.

That year I wrote over three dozen letters. It was a good feeling to learn that if I really want to do something, I *can* find the time.

This year I'm going to find time to read the books of Psalms and Proverbs. What are *you* going to find time to do?

Make me a doer, Lord, not an excuse-maker in these areas:

1. _____
2. _____
3. _____

—PATRICIA LORENZ

25 MONDAY

…Fear not: for I have redeemed thee… —ISAIAH 43:1

When I brought a twenty-three-year-old Volkswagen home, my wife said, "You're not going to leave *that* in the driveway, are you? The neighbors will think this is a junkyard." I couldn't blame her. The poor thing had been wrecked, left open to the weather for over a year, and abandoned. So I took my good car out of the garage and put the junk inside.

Little by little, piece by piece, I took it apart and started to work on it. I cleaned and polished every part that was repairable, and replaced the others with new ones. You should see it now!

Why did I do this? Well, I like working with my hands. But it's more than that. Working on that car, I could imagine myself as the Good Samaritan who rescued the man who fell among thieves. I redeemed that car from destruction, seeing it not for what it was, but for what it could be. I could see its potential, and I could help bring that potential into being.

But it's not just cars that can be fixed by loving care. Our real challenge and calling isn't to redeem junked cars, but junked people—people who seem damaged, discouraged, ignored and left looking like lost causes.

And we can begin today, too. How about volunteering, or writing a letter to a needy friend, saving up extra change for a donation or folding your hands in prayer? Like the old hymn, we can help others sing:

Touched by a loving heart, wakened in kindness,
Chords that were broken will vibrate once more.

Dear Lord, use these hands to touch some heart, as strings to make it vibrate with heavenly melody. —LEE WEBBER

 TUESDAY
...Lift up the hands which hang down...
—*HEBREWS 12:12*

The first thing my little grandson Zackie does when he walks into our house is to toddle over to me and raise his arms for me to pick him up. It's such a natural, honest gesture, and it floods me with love for him. What grandma worth her salt could possibly resist that?

Sometimes, when I'm alone, I raise my arms to God as I pray. Now I know why that feels so right! It's the natural gesture of a child reaching up to the beloved parent, wanting to be picked up!

If you feel in need of comfort today or you're overburdened and want to be carried for a while or you just need to know you're loved, raise your hands to your heavenly Father as you pray. He will pick you up.

Father, I am Your child. Take me in Your loving arms.
—MARILYN MORGAN HELLEBERG

27 WEDNESDAY
Give, and it will be given to you; good measure, pressed down, shaken together, running over, will be put into your lap. For the measure you give will be the measure you get back. —LUKE 6:38 (RSV)

For as long as I can remember, I have been a collector, for one of my fears is that I will throw away something valuable, then rue my foolishness. What I am going to do with 1963 theater ticket stubs or matches from the New York World's Fair, I don't know, but I keep them. Foremost I collect books, much to the chagrin of Shirley, who predicts that someday our house will fall—not because it was built on sand as in Jesus' parable, but from the weight of shelf after shelf of books. I also collect words of wisdom that I read and hear, and my study is overflowing with files of them. Here's something from a manila folder labeled "out of the mouths of babes":

> Love is something if you give it away, you'll end up having
>   more,
> Like a magic penny, hold it tight and you won't have any
> But lend it, spend it, and you'll have so many
> They'll roll all over the floor.

That little ditty is from my three-year-old granddaughter Jessica, who sang the lines to me on my last baby-sitting stint. She learned it at Sunday school, she told me.

If you collect meaningful sayings, maybe you'd like to file this one away. You never can tell when you'll run into someone who doesn't know that love is like a magic penny...something you can give away and still have more.

Remind us daily, Lord, that what the world saves, the Christ-follower gives away. —FRED BAUER

28 THURSDAY
A time to weep…and a time to laugh.

—*ECCLESIASTES 3:4*

Have you ever stopped to think that sometimes when you're discouraged or depressed, what you're feeling is the weight of unshed tears?

I was driving to downtown Atlanta in heavy morning traffic and I decided to slip a tape into the deck and listen to some Christian music. I'd just bought a new car so the tape player wasn't familiar to me. Keeping my eyes on the road, I picked up a tape at random, fumbled around and finally got it in.

Oh, I remembered this tape! We had recorded it live with our new tape player fourteen years ago. I hadn't heard it in many years. On the tape, my husband Jerry was alive and we were at a concert. The group sang and then one of the members talked. Some of the things he said were quite funny. Without warning Jerry was laughing—that warm, spontaneous laugh I never expected to hear again. I was jerked back in time. The effect was like an emotional whiplash. Jerry had been dead three years. Laughter had been the one thing that seemed to hold us together when all else failed. I reached for the tape but could not get it out of the deck. Jerry laughed again and seemed to be alive, in the car with me. By now I was crying and saying out loud, "Oh, please stop. Please." The tears that had refused to come for three years came now. I didn't have a tissue and I couldn't stop the tape. The traffic grew worse, and Jerry's wonderful laugh continued. Finally the tape did stop, but I cried all the way downtown—a twenty-minute ride.

It felt strangely good. Satisfying. Refreshing. God surely knew that I needed to cry. He understood, too, that some of us need a little help in releasing our carefully guarded tears, tears that bring healing and relief.

I'm glad I learned at last that it's all right if I cry, Father.

—MARION BOND WEST

29 FRIDAY

...The Lord God will wipe away tears from off all faces... —ISAIAH 25:8

As we sat in the veterinarian's waiting room, my German shepherd, Kate, seemed to sense that this wasn't a routine visit. She had been limping off and on lately and I knew we were in for bad news.

"She has dysplasia in her left hip," Dr. Gulliford said, showing me the X-ray. Dysplasia is common in large dogs, and it means the leg bone doesn't fit properly into the hip joint. It's painful and crippling.

"But Kate's only four years old!" I protested.

"It happens to young dogs, too," Dr. Gulliford said gently.

I stopped hearing him. I was remembering Trooper, my wonderful Welsh terrier, whose death at fifteen was a terrible grief. I had been so careful in choosing Kate. She was a sound, healthy puppy with a good chance for a long, happy life. I took the best care of her. Selfishly I thought, *I cannot go through the loss of another dear friend, not this soon!*

Then I looked at Kate and saw the trust in her eyes. I hugged her. God was answering my prayer for help before I could put words around it. I was grateful—yes, grateful—to be the one to look after Kate. Limping or not, healthy or disabled, this lovely animal has given me companionship, loyalty, challenge, laughter and constant support. But there is more to a loving relationship—and to life—than that. There are also tears. And when they are more than we can bear, Christ holds us up. "How can I help her?" I asked Dr. Gulliford.

Dysplasia, I learned, is not the end of a dog's life. There are surgical remedies. Kate might still limp, but she would have no pain and would run and play again. It would take a lot of postoperative work on my part, the doctor said. But I knew I could do it. When you love somebody, you find the strength to deal with the tears. God was teaching me that.

Thank You, Lord, for giving me Your strength when mine is not enough. —PHYLLIS HOBE

Spirit Lifter

THE NEW YEAR—THE ROAD

There may be curves
And turns,
Detours, perhaps,
But let's keep to THE ROAD
For the clearest view
The sure destination—
Besides,
On it, God always
Directs the traffic.

—MILDRED N. HOYER

---

30 SATURDAY   **FIRESIDE FRIEND**

And thou shalt rejoice in every good thing which the Lord thy God hath given unto thee...

—*DEUTERONOMY 26:11*

I'm one of those people who lives in the future. In my college classes, I concentrate on the grade I want to earn at the end, and don't seem to apply the material I'm supposedly learning along the way. During the summer, I can't wait for college to start again, but once it does, I'm thinking about winter break. Right now, I'm imagining opening night of the play I'm directing—a month down the road. But come opening night, I'll probably be thinking about my next theatrical challenge. I think it's called missing the joys of the present in the hope of a distant future—which never comes, because the present is the only true moment in which we're alive.

Since I've behaved this way all my life, it's hard to change and really take the time to see the joys of this moment, of today. The French writer Albert Camus once wrote, "If there is a sin against life, it consists perhaps not so much in despairing of life as in hoping for another life and in eluding the implacable grandeur of this life."

So tonight, I'm sitting down to concentrate on the blessings of today: fifty-degree weather on a January day in Minnesota, the first hearty bloom of a small violet plant a friend gave me for Christmas, a phone call from my three-year-old foster sister Alissa.

What are the joys of your "today"?

Father, today and throughout this new year, open my eyes to the many blessings around me. —TAMMY RIDER

---

31 SUNDAY
Unto him that loved us, and washed us from our sins...
—REVELATION 1:5

I'll probably never meet Kara, now four years old. But one day she made a beautiful observation that has helped me:

"We had been standing on the hillside watching the airplane's skywriting," her grandmother wrote me one day. "When the words began to disappear, she asked, 'Why, Grandma? Where do they go?' Then, as I groped for an answer, her little face brightened, and she suddenly exclaimed, 'Maybe Jesus has an eraser!'"

I smiled as I read, but my eyes filled and suddenly I wanted to hug that little girl. For that morning I had been grieving over past mistakes. A cruel thing I had said to my mother the day I left for college. And Dad...if only I'd invited him to that luncheon where I was to speak—he'd have been so proud. One tender but painful memory releases others: the time I'd punished a child unfairly, humiliated my husband, let a friend down....

No matter how much we mature as people, grow as Christians, try desperately to compensate, memories of our own failures rise up to haunt us, and sting—how they sting. For me, it's not the un-kindnesses of others that hurt so much or last so long, it's the burden of my own. Yes, I ask God to forgive me, and try to believe that I am forgiven. But the memory won't go away. And if I can't forgive myself, how can God?

Then a little girl, in her innocence and wisdom, makes me realize: Like that writing on the sky that simply disappears, Jesus has wiped away all the things I so bitterly regret. Jesus does have an eraser.

Dear Lord, thank You for that child. Now I can forget, because I am forgiven. I too have an eraser. —MARJORIE HOLMES

Thank-You Notes to God

1
2
3
4
5
6
7
8
9
10
11
12
13
14
15

16	
17	
18	
19	
20	
21	
22	
23	
24	
25	
26	
27	
28	
29	
30	
31	

S	M	T	W	T	F	S
	1	2	3	4	5	6
7	8	9	10	11	12	13
14	15	16	17	18	19	20
21	22	23	24	25	26	27
28	29					

FEBRUARY

BE A LISTENER
Your Spiritual Pilgrimage

In quietness…shall be your strength.   —*ISAIAH 30:15*

There is a deep stillness that falls upon the world with the snows of February. At night the stars blaze with frosty brilliance. Nothing stirs. The whole universe seems to be waiting, listening. There is peace in the stillness, healing in the silence.

Perhaps this month you can school yourself to be a better listener. In these long nights and short days, try really listening to those around you. Not just to their words. Listen for the unspoken plea for reassurance. Listen for the silent cry for help.

Listen—and respond.

Tandem Power for February

| 1 | LOVE—THE ACTION VERB

...Let us not love in word, neither in tongue; but in deed and in truth.   —*I JOHN 3:18*

With a whirring sound and a spinning miniature hacksaw, the jeweler carefully slices through the band of my wedding ring and slides it off my finger—for the first time since our wedding day twenty years ago when we discovered that the ring was too small. I vividly remember that moment in the restroom between the ceremony and reception when I painfully jammed it over my knuckle, with the help of some cream and a surge of adrenalin. I have never gotten it off again...until today. And today, as twenty years ago, my husband Lynn is by my side. A new ring, using the old gem, is to be my anniversary present.

"You've got a nice gem here," the jeweler tells us. "But you will be amazed how our polishing process will make it sparkle." Suddenly I realize that love is more than something we *feel.* It is something we *do.* Love is a polishing process. It is an action verb.

I make a decision. February is a month traditionally dedicated to love. So, while my finger is ring-less and my gem is at the jewelry store being polished, I will work all month at polishing the love in the relationships all around me. With the extra Leap Year day, that means I need twenty-nine action-ideas, so I start a mental list: Get a box of valentines and tuck them into surprise spots all month long, like brown-bag lunches, a sock drawer, a pillow case or a suitcase. Take a heart-shaped thank-you cake to a special friend. Write a love letter, using the messages on candy hearts. Have lunch at school with a ten-year-old. Give out ice cream cone coupons. Go a whole day without a single grumble. Swallow a grudge.

Have you got some ideas? God wants to show His love through our actions. When we cooperate and let His love flow freely through us, we are using Tandem Power. And together, we polish His sparkle into the relationships all around us.

Heavenly Father, let us link our love with Your love and pass it on at least once a day, in twenty-nine unexpected ways this month.   —CAROL KUYKENDALL

2 TUESDAY
For God, who commanded the light to shine out of darkness, hath shined in our hearts, to give the light of the knowledge of the glory of God in the face of Jesus Christ. —II CORINTHIANS 4:6

The lowly woodchuck has elevated two Pennsylvania towns to celebrity status. Both Punxsutawney and Quarryville mark the emergence of the groundhog/woodchuck as the key to when spring will arrive.

The legend, dating back to early German settlers, was that if an animal saw its shadow on Candlemas Day (February 2), there would be six more weeks of bad weather; but if no shadow, an early spring.

Punxsutawney first celebrated the event a hundred years ago when a small delegation hiked to the woods in 1887 to observe the movements of Punxsutawney Phil, as he came to be known. The annual trek bloomed into a major media event and its Groundhog Club now numbers thousands of members.

In Quarryville, according to James E. Pennington, Hibernating Governor of Slumbering Lodge, it was such a special event that uniforms were designated: top hats, signifying the dignity of the groundhog, and nightshirts, symbolic of hibernation. Quarryville has been celebrating the event since 1908.

On this Groundhog Day, I ask myself—and you, too—how many of us, like Phil, duck back into our holes to sit out the shadowy periods of our lives? Or retreat in fear and defeat at our first failure or disappointment, or even a good challenge? Maybe we'd be better served if we put our faith in the Author of all weather, rather than in an oversized rodent who doesn't see too well and actually is afraid of his shadow!

Lord, don't let me cling to darkness; help turn my fear to faith by trusting Your light today. —SAM JUSTICE

3 WEDNESDAY
Blessed is the people that know the joyful sound: they shall walk, O Lord, in the light of thy countenance. —PSALM 89:15

Like most people, we have radios scattered all over the house. But my favorite is the little one in the kitchen, tuned always to the good music station, ready to provide symphonies, singers or jazz as I work. Pavarotti as I peel potatoes, Benny Goodman as I scrub the floor. Whether I'm cleaning cupboards or cooking, the miracle of music is there to enjoy just by turning a knob.

Our kitchen radio has one peculiarity, however. The music comes in better whenever I am near the set. As I move away from it, it fades out or other stations come in, clamoring for attention. Chattering voices, commercials—annoyed, I must stop what I am doing and try to tune out this interference. Calm is restored, the music flows again sweet and clear. But only so long as I remain close to the source.

Finally, it dawns on me: Move the instrument. Instead of keeping it tucked away in its usual corner, try bringing it out to the center of the kitchen table, where I will never be far away from it. A simple bit of common sense I should have thought of before. Because now the problem is resolved. No matter where I am in the kitchen, the beautiful music I need to feed my spirit now flows all around me.

And it occurred to me only last night, preparing dinner while listening to Brahms: God is like that, too. He wants us to be near Him. The closer we are, the clearer we hear the music of His spirit, shutting out the clamor and pain of life's irritations and problems, giving us peace and joy. He can't be hidden away in a corner; He must be the very center of our lives if we are truly to hear His harmony.

Dear Father, how You must love us to give us music and all the wonderful instruments that bring it to us. Help us to stay near to You, its Source. —MARJORIE HOLMES

THURSDAY

Know ye not that ye are the temple of God, and that the Spirit of God dwelleth in you? —I CORINTHIANS 3:16

Clay was not meant to be a city dog. He was a bird dog, a pointer, a hunter who never hunted. He was never trained, yet the genius of his ancestors could not be denied in him. On our dawn runs through Central Park he would always find something worth a point or two. Once I even found him "honoring" the point of an Irish setter honoring that of another setter. But pigeons, no. Clay was bright enough to give up on these early in life—our city streets were too full of them.

One morning we were trotting along the bridle path when I saw Clay stop, his right forefoot curled into a familiar hook, his head, body and tail frozen in a level line. What had he found this time? I could see nothing. Clay waited for me to approach, then began his slow, taut advance. Then I saw what he saw, a squat bird with a tiny head.

"Why, Clay," I laughed, "it's a pigeon!"

Yet a wounded pigeon. It lay in the brush, its wing torn, its eyes looking up at us in a frightened stare. Gently I scooped the bird up and headed home with it, Clay alongside, a pleased wag to his tail. Back in the apartment I did what I could, but the creature died before nightfall.

I've never forgotten that pigeon, or Clay's reaction to it. Did he really sense that the bird was wounded? Who's to say? To me it was just one more example of the mysterious instinct bred into these so-called lesser creatures over whom God gave us dominion. It has always made me wonder about the instincts bred into me. What am I doing with the genius of *my* ancestors? Am I using my mind more? Am I more caring? More loving of the God in Whose likeness I am made? Are you?

Father, I was born with great good in me; help me always to make good use of it. —VAN VARNER

FRIDAY **FIRESIDE FRIEND**
...I am come that they might have life, and that they might have it more abundantly. —JOHN 10:10

"Have you ever noticed what people *do* on TV?" my husband Michael asked me one night. "They don't watch TV!"

I thought about the few shows we see often, mostly family situation comedies. Mike's right. The characters go on a camping trip or work on a school project or bake a birthday cake. A father and teenage son shoot baskets, and the son "comes of age" by winning for the first time. Children have pajama parties or look at photograph albums (a handy device for flashbacks). They laugh, they cry, they argue, they reconcile. *But they do not sit around passively watching other people in a box!*

That fits in with what James tells us. We are to be doers of the word and not hearers only (1:22). Because we are renewed in Christ, we want to do good works as a result.

But the instruction also motivates our family to find alternative activities that help us grow and enjoy one another. For instance, we often go for a walk on a nearby levee, play board games like *Uno*, or fly kites at a local park.

Our family calendar's filling up and so is our enthusiasm for one another—because there's more to life than being spectators.

Lord, help us to be doers—not just viewers—in life, and to be truly a "family."   —B. J. CONNOR

---

6 SATURDAY
How precious to me are thy thoughts, O God!
—PSALM 139:17 (RSV)

Brain Power.

That was the topic of the talk I attended last evening: to learn how our brains work and how we can improve our memories. One suggestion intrigued me. "If you want to remember something painlessly," the speaker told us, "read it just before going to sleep and let your subconscious work on it all night long."

When I got home, I looked at the stack of magazines and half-finished books piled beside my bed. On top was an article about dieting I had fallen asleep reading the night before. So what was my last thought? I'd eaten too much of the wrong foods that day. No wonder I awoke feeling grumpy and mad at myself before I even put my feet on the floor. My subconscious had worked on those negative thoughts all night.

So before bed, I decided to try her experiment. I got out a book of Biblical promises and glanced through the pages. "Glory be to God who by his mighty power at work within us is able to do far more than we would ever dare to ask or even dream of," I read from Ephesians 3:20 (LB). As I fell asleep, I turned the words over in my mind and pictured God at work within me. And this is what really happened: When I woke up this morning, I did not feel the usual vague sense of dread about the day's responsibilities. Instead, I felt fueled with His presence and excited about the potential of the hours that stretched before me. I could start a new diet or practice more patience or complete a home fix-it project. After all, I was equipped with the power of His promise.

Tonight, why don't you try tucking one of God's promises into your brain just before falling asleep? It seems to bathe the unborn day in His power all night long!

Lord, help me fill my thoughts with Your thoughts even while I sleep. —CAROL KUYKENDALL

| 7 | SUNDAY | FIRESIDE FRIEND |

Consider the lilies of the field, how they grow; they toil not, neither do they spin. —MATTHEW 6:28

It was drizzling lightly that Sunday morning as we drove to church. Our son Eric asked a rather simple question: "Why is it raining?" My wife and I looked at each other for support as we searched for an answer that would satisfy the curiosity of a six-year-old. Before one of us could respond, Eric blurted out, "I know why! It's raining because the trees asked God for the rain."

As we drove along, I thought of how many examples there are in nature that show God's ability to meet the needs of all His creation. God uses these to help us to deepen our relationship with Him. What clearer example of faith, trust and answered prayer than that some trees were in need of rain, at least in a little boy's opinion.

The next time the dark clouds form, perhaps you will remember with me that God is not trying to spoil our day with rain, but that what He's really doing is preparing to answer the prayers of some thirsty trees!

Praise You, God, for using nature to show us the sensitivity of Your care. —ERIC W. THOMAS

| 8 | MONDAY |

...Let us not be weary in well doing: for in due season we shall reap... —GALATIANS 6:9

You know the feeling. Once in a while you wake up with a small dark cloud hanging over your head. Nothing definite—just a feeling of weariness, a "down" feeling. When my morning starts off like that, I know a cure—and my prescription works!

My first stop is my church. Just stepping inside brings a feeling of relaxation and security, for this is God's house, where I know I'll be welcome. Being close to Him and talking with Him is the beginning of my recovery.

As I sit there in the quietness, I try to think of something I can do to help others. How about calling my nephew who's away at his first semester at college? How long has it been since I've taken magazines to the nursing home? What have I left undone? What promises have I made but failed to keep?

I plan my day. By nighttime I'm tired, physically and mentally, but I have the satisfaction of knowing that those hours have been well spent. During that time I've forgotten myself and thought of others. The next morning the "blues" have passed, and I'm ready to face the world again.

Do you have a block of some kind? Are you depressed? Do you think you've reached a dead end in your job, or with your family, or—more importantly—with yourself? Make your first step a visit to God's house.

When I am sunk deep inside myself, God, please touch me so that I can come out and can find ways to help others.

—WALTER HARTER

9	TUESDAY

...Who for the joy that was set before him endured the cross... —HEBREWS 12:2

Our younger daughter Natalie was born a nervous child. Night after miserable night she whimpered and cried unless we held her.

"I don't know what else to do for her," my wife Sharon confessed. "I've tried everything." She was puzzled but very patient.

Worn from loss of sleep, I was angry. *How could Sharon be so calm about it,* I wondered.

The next night was the same. I elbowed Sharon and said, "Your turn. She's crying again." Obediently she staggered up the stairs, and soon the cries subsided. Hours later I woke to find that Sharon had not returned. When I went into Natalie's bedroom, I saw Sharon slumped in the old oak rocker with Natalie curled up in her lap. Sharon was asleep, her face lined with fatigue and her hair standing out like weeds. But on her face was an unforgettable smile!

In that moment I understood why Sharon seldom complained. She too was suffering, but she was doing it for someone she loved. That gave meaning to it, while I had been thinking only of my own discomfort.

The sky was pink, so I dressed and fixed breakfast. When Sharon stumbled into the kitchen, I held her close and brushed the hair from her eyes. "Tomorrow night," I said, "I get to sit up with Natalie."

Lord, as You gave Yourself to us, help us to give ourselves to one another. —DANIEL SCHANTZ

10	WEDNESDAY

Love bears all things… —I CORINTHIANS 13:7 (RSV)

It happened one year at the zoo. My daughter and I stood beside a grandmother and a little girl whose face was sprinkled with bright red freckles. The children were waiting in line to get their cheeks painted by a local artist who was decorating them with tiger paws.

"You've got so many freckles, there's no place to paint," a boy in the line cried. Embarrassed, the little girl beside me dropped her head.

Her grandmother knelt down next to her. "I love your freckles," she said.

"Not me," the girl replied.

"Well, when I was a little girl I always wanted freckles," she said, tracing a finger across the child's cheek. "Freckles are beautiful!"

The girl looked up. "Really?"

"Of course," said the grandmother. "Why, just name me one thing that's prettier than freckles."

The little girl peered into the old woman's smiling face. "Wrinkles," she answered softly.

That moment has whispered something to me ever since. If I look at others with the eyes of love, I will not see blemishes. Only beauty.

Help me to see beyond the "wrinkles" and "freckles" of others to the loveliness within. —SUE MONK KIDD

11	THURSDAY

...He leadeth me in the paths of righteousness...
—PSALM 23:3

In Savannah, Georgia, where I live, tomorrow is celebrated as Georgia Day because this was the day in 1733 when a little band of Englishmen climbed the bluff overlooking the Savannah River and established the thirteenth British colony in the New World. Usually on Georgia Day a special tribute is paid to some distinguished Georgian. Last year it was Juliette Gordon Low, who founded the Girl Scouts of America here in 1912. Since she was my aunt, I was asked to share some recollections of her at the Georgia Day luncheon.

This was easy to do because Aunt Daisy, as we called her, was such a colorful and dynamic person. Amusing stories about her are numerous, and we all laughed at some of them. Then I talked about her tenacity of purpose and the high ideals she brought to Scouting. At the end I quoted a little verse that I thought summed up her life and character very well. Those four simple lines, written years ago by Adam Lindsay Gordon, made more of an impression on the audience than anything else I said. Later, quite a few people asked me to write them down so they could memorize them.

Perhaps you may find them memorable, too:

> Life is mostly froth and bubbles;
> Two things stand like stone:
> Kindness in another's troubles;
> Courage in your own.

Let these words illuminate our hearts and minds, dear Lord.
—ARTHUR GORDON

12 FRIDAY
...*Be prepared*...   —*MATTHEW 24:42 (LB)*

Nothing measures human character and fortitude better than adversity. Some people are broken by their trials and defeats; others, like an archer's bow bend under pressure, but resiliently bounce back again and again. On this day in 1809, Abraham Lincoln was born. Few people of greatness have been more sorely tested.

Among the troubles that visited Lincoln: the death of his mother when he was but nine, rejection by his first love, the bankruptcy of his first business venture, defeat the first time he sought public office. And even when he finally made it to Congress, he lasted only one term, being so unpopular that reelection was out of the question. But he did not consider the setback final or fatal. Returning to his Springfield, Illinois, law practice, he reportedly told a friend, "I will get ready. My time will come." His faith was justified.

When we are tested by adversity's fire, when friends are scarce as hen's teeth and defeats come in bunches, when our tank of self-esteem is on empty and hope has taken a holiday, it is helpful to remember Lincoln's statement. In it are two keys to a better tomorrow: positive action and quiet faith. Next to trusting God with what lies ahead and praying, "Thy will be done," I can think of no better affirmation of faith than "I will get ready. My time will come."

When we can see nothing but fading sunsets, Lord, turn us around.   —FRED BAUER

13 SATURDAY   **FIRESIDE FRIEND**
I love thee, O Lord, my strength.   —*PSALM 18:1 (RSV)*

A bevy of valentines, suspended by slender threads from the ceiling, caught my eye as I walked into the classroom of a small Christian school, where I was visiting. Red hearts, pink hearts, lace-trimmed hearts, hearts bearing pictures cut from magazines, hearts adorned with paper doilies. They looked so pretty that I couldn't help mentioning them to the teacher.

"Oh," she explained, "these are the valentines that the children made for God."

What a beautiful thought!

FEBRUARY 1988

Every February I send valentines to my family and friends to express my love for them. But I will have to confess that I have seldom thought to tell God that I love Him.

Do you suppose He longs to be loved, as we do?

Since visiting that classroom, I've been concluding my morning prayers with a verbal valentine, a simple, "I love You," to the One Who loves me most of all.

Have you told Him lately that you love Him?

Dear God, I love You very much. Amen.

—ROBERTA DONOVAN

 SUNDAY

So faith, hope, love abide, these three; but the greatest of these is love. —*I CORINTHIANS 13:13 (RSV)*

Today is Valentine's Day, that warm and wonderful day for telling others that we love them. But why limit those expressions of affection to a single day? Why not say something *every* day that will convey the same message?

It's not hard, really. A single sentence, a single phrase can do. For example:

"I'm so proud of you."

"My self-confidence is higher when I'm with you."

"I truly believe you put my happiness ahead of your own."

"You have a wonderful way of making me laugh."

"You keep me from making foolish mistakes."

"I'm so glad you're back!"

"Thank you for being you."

See how simple it is? Why not invent some phrases of your own to add to this list. There's no reason why you can't keep Valentine's Day going right through the year.

Today, Lord, help me express my love in simple ways.

—RUTH STAFFORD PEALE

Spirit Lifter
WHAT IS LOVE?
It is Silence—when your words would hurt.
It is Patience—when your neighbor's curt.
It is Deafness—when a scandal flows.
It is Thoughtfulness—for others' woes.
It is Promptness—when stern duty calls.
It is Courage—when misfortune falls.
—AUTHOR UNKNOWN

---

15 MONDAY
For he loveth our nation...   —LUKE 7:5

During a trip to New York a few years ago I visited one of its famous museums. On a self-guided tour, I was thunderstruck by a massive painting covering an entire wall, the famous *Washington Crossing the Delaware.*

I stood in awe of the lifelike color, the feeling of movement, the sheer size of it. I studied the determined expressions on the faces of Washington and his men as they pushed through the ice with wooden oars that cold Christmas night in 1776.

But what really struck me was the artist's name, Emanuel Gottlieb Leutze. Had a German painter created one of America's most treasured historical paintings? Later I learned that Leutze was born in Germany in 1816, immigrated to Philadelphia with his parents when he was nine years old, grew up and studied painting in his adopted homeland. At age thirty-five, he captured this piece of American history on canvas.

Would it surprise George Washington to learn that a young German had created a quintessentially American treasure? Surely not. After all, hadn't Washington fought for American liberty with the assistance of fellow patriots with names like Lafayette and Pulaski, Von Steuben and Salomon? And didn't George Washington value the "melting pot" quality that America had been founded upon?

49

No, when George Washington led his men into battle, it was to fight for an America of richness and diversity and true freedom for all.

Father, as we remember our founding fathers on Presidents' Day, let me keep alive in my heart and life their spirit of freedom, tolerance and justice for all Americans.

—PATRICIA LORENZ

Family Time

| 16 | TAKING CHARGE

...We are well able to do it; even to ourselves we looked like grasshoppers. —NUMBERS 13:30, 33

Two men said it could be done; ten men didn't believe it. Two men saw themselves as winners; ten men pictured themselves as losers—"we looked like grasshoppers."

You remember the story. With a mighty show of power God delivered the Israelites from Egyptian slavery. A little later they watched as God piled up the waters of the Red Sea so they could cross and escape from the pursuing Egyptian army. Then, as soon as they were safe on the other side, they saw the water surge back into place and destroy Pharaoh's army.

The Israelites then witnessed God's presence during their encampment at Mount Sinai. And from there they marched north to an invasion point on the southern border of Canaan, where the Lord told Moses to send twelve spies into the Land of Promise to scout things out.

Upon their return a month and a half later the twelve spies reported that it was a rich and lush land "flowing with milk and honey." Two of them exuded confidence and said they could conquer the land. But the other ten were negative thinkers who pictured themselves not as men but as grasshoppers. Now, you'd think that after seeing all that God had done for them, they wouldn't be ready to turn tail and run. But they were, and they did.

With our twenty-twenty hindsight vision we find it easy to criticize those unbelieving Hebrews. And yet three thousand five hundred years later we so often find ourselves looking on the dark side of things, ready to believe the bad news—we see ourselves as grasshoppers in a world full of giant difficulties. We're all set to sound retreat, even after seeing all the Lord has done for us. As we pick our way steadily through the days and months of this year, the choice is ours. Do we "go up and conquer" or muddle around in our wilderness? When we look in the mirror, do we see "grasshoppers" staring back at us?

That's not what the psalmist saw, for he wrote, "Yet thou hast made him [you and me] a little less than God...thou hast put all things under his feet" (Psalm 8:5–6, RSV). The good news for us this year is that God wants us to be in charge of our days. And Paul gave us the grand affirmation that makes this possible: "I can do all things in him who strengthens me" (Philippians 4:13, RSV). Write these words on a card and tape it to the bathroom mirror. Read them out loud every morning and "conquer."

Father in heaven, help me to act each day like a person made in Your image.   —FLOYD AND HARRIETT THATCHER

Spirit Lifter
A happy family is but an earlier heaven.
—SIR JOHN BOWRING

---

17 WEDNESDAY
...Having nothing, and yet possessing all things.
—II CORINTHIANS 6:10

I've been feeling overloaded lately, the way I feel when I travel with too much luggage. That's why I really needed to hear what a wonderfully wise lady at the nursing home told me this morning. Mrs. Elliot said that when her home was sold and she had to give up the accumulations of a lifetime, she'd thought that she "just couldn't get along without all of those *things*. But you know," she said, "a rather amazing thing happened. Once I let go of all of that, I found a new sense of inner freedom. It was as if I had exchanged certain material blessings

51

FEBRUARY 1988

(which were only clutter, really) for spiritual blessings, which are infinitely more valuable."

It's a good lesson for me to ask on this Ash Wednesday. Oh, I'm not going to go out and sell all of my possessions, but I *am* going to examine my life to see what's cluttering it up. Maybe I don't really need to go to all of those meetings. And wouldn't it be nice not to have to dust so many knickknacks? Perhaps I *could* even turn down a few social engagements. In place of these, maybe I could spend more quiet time with God. Because Mrs. Elliot is right: Spiritual blessings *are* infinitely more valuable than any external things.

Lord, during this Lenten season, help me to let go of things and occupations that keep me far from You. Instead, create in me a constant desire to draw close to You.
—MARILYN MORGAN HELLEBERG

| 18 | THURSDAY
Casting all your care upon him; for he careth for you.
—*I PETER 5:7*

Recently I read of an experiment where a group of college students wrote in diaries for twenty minutes daily, concentrating on unresolved problems and painful events in their lives. Results indicated that this activity significantly improved the efficiency of their immune systems. During the following six months they required medical treatment far fewer times than a similar group who wrote about trivial matters.

I was intrigued. But I dislike cluttering my diary with dismal subjects. So instead I began writing daily twenty-minute letters to God. I include everything that's troubling me: fears, worries, self-pity, jealousy, resentments, things I could never reveal to a counselor or close friend.

I'm not sure, yet, what it's done for my immune system—though I haven't been ill since I started. But I do know that, after the writing stint, I'm relaxed and at peace. After all, I should be. I've just assigned all my problems to the world's greatest Physician.

Would you care to join me in an experiment? The "Thank-You-Notes-to-God" sections at the end of each month is a good place to begin. Don't let the time factor hinder you. Maybe five or ten minutes a day will serve you better. You can always vary the amount of time and gradually increase it. *But begin*—steadily, solidly, simply. You can use a looseleaf or spiral notebook if you'd like to take this letter-writing to God more deeply. Then in three months—mark your calendar for May 18—why not drop a line to Daily Guideposts Editor, Carmel, N.Y. 10512, and share with us the results of your diary experiment?

Dear Father, thank You for listening to my troubles and for giving me the faith to leave them with You.
—ALETHA JANE LINDSTROM

19 FRIDAY

...If thou wilt diligently hearken to the voice of the Lord thy God... —EXODUS 15:26

Maybe you already know this about me, but for those of you who don't, I have a hearing problem. I rely to a great extent on lipreading, but I do have *some* hearing capacity and I try to enhance this by going to an auditory training class. The instructor holds a sheet of paper in front of her mouth so I cannot lipread. Then she repeats similar-sounding words, like *buy, my, try*. Or sentences. You have to blot out everything else and listen with all your might. It takes tremendous concentration. After one of these sessions I am usually exhausted.

The other day I was leaving church with a friend who was comparing herself, a bit wistfully, with the other Christians who never seem to have trouble hearing God's voice. "I hear them say things like, 'During my prayer time this morning God told me....' Or, 'I asked the Lord what to do about this problem and He said....'" Why, she wanted to know, didn't this ever happen to her?

So I told her about my auditory training class. How I had to concentrate, how I had to screen out everything else. "Maybe you need to *practice* listening for God's voice," I suggested. "It's a still, small voice, you know. But you can learn to hear it if you really try."

"What must I do?" she asked.

"Set aside a regular quiet time when you tune out the world completely and tune in to God," I answered.

So she said she would try harder. And I think she'll be successful. How about you?

Lord, help me to listen diligently to Your voice.

—ELEANOR SASS

 SATURDAY

He that observeth the wind shall not sow; and he that regardeth the clouds shall not reap.

—*ECCLESIASTES 11:4*

As a boy I lived at the edge of a small, dull town. At the corner of our lot a massive pine tree pointed to the clouds as if to say, "This way to adventure." Naturally, one day I obeyed the invitation, clawing my way up through the fragrant limbs until my heart raced and my breath came in gasps. Near the top I paused to look around, then I realized that I was much higher than I had thought. I was terrified. Tears came to my eyes, and I prayed fervently, "Lord, please get me down safely and I will never do this again."

Somehow I managed to get down and for the next few days I stayed at a safe level in my tree-climbing activities. But gradually I became aware that something was missing. Danger, excitement were missing. And adventure. So gradually, hesitantly, I started to climb higher again, and at once the thrill, the magic, began to come back.

Now, years later, I believe God was using that tree to teach me a valuable lesson. We humans need both security and adventure, but the need for adventure may well be the greater one. When life is perfectly safe it can also be perfectly dull. In a world preoccupied with security, I often think of that tree. I try always to climb a little higher than I think I can, and I seldom regret it. The view is marvelous.

Father, help me to obey that urge to do a little more than I think is possible. Guide my reach, hold firm my grasp.

—DANIEL SCHANTZ

21 SUNDAY

The purpose of tithing is to teach you always to put God first in your lives. —*DEUTERONOMY 14:23 (LB)*

When my mother died a few years ago, Dad gave me a box of papers from her desk. Included were her down-to-the-penny household statements for each month during my childhood years.

Every month she paid eleven bills by check: house payments, taxes, insurance, utilities, groceries, etc. The rest of the family income was placed in ten separate envelopes labeled: church, school expenses, clothes, gifts, repair and improvement, dues and licenses, doctor-dentist, Dad's allowance, Mom's allowance and savings.

The June 3, 1960 ledger states that she wrote $274 in checks. The cash in the envelopes totaled $130. Our family of five was living on $404 a month. In spite of the tight budget, Mother and Dad were giving more to the church than they were keeping for themselves. Mom kept $10, Dad kept $10...and $24 went to the church.

Have I followed in my parents' footsteps? Hardly. The excuses come too easily. Four children to put through college. A big mortgage. An emergency that might come up. The vacation fund.

As a child I never had the slightest notion that my parents inched their way through on such a tight budget. Yet every month they gave no thought to doing any less for the church than the absolute maximum that their tiny budget could stand. Maybe that's why I felt so rich as a kid.

Lord, give me the courage to tithe and then to trust my budget concerns to You. —PATRICIA LORENZ

22 MONDAY

And do not seek what you are to eat and what you are to drink, nor be of anxious mind. For...your Father knows that you need them. —*LUKE 12:29-30 (RSV)*

There are many puzzling verses in the Bible, but one that always used to stop me was a phrase in Christ's Sermon on the Mount where He advises His followers "to take no thought for the morrow" (Matthew 6:34). Like a tenacious bulldog that once latched onto my pantleg and wouldn't let go, that verse had grating teeth. I didn't question the point Christ was making, to trust God with our future, but I was always taught that it's wise to pray as if everything depended upon God and work as if everything depended upon us. Or as an old evangelist once said, "God provides for the birds, but he does not throw food into their nests."

All my ruminating was resolved one day when I discovered the Revised Standard Version, which translates the verse, "do not be *anxious* about tomorrow." That one word made a ton of difference. Yes, of course, make provisions for tomorrow, but don't wring your hands about it. Your heavenly Father Who looks after the birds of the air and the animals of the fields will surely take care of you.

All of this came to mind because of something I read yesterday from Dr. Robert S. Elliot, the founder of the Department of Preventative Medicine at the University of Nebraska Medical Center. Dr. Elliot has devised a two-pronged formula for dealing with stressful problems, present and future: "Rule #1: Don't sweat the small stuff. Rule #2: It's all small stuff."

Help me put life in perspective, Lord, so I don't discover at the end I've missed the point. —FRED BAUER

---

23 TUESDAY
Hope deferred makes the heart sick, but a desire fulfilled is a tree of life. —PROVERBS 13:12 (RSV)

A little while ago my doctor prescribed for me some strong medicine for my heart condition. As I read about this new medicine, I found that it could cause depression and even suicidal tendencies. The instructions even said that if suicidal tendencies develop, the medicine should be discontinued. Well, I should hope so!

I'm normally an optimist, but the medicine created a negative reaction in me. I found myself dredging up negative experiences from the past: times I'd failed, times things had gone wrong, times I'd done things I shouldn't have. I also worried about my health. Finally, I got so depressed, I got on my knees and said, "God, I have to fight back. I know You don't want me to live like this. Please help me."

The next day I decided to try a new approach. I'd do positive things to crowd out the negative feelings. So, every day, I made time to listen to good music, to read a good book or informative article, to work on some interesting projects and to get some good exercise. But most importantly, every day I took time to read the Word of God and pray. And slowly I began to find that despite the medication, I could control the down effects.

Do you struggle with depression or a habit that is causing you bad health? There are things you can do. First, get professional counseling. And then, make up a series of steps that reinforce what makes you glad to be alive. Take a drive in the country. Cook up a favorite recipe. See a good movie. Force yourself to enjoy life. And see how much you can make your own happiness—with God's help.

Dear Lord, help me to shut the door on dark and negative things, and open the windows of my mind to the sunlight of beautiful things. Amen. —LEE WEBBER

 WEDNESDAY
Surely he has borne our griefs and carried our sorrows... —ISAIAH 53:4 (RSV)

I said good-bye today and it was just about the hardest thing I've ever done. Time had run out for Bridget, our border collie, companion and friend for more than fifteen years.

My mind accepted that she was suffering, that putting her to sleep was a kindness, but my heart agonized at letting go. This was our Bridget, the dog we grew up with as young newlyweds, the one who had gone everywhere, done everything with us...who still loved us best.

I sat beside her on the kitchen floor glancing anxiously at the clock, dreading every disappearing minute that hastened our appointment at the veterinary hospital. How could I possibly go through with it?

Very quietly a Voice inside me said, "You can't. Give your grief to Me." It was Jesus, the one Friend Who wasn't ever leaving me.

"Okay, Lord. That seems the right thing to do."

There, huddled over Bridget, crying into her graying muzzle, I offered my sorrow to Jesus. I opened every hurting, aching pore. As I did, I felt Him enter my suffering and absorb it until it became His pain, too. I no longer carried this heavy sadness alone. Straightening up I spoke gently. "Come on, old girl. It's time to go"...and something like courage stirred in my voice.

Are you grieving today? Try letting Jesus into your hurt. He will share it with you and make it bearable.

Precious Lord, truly You have borne our griefs and carried our sorrows.
— CAROL KNAPP

25	**THURSDAY**

And suddenly there came a sound from heaven as of a rushing mighty wind... —ACTS 2:2

The Walla Walla valley in Washington State, where I live, is famous for *chinooks*, warm, dry winds that blow down the slopes of our Blue Mountains. A chinook's temperature increases by about one degree for every one hundred eighty feet of descent. As it blows, it takes up moisture by evaporation. We've gone to bed with six to eight inches of snow outside our front door and awakened the next morning to bare ground! The first year we lived here, we went to a movie in thirty-degree weather. During the two-hour show, a chinook started to blow, and when we came out of the theater, the temperature had risen to sixty degrees!

My good friend Donna is a little like a chinook; she always knows how to warm me. When I was very disappointed because a class I was going to teach was cancelled or a retreat cost more money than we could afford, Donna reassured me that there would be other opportunities. When I moped because my college son chose not to come home one weekend, Donna reminded, "He loves you; he just needs his friends now." I spoke with Donna when my now-grown children showed no inclination to find a church home. "Give them time," she counseled. "They have to find their own way."

Donna seems to have a way of blowing a warm breath of hope on all the discouragements I encounter. In an extraordinary way, I hear

God speaking through her words of caring. It makes me think: *Do I do that for others?* The next time I walk down the street to visit a shut-in neighbor or that young mother on the next block, I'm going to say a quick prayer for God to be with me, through my words and my actions.

Father, let rushing warm winds of encouragement and love for others rush through me. —SHIRLEY POPE WAITE

26 FRIDAY
...He that is without sin among you, let him first cast a stone at her. —JOHN 8:7

At church camp when I was a teenager, an ugly rumor about two of our counselors quickly became the talk of the camp. The next day, at morning prayer, the minister read the story of the adulterous woman, in which Jesus told the crowd that any person who had no sin could cast the first stone. And one by one, those who had come to stone her to death walked away.

Then the minister passed around a bucket of stones and insisted that we each take one and carry it in our pocket throughout the remainder of camp. Any time we felt like criticizing someone else, or talking behind another's back or passing on an ugly rumor, we were to reach into the pocket, touch the stone and ask ourselves if we were without sin.

It's so easy to criticize others, but only God knows a person's heart. Would you try something with me? Today, let's each find a small stone to carry in our pocket or purse as a reminder that we are not to judge others.

Lord, prevent me from casting stones.
—MARILYN MORGAN HELLEBERG

| 27 | SATURDAY | FIRESIDE FRIEND |

These all...confessed that they were strangers and pilgrims on the earth. For those who say such things declare plainly that they seek a homeland.
—*HEBREWS 11:13–14 (New KJV)*

I have recently moved back east to a very urban part of the country. After twenty years of having lots of grass, shrubs and trees to enjoy (and take care of), I now live in an upstairs apartment, with no access to any yard or lawn. That is just one aspect of the change. I no longer have a home of my own; I left behind good friends and activities that nourished me. And trees and grass are scarce both where I live and where I work. At times I feel out of place!

This morning before I had my glasses on, I looked out of my kitchen window and saw a strange-shaped gray animal in my neighbor's backyard eating the crusts she puts out for the pigeons. Somehow it didn't look like a cat, and I ran for my glasses. It was an opossum! In the middle of a crowded city, a long way from any woods or open country.

As I watched the possum sneak another crust and retire to his corner, a scraggly thicket of trees behind the row of garages, I realized that the possum had the secret of being at home wherever he (or she) was. It had *made* a home in the crowded city and had learned to live on what was there. In fact it lives pretty well, because it had a rather stout figure!

I enjoyed seeing the possum this morning. And I'm going to put into practice the lesson it taught me: to take advantage of the many opportunities that are here in this metropolitan area for meeting new people and for finding activities that will sustain and refresh my spirit. If I'll get out and "scrounge," I can find myself at home here, or anywhere.

Dear Lord, help me remember that ultimately You are my home, and when I am at home with You, I can be at home anywhere. Thank You. —MARY RUTH HOWES

28	SUNDAY

...If thou canst believe, all things are possible...

—MARK 9:23

I shuffled through the hospital corridor one afternoon on my way to visit a friend who'd had spinal surgery. She wasn't healing well and there were doubts that she would ever walk on her own again.

I found her room empty and was informed she'd gone to physical therapy. As I waited, I noticed a slip of paper taped to her bedside table. It said:

Three times a day—
1. Yield yourself to the flow of God's power.
2. Picture yourself walking without aid.
3. Counter every negative with a positive.
4. Give thanks.

When she returned I asked her about the list. "That's my own prescription for getting well," she said, smiling. "It takes more than *physical* therapy, you know. It takes *spiritual* therapy, too." In no time she was home, walking without crutches.

Her comment reminds me how indelibly the mind, body and spirit are intertwined, how deeply they affect one another. Whether I'm trying to get well, or simply trying to stay well, I often recall her prescription. It's good medicine anytime.

Father, teach me to keep my spirit healthy with positive thoughts. —SUE MONK KIDD

29	MONDAY

Boast not thyself of tomorrow; for thou knowest not what a day may bring forth. —PROVERBS 27:1

The story is told of a time when the devil called a meeting of his imps to discuss some better method of recruiting souls for his kingdom of darkness.

"Tell the people God doesn't exist," one suggested.

"No," the devil replied. "Even I can see evidence of Him all about me."

"Promise them great wealth such as they won't know as Christians," another said.

The devil shook his head. "No good. They look forward to eternal riches."

"I know what to do," a third said. "Tell them that God exists and that they can count on eternal riches, but they don't have to worry about that today. Tomorrow will be plenty of time."

The entire clan of demons applauded that suggestion. "Perfect!" the devil exclaimed. "Tell them there is no hurry. Delay them long enough and we can surely get them."

My dictionary defines procrastination as the "act of putting off until another day or time." And procrastination is the devil's greatest tool. But my Bible warns, "Boast not thyself of tomorrow, for thou knowest not what a day may bring forth" (Proverbs 27:1). The things that I plan to do for Jesus—the acts of kindness, the words of love, the forgiveness of hurts—I must do *now*. Any delay may allow the evil one to cheat me out of the joy that is mine with my Lord today.

Guide my every day, Father, that it may be spent in Your presence. Amen.   —DRUE DUKE

Thank-You Notes to God

1

2

3

4

5

6

7

8

9

10

11

12

13

14

15

16	
17	
18	
19	
20	
21	
22	
23	
24	
25	
26	
27	
28	
29	

S	M	T	W	T	F	S
		1	2	3	4	5
6	7	8	9	10	11	12
13	14	15	16	17	18	19
20	21	22	23	24	25	26
27	28	29	30	31		

MARCH

BE A HOPER
Your Spiritual Pilgrimage

Faith is the substance of things hoped for...

—HEBREWS 11:1

March is boisterous, unpredictable.

Sunshine and sleet. Lion and lamb. But one thing is certain: March is full of hope. A crocus here. A snowdrop there. Maybe even a jonquil or two, all saying, "Don't give up hope. Spring is coming!"

So why not practice hope this month? Tell yourself that things are getting better. Tell other people they have what it takes to overcome difficulties.

Spread hope around like "a host of golden daffodils." You'll brighten a lot of lives. Including your own.

Tandem Power for March

1

A MIND-FULL OF JESUS

I sought the Lord, and he heard me, and delivered me from all my fears. —PSALM 34:4

Momentarily I am alone, lying on a narrow steel bed in a sterile white room at Community Hospital. I am a "one-day surgery" patient, and soon nurses will prepare me for the procedure. Though the surgery is relatively minor, I can't control my rising fear. I've never had surgery before. Other than the deliveries of our three children, I've never been a hospital patient. And if I boil my fear right down to the raw bones, it is this: I am afraid of needles. And general anesthetics. I know these are irrational fears, but at this minute, I feel on the brink of losing control because I am afraid. I long to hold my husband's hand but he is down the hall registering me.

To prepare for this moment, I studied several people in the Bible who steeled themselves against excruciating external pain with their unwavering internal strength. Stephen, who was stoned to death; Paul, who was beaten and left for dead; and especially Jesus, Who endured the nails being pounded into His hands. I think how they withstood suffering with seeming calmness, not because they were numb to the pain, but because they drew upon their internal peace and power that was stronger than their fear of the external circumstances.

That's what I intended to do. I would fill my mind with positive images that would crowd out all the fears. And I would concentrate on those images. Stephen. Paul. Jesus. Soon my husband Lynn returns, and then a nurse, and I am being wheeled down a long, empty hallway and into a bright cold room, and one nurse is holding my hand, and another is holding my arm for the needle, and I fill my mind with Jesus and somewhere far away I feel a slight prick...and then a fuzzy voice says, "It is all over."

If you face pain or fear this month, why don't you fill your mind with pictures of Jesus praying in Gethsemane or embracing little children or enduring physical hurts with spiritual strength? These images can ignite the power of peace God places within us to comfort us in times of need. He is there. We only need to focus on Him and respond to His presence. That is using Tandem Power!

Dear God, You equip me with Your presence. Please help me

learn to focus on Your presence in times of need by filling my mind with Jesus. —CAROL KUYKENDALL

I am the good shepherd... —*JOHN 10:11*

One of the built-in graces of parenthood, unappreciated by me at the time, I confess, was that it served as a greenhouse for the steady growth and flowering of my prayer life. There were fervent prayers for each child on that first walk to school unaccompanied, the first bicycle, the first car, in illness and emergency, in conflict and challenge.

The frantic prayers came when my son, nicknamed Koko, was well into his teens. Koko had stated his creed early on: "I want to be Daniel Boone and nobody will let me," but he went right on trying. By the time he could afford his own car, distances, curfews and penalties were as naught when he went adventuring. Meanwhile I, a single parent, sat at home watching the clock, listening for the phone and praying myself into a panic.

Finally I sought help from the wise pastor at our church, himself a father and grandfather. "He's so young to be all alone out there," I cried. He suggested that daily and in times of stress I repeat the Twenty-third Psalm, inserting my son's name: "The Lord is *Koko's* shepherd...he leadeth *Koko* beside the still waters...surely goodness and mercy shall follow *Koko* all the days of his life...."

It didn't work instant miracles in my son's conduct of life—I was still repeating it when he enlisted in the service and was sent to Lebanon—but it strengthened me to know he was not "all alone out there." Today "Koko" is George, a father himself, and a pillar in his community, but I still pray the Twenty-third Psalm Koko-fashion for those I'm troubled about.

If you have stragglers or strays on your prayer list, see if it will not bless you both to invoke the Good Shepherd to lead them back to the fold.

Thank You, Lord, for Your Shepherd's heart.
—ELAINE ST. JOHNS

MARCH 1988

| 3 | THURSDAY |

When anxiety was great within me, your consolation brought joy to my soul. —PSALM 94:19 (NIV)

I've noticed that when I'm too busy to spend time with God, I get very tired. And there's a reason: My own energy isn't enough to get me through the day.

A few weeks ago my car wouldn't start. Tom Yeager, my mechanic, couldn't find anything wrong. The battery was new, and all parts were in good shape. "Then why did my battery run down?" I asked.

"Maybe you're not giving it a chance to store up extra energy," Tom suggested. "Cold weather puts a lot of stress on an engine. Try letting it run at least ten minutes before you drive."

Ten minutes is a long time to sit when you're in a hurry to go somewhere. Nevertheless, I took Tom's advice and my car now starts up beautifully.

But it made a difference in my life, because in many ways I was like that battery running out of energy. I was trying to do too much— all by myself. Well, suddenly I had the gift of ten minutes every morning, and I decided to spend them with God—sitting there in the car, with no phone to interrupt, no one else present, no things for me to do. Sometimes I pray, sometimes I share my thoughts and feelings about the things that concern me, and sometimes I just enjoy His presence. It gives me the extra spiritual energy I need to get through the day.

Lord, help me to use the unexpected moments of quiet or waiting in my day to replenish my spiritual reserves.

—PHYLLIS HOBE

| 4 | FRIDAY |

…The Lord shall be thine everlasting light…

—ISAIAH 60:20

Perhaps you'll recall that last year I wrote about a cat who slept in the window of a bookshop that I pass every evening after work. The Orange Cat became a little grace note at the end of each day. I looked forward to seeing what book he had chosen to bed down on or what ridiculous sleeping posture he had assumed.

Then came the time when the Orange Cat was not there. Day after day I looked for him, but he did not appear. Often I was tempted to ask about him, but I'd stop, for I was in a period of my life when things were going wrong; I was fearful of more bad news. Then, on the afternoon of New Year's Eve, just when I'd decided that I *had* to know about him, just when I most needed some good augury, there the Orange Cat was, asleep in the pale winter sunlight, sublimely supine.

This past winter I went into the shop for a book. I hadn't seen the Orange Cat for some time and so I asked a clerk where he was.

"Who, Mitchell Kennerley? He's probably in the back somewhere."

In a back room, a man sat working at a desk whose top was crowded with a telephone, a pile of books and, stretched out directly under the bright light of a desk lamp, my Orange Cat.

"How does he decide where he's going to sleep?" I asked the man.

"Oh," he said, "wherever he can be warm. Sometimes it's the sun in the window, sometimes under the light from this lamp."

That sounded logical enough. Until I happened to mention it to a friend who said, "How do you know that it's the warmth and not the light that attracts your Orange Cat?"

"That's rather obvious. After all, most of the time when I see him his eyes are shut. Why would he need the light?"

"Maybe he's like us humans," my friend replied, a bit grandly I thought. "A lot of us close our eyes to the Light, but we seek It anyway."

It seems that the Orange Cat is always giving me something to think about.

Jesus, I know that You are the Light of the world, and I do seek You. —VAN VARNER

| 5 | SATURDAY |

...And a little child shall lead them. —ISAIAH 11:6

"Mommy, let's walk to the park," four-year-old Andrew begged that first warm day after a long Wisconsin winter. I wasn't really up for it, but Andrew persuaded me to abandon chores in favor of Mother Nature. He scampered out the door—and I ran after him.

"Let's climb that hill!" he squealed.

I stalled. "There are too many tall weeds."

"There's a path!"

At the top he turned to run down. Before I could caution him to slow down he'd fallen face down, then rolled the length of the hill. I expected tears and loud wails.

"Hey Jill! I went up to get a pail of water and I fell down and broke my crown!" His laughter was contagious.

The path led into the woods. Andrew stopped cold. "Gretel, I think we're lost. Did you bring any bread crumbs to drop on the path? What if the wicked witch gets us?"

"Oh, Hansel, the birds ate all the bread crumbs. You'll have to take care of that witch if we meet her."

We came to the footbridge that spanned the creek. Andrew scampered down the bank underneath the bridge. "Mommy, walk across the bridge."

I obeyed, wondering what he was up to now. Then a wee voice trying to sound mean and ornery shouted, "Who's that tramping on my bridge?"

I followed my cue. "It's just the littlest billy goat gruff. Don't eat me up!"

Walking home, the late afternoon shadows were taller than we were. Andrew put his little hand in mine and said out loud, "I love you, Mommy!"

Today, why don't you create some magic with a little friend and discover God's beautiful springtime world?

Lord, thank You for little children who can talk us into spring-time walks…even when we think we "don't have time."

—PATRICIA LORENZ

 6 SUNDAY   **FIRESIDE FRIEND**
…And there went with him a band of men, whose hearts God had touched.   —I SAMUEL 10:26

One Sunday while waiting to serve communion, I sat in the front pew. From there I noticed how dry and lifeless the wood had become on the minister's podium, except for two areas that looked as if they had been polished and buffed. I was curious. What could account for their smooth glow?

When the minister began to speak, it became clear. He gently curled his hands over the edges of the podium, exactly where the podium was glossy and bright. Evidently the oil from his fingertips, rubbing the edges of the podium Sunday after Sunday, had polished the wood to a deep satiny shine over the years.

I discover I am like that podium. Sometimes I feel dull and lifeless. And it is only when and where I allow God to curl His hands over the edges of my existence that I am transformed. Patiently and repeatedly the Creator offers His hand...because He knows that His touch will bring life to the lifeless.

Lord, I need Your touch to bring out the shine and luster of my life today. —TERRY HELWIG

 7 MONDAY
To every thing there is...a time to embrace...
—*ECCLESIASTES 3:1,5*

It was dusk and the snow falling outside the window cast a blue glow into the hospital room. I sat slouched in the corner chair listening to my father's labored breathing as he struggled against terminal cancer. As a physician I am forced, on occasion, to face death with one of my patients. But clinical detachment was impossible now—Dad had asked that I be involved in his care.

He knew there was no hope of recovery. We talked for hours, honest discussions that brought us closer together. As we prayed together and he shared his strength with me, the thought of losing him became even more difficult to bear.

You are not the first son to lose a father, I told myself as I walked down the hall to the elevator.

"Sorry about your dad," one of the hospital nurses murmured as I walked by.

I barely knew this nurse. She had always seemed quite shy.

"Thanks," I mumbled. "I'm sorry too."

Abruptly she turned, then walked to where I was leaning against the wall. "You really look like you need a hug," she said gently.

My arms hung at my sides as her tight squeeze forced warmth

and life back inside me. The elevator doors suddenly opened. We both took a few steps back. She smiled, nodded in satisfaction, turned and went back to caring for the other sick in her world.

I straightened my shoulders, ready to face my other patients with newfound strength.

Thank You, dear Lord, for Your healing, and those who are a part of it. Use me also. —SCOTT HARRISON

| 8 | TUESDAY |

But thou, when thou prayest, enter into thy closet…
—*MATTHEW 6:6*

We haven't told anybody yet, although the clues should be fairly obvious. Carol drinks three glasses of milk a day, she's bought a lot of vitamins high in calcium and she's taken to banana milkshakes (something recommended in one of the books she's read). She gets pretty tired in the morning, but goes window shopping in the afternoon for dresses at a maternity store. Privately we've speculated on names and godparents and whether it will be a boy or a girl. Short of indulging in pickles and ice cream, we've done everything that's said of expectant parents.

In a month or two the news will be out and Carol's friends will give her a shower and our parents will offer sound advice. We'll buy a crib and a carriage and a changing table and we'll paint the extra bedroom a different color—maybe with stars and a moon and a cow jumping over it. But for now it's our secret.

"But thou, when thou prayest, enter into thy closet, and when thou hast shut thy door, pray to thy Father which is in secret…." In saying this Jesus showed His understanding of the creative power of secrecy. Hopes and dreams in their infancy need quiet nurturing—not a lot of talk. I think of Carol and me, preparing for this big step in our lives, encouraging each other with a squeezed hand at a party, a knowing smile and a reassuring prayer. Maybe the source of the reassurance is that the best secrets held between two Christians are automatically shared with a third.

Or perhaps in this case, I should say a fourth.

Lord, I pray that the secrets in my heart be part of Your will.
—RICK HAMLIN

9 | WEDNESDAY

...Inasmuch as ye did it not to one of the least of these, ye did it not to me. —MATTHEW 25:45

I've always felt unsure about giving money to beggars on the street. Sometimes, averting my eyes, I ask myself, *Would I just be financing his purchase of liquor?* Sometimes, thrusting money into the hands of a plaintive young man, I lecture myself, *A Christian should be charitable.* I'm never sure that I am doing the right thing.

Last week as a friend and I were walking to our car on a busy urban street we were stopped by a young woman. "Please sir, madam. Can you give me some money? I need to buy milk for my children." *Oh, dear,* I thought. *Is she telling the truth? Her eyes look funny. Is she on drugs? Would money help her or hurt her?* My indecision immobilized me. But my friend had already taken out his wallet and removed several dollars. "Here," he said. "Buy the milk...and some meat for yourself. God bless you."

"How do you know she won't spend that money on drugs?" I asked my friend as I followed him to the car.

"I don't," he said. "Only God does. The issue is not what *she* does with the money—it's what *I* do with *mine.*"

I've thought a lot about my friend's words. And I've started stuffing a few small bills and some change into my coat pockets whenever I go out. *It's what I do with mine.*

I don't know if my little gifts will save any souls. That's God's business. But they just might help save mine.

Today, Jesus, I will look for You in my brother's eyes.
—MARILYN MOORE JENSEN

10 | THURSDAY   FIRESIDE FRIEND

Let your light so shine before men, that they may see your good works, and glorify your Father which is in heaven. —MATTHEW 5:16

"Oh, you're such a saint!" How my mother dreaded hearing those words. Yet hear them she did as soon as anyone found out that she was a foster parent who had cared for over forty children, many of them handicapped. "I'm no saint," she'd protest to me in private. I'd nod in agreement; she was a normal mother to me, occasionally losing her patience, often a caring and supportive friend.

One day someone told me the story of a little boy who was asked in Sunday school to define a saint. The little boy thought hard, then remembered the stained glass windows in the sanctuary, the ones depicting various saints. "A saint," he answered, "is a person the light shines through!"

That definition was true of my mother, and it can be true of each one of us. We can let God's light shine through us. Today, perhaps you can take the time to talk with the stranger in the check-out line, the one who reveals that she and her husband have just moved to town. Or perhaps you'll find a way to be patient when a child asks "Why?" for the umpteenth time. I'm going to find a way to let my faith shine, and I know you will, too.

Father, Your light can change the world, if we just share what You've given us. —TAMMY RIDER

| 11 | FRIDAY
A wise man will hear, and will increase learning; and a man of understanding shall attain unto wise counsels.
—PROVERBS 1:5

One of my relatives, Marge, is a non-stop talker who always greets us with a barrage of trivia when we visit. For example, she might announce that on Tuesday her Meals on Wheels arrived late, and the mashed potatoes were cold. That would lead to her aunt who always served mashed potatoes cold and only her husband ate them—because he got them cold in the Army. Which in turn reminds her that Uncle Bob wouldn't eat potatoes mashed, insisting they be home-fried. You get the idea: she can go on and on....

As she talks, I nod my head, and sometimes I just nod off. Once, I woke up to hear her going over our bank statement with my wife Ginny. Marge had worked in the actuarial section of a major life insurance company and is a whiz at figures.

"Maybe you could straighten out our checkbook," I ventured.

"It's a mess," Ginny added. "Nothing seems to balance."

Marge rose to the challenge and quickly found the problem—a

deposit that had been entered twice. She spent the next hour carefully showing us a more efficient way of keeping accurate records.

And I didn't know this: But Marge is an expert in other essential areas, too. On subsequent visits, she helped us interpret an insurance policy that we found needed updating. One day we talked a little about wills and trusts. And with tax time approaching, maybe Marge could answer a question or two for me....

Father, show me the joys—and rewards—of moving beyond snap judgments to discovering the real gifts others can bring us. —SAM JUSTICE

Spirit Lifter
BELIEF, HOPE, AND LOVE:
THE ESSENTIAL THREE
All things are possible to him who believes; they are less difficult to him who hopes; they are easy to him who loves; and they are simple to anyone who does all three.
—BROTHER LAWRENCE

---

12 SATURDAY
Who satisfieth thy mouth with good things; so that thy youth is renewed like the eagle's. —PSALM 103:5

One month after I graduated from college I was seriously hurt in an industrial accident. I awoke in a hospital bed to find my lifeless right arm suspended above my head in traction and the prognosis listed as "probable amputation." My mind instantly translated that into surgery performed. Furthermore, I figured no one would want a one-armed journalist, so I gave up my career hopes in despair.

I should have waited on the Lord. First of all, with Jesus, the "probable" became "unnecessary." My right arm is still quite crooked, but I can punch out fifty-five words per minute. Secondly, before I learned that things might work out okay, I finally did give my fear over to Jesus and accept the possibilities. When I did that, I learned the wonderful lesson that with faith, a life with one arm could be fantastic.

Are you facing some fearful problem? May I suggest you take Isaiah's advice and wait on the Lord. Just hang on and give Him a little more time. He will restore your strength and give you eagle's wings to soar above any trouble.

Lord, give me the patience to wait for my wings.
—ERIC FELLMAN

---

13 SUNDAY
Train up a child in the way he should go: and when he is old, he will not depart from it. —PROVERBS 22:6

As I sat on a park bench to rest for a few minutes, I caught sight of a small boy on a bicycle coming along the path. As he passed in front of me, he hit a stone, and the bicycle wobbled from side to side. He would have tumbled over, but the two small wheels at the side of his rear wheel kept his bicycle from falling. As I watched him go on his way, upright and secure, I recalled the name of those balance aids: training wheels.

The day was balmy, so I continued to sit on the bench and think about what made *me* keep upright and secure. What were the two "training wheels" in my life that had helped me keep my balance over these many years?

One was my church. The Bible says, "Train a child in the way he should go," and I never did depart from its teachings. Caring Christians were there to help guide me, to give me balance.

The other "training wheel" was my family. I've learned so much from them—from my parents, my wife, my children—and their love has given my life a sense of equilibrium and harmony.

Balance, training, security—these words raced around in my mind as I got up and headed for home.

God, as I continue down life's path, provide me with balance and wisdom so that I can do Your will. —WALTER HARTER

14 MONDAY
Trust in the Lord for ever, for the Lord God is an ever-lasting rock. —ISAIAH 26:4 (RSV)

We were loading the airplane for the flight home after spending an idyllic weekend with friends at their remote chalet in the Alaskan bush. I kept glancing back at the cabin set among the trees, staunchly shouldering five feet of snow. *A person could hide away from life's problems in a place like that,* I thought. Since our arrival two days earlier I hadn't worried once about our struggling business. I had even managed to forget the bare pantry shelves at home. Now I was flying back to grim reality. No wonder I was reluctant to leave.

Skis bounced along the makeshift runway lifting us effortlessly into blue sky. Below us frozen rivers glistened in the sun. Forests of dark spruce spread across boundless stretches of windblown snow. Occasionally the blurred shape of a moose emerged from the trees. A miniature sled dog team steadily wove a trail through a winding mountain pass.

Looming in the distance, overseeing all this vast domain, towered Mt. McKinley or Denali, the "Great One." It made me think of God and His greatness. Names like Rock...Shield...Fortress...Stronghold marched through my mind. My worries seemed to shrink beneath the gaze of the immense mountain with the broad sweep of wilderness sprawling at its feet.

I thought how insurmountable my problems appear to me, on the ground, and how temporary they must look to God Who sees my life from eternity's heights. Like Denali, God is a Rock rising high above His vast creation...but unlike Denali, our Great One is alive and endures evermore!

God, You are the solid Rock Who overshadows and outlasts life's every rocky twist. —CAROL KNAPP

Family Time

15 DREAM YOUR DREAMS
All things are possible to the believer. —MARK 9:23

As families go, ours was quite normal. Floyd and I worked five days a week, and our daughter was in college. Each day we traveled the same streets, shopped in the same stores, ate by the same schedule. At night we watched the same television programs and went to bed right after the late news.

If you had asked us, we would have said, "We have a comfortable life." But in retrospect, we were dull and sterile in our routines. Rip Van Winkle had nothing on us except our eyes had been open during those first twenty years of our marriage; his had been closed during his twenty years of sleep. But the results were pretty much the same.

Then something happened! A speaker and a book inspired us to struggle out of our comfortable but boring ruts. We heard it loud and clear: You're never too old to dream of new and better things. And with that, the wisdom writer's words took on new meaning, "Where there is no vision, the people perish" (Proverbs 29:18). It was then that we saw that this vision could help us to set reasonable goals and to come alive as Christians.

We began to put our dreams—our goals—into writing. Our index card affirmations became a regular part of our lives—in my purse and in Floyd's shirt pocket. Our mood was set each day by the card that read, "This is the day which the Lord hath made; let us rejoice and be glad in it" (Psalm 118:24, RSV). These written words, repeated every morning, revolutionized our attitudes and our days.

Each of us carried cards with positive affirmations. I remember one of Floyd's. Because he was introverted and inclined to be critical, he wrote, "I am open and friendly and always see the good in others." To offset my tendency to worry and be anxious, one of mine read, "I am a positive person who knows that everything works out for my good." Then each of us carried a card that read, "We are a warm and loving family that trusts and builds up each other."

Repeated several times a day, our dream-goals began to take shape. This new discovery wasn't a panacea, and it wasn't a magic formula for getting everything we wanted. But over the years we've begun to learn a little about the truth expressed in Proverbs—we are what we think about (23:7). We move toward, *we become*, our dreams and our goals simply because that's the way the Lord made us.

We know that 1988 can be the best year of your lives if you will dream together as persons and as a family. Dream spiritual dreams, set personal goals, picture exciting things happening. Write them down, repeat them several times a day—and *believe*. Picture yourself living those dreams, and once a month on "family night" share openly with each other what God has been teaching you.

Help us, Lord, to dream Your dreams for us.
                                        —HARRIETT AND FLOYD THATCHER

| 16 | WEDNESDAY |

...What things soever ye desire, when ye pray, believe that ye receive them, and ye shall have them.
                                        —MARK 11:24

Everything seemed to go wrong this morning. Trying to unclog a tube of toothpaste, I squirted a glob right into my eye, there was no hot water when I jumped in the shower and, to top it off, I'd run out of shampoo and so resorted to a bar of soap. Well, that was my morning! No wonder by the time I sat down to talk to the Lord, the day already seemed out of control. And that's exactly how my prayer seemed to go. Out of control in ten different directions.

Usually I use the "ACTS" formula for prayer: A-doration; C-onfession; T-hanksgiving; S-upplication. But wouldn't you know it...today my mind kept wandering off. The reality of middle age. The pain in my eye. The lack of consideration that causes others to use up the hot water. "Drats," I scolded myself. "Prayer failure. One more thing wrong with the morning." Then I remembered what our minister said about wandering prayers.

"Worry not," he advised. "Simply embrace every wandering thought into your prayer. A person flashes into your mind? Pray for him. What to fix for dinner? Pray for the preparation time. A tempting pair of shoes on sale? Turn the material desires of your heart over to God. Turn interrupting thoughts into parts of your prayer...and then get back on track."

It worked for me this morning, and soon afterward the day looked better. Through my one good eye.

Father, You know my every flaw and love me still and lift me up. Thank You.   —CAROL KUYKENDALL

17 THURSDAY
Oh that men would praise the Lord for his goodness,
and for his wonderful works to the children of men!
—*PSALM 107:8*

Every March 17, I sit down and read Psalm 107.

Long ago, when a writer-friend of mine, Paul Gallico, was leaving for Ireland to research a biography of St. Patrick, I complained to him, "You can't have a real saint without miracles. Patrick has been stripped down to super-missionary status—no fire duel at Tara because he didn't do magic, no charming the snakes off the Emerald Isle because there weren't any there." The final indignity to me, with great-grandmothers named O'Mahoney and Taggart, was that he wasn't even Irish. "So what's to write about?" I demanded. "A Roman Briton named Magonus Sucatus Patricus who converted a pagan nation to Christianity in the fifth century. Period."

In defense of Patrick, Paul sent me back snippets from his research: "It's true that he himself laid no claim to miracles, but he had no doubt that he received messages from his Creator—dreams, visions, voices." In response to which, after being kidnapped from Britain at sixteen and enslaved by Irish raiders, he escaped at twenty-two, roamed penniless through Italy and France, became a priest at Auxerre, went home to Britain, and at forty-nine returned somewhat reluctantly to Ireland to face his great mission. "The question is," Paul wrote, "which was the miracle? That he got messages—which I suspect we all do one way or another—or that he steadfastly obeyed them?"

I had to think about that.

Later he wrote: "Do you realize that one thousand five hundred years ago Patrick, in response to his visions, was as modern as tomorrow? He bought and freed slaves as he Christianized. He also advocated mass education and literacy, previously restricted. He introduced the written Gospels, book culture and the Latin alphabet, and insisted that his converts learn and teach. Just in time, too, for when the Dark Ages engulfed Western Europe it was mainly Patrick's converts beyond the Irish Sea who kept the flame of Christianity and culture alight.

"You've been looking in the wrong direction for miracles, my girl," he concluded kindly. "Love, (and read Psalm 107)."

Lord, let me this day look in the right direction, and give thanks that Your miracles abound. —ELAINE ST. JOHNS

| 18 | FRIDAY |

I will say of the Lord, He is my refuge…in him will I trust. —PSALM 91:2

Sam was my best dog, ever. A field trial dog who found birds and pointed them with contagious enthusiasm, Sam taught me the joy of becoming part of nature. If his point said a bird was hiding in a clump of bushes, it was there. He was much more than a bird dog, though. Often we'd share together lazy lunches in an abandoned apple orchard, and the snooze that followed.

Late one afternoon, Sam and I became separated. Neither of us was familiar with the area. I called and whistled. No sign of Sam. I had to get back to town for an important appointment. But how could I leave Sam? If he finally came back and I wasn't there, would I lose him for good?

Then I remembered a trick an old dog trainer had passed on. I unbuttoned my jacket, removed my shirt and laid it on the ground under the branches of a small bush.

I worried all night. But when I returned the next morning, there was Sam curled up with his nose under the sleeve of my shirt. He looked up and wagged his tail. "Where've you been, friend?" his eyes seemed to say. "I've been waiting for you all night. But I knew you'd come back."

Later I wondered. When I get lost, do I have the trust to look for some part of God's word and curl up in it? To wait patiently, knowing that my Friend will find me if I just have faith in Him?

Father, give me the simple faith to know that, even when I feel lost, You are always there, seeking me. —SCOTT HARRISON

19 SATURDAY   **FIRESIDE FRIEND**

...The Lord gave, and the Lord hath taken away; blessed be the name of the Lord.   —*JOB 1:21*

My friend Mercy Parkhill came over one sunlit morning not long after my father's death, bringing a coffee cake, and, I expected, her condolences. Instead, as I brewed a pot of coffee, she sat at my kitchen table and said, "Well, Gail, now is the time to count your blessings."

I turned and stared. *Count my blessings? Dad had just died!*

She looked straight at me. "I know it sounds odd," she said. "But just think about it."

Later, I took my wise friend's advice—I sat down with a pencil and paper and tried to list good things that had come out of Dad's life. The honesty that made him so respected in our community. The encouragement he gave us to seek and value education. The support he always gave when I needed it. His being firm when we were wrong, too. As I worked on my list, sorrow began to dwindle to its proper size.

Mercy's suggestion has become a useful tool for other kinds of disappointment, too. When I have a fight with my kids, I make myself think of the love and laughter they've brought into my life. When a friend forgets my birthday, I try to remember the many times she has been there to give me support.

Is there some sorrow or disappointment that seems to be lingering in your life? Maybe, like me, you need to do a "silver-lining" search. I know it sounds odd. But just think about it.

Dear Father, it is hard to let go of my problems, but here are some reasons I feel grateful:

1. _____

2. _____

3. _____

—GAIL BROOK BURKET

20 SUNDAY

...Choose this day whom you will serve...but as for me and my house, we will serve the Lord.

—*JOSHUA 24:15 (RSV)*

For several years now, I've tried unsuccessfully to grow grass in inhospitable spots. "You can't have as many trees as you've got," a wise old neighbor told me, "and have grass, too. Take your choice: trees or grass." I'm stubborn, and also greedy; I wanted both.

So I called in an expert, a man whose specialty is doctoring sick lawns. I paid him to tell me what my neighbor had given for free. "Take your choice," he counseled, "trees or grass." So, resignedly, I've started wheelbarrowing myrtle from the woods to use as ground cover for the bald places under trees. It won't win any *House and Garden* prizes, but it beats cutting down beautiful air-cleaning, sun-cooling, peace-giving trees.

Choosing between a sunlit, grassy yard and a less green, shady one suggests a spiritual parallel to me. Christ told His disciples that they could not serve two masters, and what was true then is true today. We all have to choose between light and darkness, else when we come to the end and God, like a shepherd, will separate the sheep from the goats (Matthew 25:32), we could learn we have made a mistake of eternal proportions.

So spring, a season of resurrections, is a good time for reassessing our lives, a good time for review and recommitment, a good time for putting our houses in order—spiritual and otherwise.

Send Your light, Lord, Your blessed Gospel light.

—FRED BAUER

| 21 | MONDAY
Jesus saith…Feed my sheep. —JOHN 21:17

Monday. From the window I notice a small brown wren huddled on the grass beneath the bird feeder, struggling to fly. The frigid wind bends the branches of the crabapple tree. Fifteen minutes pass. He cannot seem to find the strength. Is he sick? Too young? Too weak? It seems sad. But I suppose there is little I can do for him.

Suddenly my attention is drawn to another wren that flies to the feeder. I am astonished as she begins to toss seed with her beak from the ledge of the feeder down to the grass below. It falls like kernels of grace upon the little bird, satisfying his hunger. The next time I pass the window he's gone.

Tuesday. I watch the wrens pecking at the feeder, thinking of the lesson they have taught me. We are put here not only to partake, but to feed the hungers of those around us. I look at the feeder. *Drop seed*, God whispers. *Drop seed.*

Lord, teach me to see life as a community of sharing, and help me to be an active participant. —SUE MONK KIDD

22 TUESDAY
Take us the foxes, the little foxes, that spoil the vines: for our vines have tender grapes.

—SONG OF SOLOMON 2:15

Fifty feet from our front door is my favorite hazelnut tree. Last spring, while other trees were bursting with buds, it displayed only a few dispirited sprigs of green. In early summer, I asked my uncle to come look at the tree and to give me some advice. Even though the hazelnut was almost three feet in diameter and over one hundred fifty feet high, it stood gray and desolate amidst the leafy grandeur of its neighbors.

My uncle said, "You don't need to cut down the tree; you need to cut down these bushes," pointing to some plantings around the base of the tree.

"How can these little bushes bother the tree?" I asked.

"You cut them down, and pull out the roots, and I guarantee the tree will be okay," he replied. "They are sapping its strength."

Uncle Jack was right. That day I pulled out the bushes. By the end of the summer almost every branch of the hazelnut had healthy leaves and that fall we had a bumper crop of nuts.

Now when I look at that tree, I'm reminded of how little things can tear at us and sap our strength. Perhaps you've found, as I have, that blaming yourself over and over for a simple mistake prevents you from moving on to more important things. Perhaps right now a small resentment is taking a lot of your time and energy. Perhaps you need to forgive yourself or someone else today so that you can move on to the fullness that God has promised.

Lord, reveal to each one of us the small things in our lives that prevent us from blossoming forth as You have planned.

—ERIC FELLMAN

23 WEDNESDAY
*...Ye shall find a colt tied, whereon never man sat....the
Lord hath need of him...* —MARK 11:2-3

Often I study my Bible and get a fresh new insight into a passage I
have read many times before. Such was my experience this morning.
As I read the above Scripture, one phrase leaped out at me: "whereon
never man sat."

I have seen enough Western movies and read enough books on
animals to know that breaking a horse can be a tedious job. The animal who has never been ridden will buck and pitch and make every
effort to throw a person from its back. Yet this unbroken colt was
submissive and accepted the Master with no struggle when the Lord
had need of him.

How wildly I struggle sometimes when my Lord has need of me!
Too busy, I argue when asked to serve on a committee at church. *I
have no talent for that*, when needed to take charge of a program. Or
I don't know how to do it. Get someone younger is always a good out. Or *I
did it last time, it's someone else's turn.* Or...

On and on I go like the stubborn animals that refuse to be broken.
Why can't I humbly submit to Him and let Him use me as He needs?

Surely, if I try hard, I can do that...just for *this* day!

*Forgive my stubbornness, Lord, and help me to overcome my
rebellious nature. Amen.* —DRUE DUKE

24 THURSDAY **FIRESIDE FRIEND**
*The grass withereth, the flower fadeth: but the word of
our God shall stand for ever.* —ISAIAH 40:8

Most of my time these past two weeks before Easter has been spent
weeping. I find myself saying, "Come on, Mary Jane, be a big girl," only
to shed more tears. Then think, when someone you love is suffering,
that is reason enough to cry.

There are many kinds of grief, and I am weeping for my mother.
Today she is entering a facility for the aged, her spark and keen enthusiasm for life greatly diminished. And, while she has reluctantly accepted her circumstances, I have not—and so I weep, the way Jesus

must have wept out of love for Mary and Martha when they sorrowed after the death of their brother Lazarus.

I have decided the time for being a big girl will come later, when my tears have served their intended purpose of healing; then I, too, will reluctantly accept Mother's circumstances and I can get on with loving her as I have in the past—with joy.

If you are weeping for a loved one today, remember with me for a moment a greater truth than our troubles and sorrows: that Easter brings with it no promise to remove life's pain and suffering, but it does bring the promise of life eternal.

Father, help me to live this day with renewed hope in the blessed assurance of Your great love and Christ's victory on the cross. —MARY JANE MEYER

 FRIDAY

And he went a little farther, and fell on his face, and prayed, saying, O my Father, if it be possible, let this cup pass from me: nevertheless not as I will, but as thou wilt. —MATTHEW 26:39

The day dawned with another month of Milwaukee's blustery cold weather ahead. I was out of wood for the woodburner. I'd never split logs or used a chain saw before, but we certainly needed the wood. Could I do it?

I was afraid to use the heavy, sharp equipment. Finally I heaved the heavy ax down over my head and slammed it into one log after another on the chopping block. Most times I missed the log completely. My shoulders ached, my hands shook. But two hours later there was a pile of wood ready to be cut to sixteen-inch lengths with the chain saw.

Terrified that I would cut through the electric cord or myself, I started the saw. Sawdust blew everywhere…on my neck, in my face. I worked on, sweating, aching. A blister developed on my thumb and the pain in my lower back brought me to tears.

Oh God, where are You?

Several hours later, the wood pile was restocked…and I'd learned something more valuable than how to work a chain saw. I'd learned that with determination and inspiration we can do anything. Anything! Christ on the Cross gave us all the inspiration we need.

Is there something in your life that you're afraid to attempt because you don't think you can? In his classic *The Conquest of Fear*, the writer Basil King says:

"Be bold and mighty forces will come to your aid."

Lord, give me the courage to try new things. Stick with me when I'm discouraged. And thank You for the inspiration of the Cross. —PATRICIA LORENZ

Spirit Lifter

Our Lord has written the promise of the Resurrection, not in books alone, but in every leaf in springtime.
—MARTIN LUTHER

---

26 SATURDAY
[Charity] doth not behave itself unseemly, seeketh not her own, is not easily provoked, thinketh no evil.
—*I CORINTHIANS 13:5*

We have a Japanese "daughter," whom we first met when we hosted her and a classmate during a student exchange program. Later we were able to visit Sayuri and her family in Kamakura, Japan.

Our guidebook had told us that the Japanese are a very correct, proper people and offense is easily taken. So we were a little surprised when the family said good-bye with such emotion. Sayuri shed tears and pointed to her watch, which she kept set at Walla Walla time.

Our surprise continued when we received the next letter from Sayuri. She ended with these words, "Can I write 'love'? Is it rudeness? But, I love you."

Yes, Sayuri, you may write *love* any time you want. Love is never rudeness. In fact, many translations of I Corinthians 13 state, "Love... is not rude...." Love transcends all cultures, races, nationalities and social status.

We love you too, dear Sayuri, our Japanese "daughter"!

Dear Father, thank You for loving us, and teaching us to love one another, for You are Love. —SHIRLEY POPE WAITE

EVERYDAY EMBLEMS OF HOLY WEEK
The Wonder of Easter

Every Bible reader knows that Jesus used objects from everyday life to illustrate His parables. A mustard seed. A needle. A lost coin. Through ordinary objects, His marvelous insights were made clear and vivid to all His hearers—even children.

In the pages that follow, Linda Ching Sledge recreates some of the special events of Holy Week through ordinary objects. Simple things she discovers around her home remind her of Jesus and His final days on earth, from His entrance into Jerusalem to His triumph over the grave: A rock. A coin. A tree. A table. A cup. A wooden beam. A curtain. A pinch of spice.

This Holy Week look for traces of God in other homely places. Search for things that remind you of the man from Nazareth, the humble carpenter into Whose hands God put the fate of the world.

Open your eyes—and let the everyday wonder of Easter come through. —THE EDITORS

DAY ONE—ROCK OF AGES

27 PALM SUNDAY

And when he drew near and saw the city he wept over it, saying, "Would that even today you knew the things that make for peace! But now they are hid from your eyes." —LUKE 19:41–42 (RSV)

I keep a stone from Germany to remind me of a trip I took with my husband seventeen years ago. It came from a ruined castle where stones from the shattered turrets were left in jagged piles exactly as they had fallen. Sometimes when I look at this fragment of lost grandeur, I think of

Jerusalem as that great city must have seemed two thousand years ago.

Rich, impregnable and proud, the citadel of the Israelites sprawled self-righteously upon a range of mountains. Its kings had built its stone walls high and thick enough to repel the most persistent invaders. Behind its massive gates, David's temple and the palace of Herod reached up into the clouds. This was the brilliant city to which Jesus came to die.

The miracles He had performed in the villages had made Him famous. Now the news spread through the city like fire: The Messiah was coming.

While He was yet far off, they saw Him! Mounted on a donkey, He was leading a great procession. The crowd surged out the gates to greet Him. They spread their garments on the road outside the city and waved green boughs in welcome. They sang and chanted His praises: "Blessed is the King Who comes in the name of the Lord!"

Christ knew the triumph of that moment would soon turn to tragedy. In thirty years, Jerusalem would fall to the Roman legions, who would smash its Temple and towers to rubble. Lifting up His voice, He mourned the fate of the fickle people who would welcome Him as King. He mourned the destruction of the proud city that would reject Him, the cornerstone of their salvation.

"And they will not leave one stone upon another in you," He lamented, "because you did not know the time of your visitation."

Thus weeping for Jerusalem, Christ passed among the cheering crowds and entered the mighty city.

Man of sorrows, my rock and my salvation. The road is smooth, the path made straight. I lay my passions and my pride before You. —LINDA CHING SLEDGE

DAY TWO—HIDDEN TREASURE

28 MONDAY

And Jesus entered the temple...and overturned the tables of the moneychangers and the seats of those who were selling doves. —MATTHEW 21:12 (NAS)

We bought an old table at a rummage sale when a church moved its offices. It cost us only ten dollars, so we treated it casually, cluttered it with

junk, even considered throwing it out. We preferred our other, more mod-ern tables.

Twelve years after we bought it, a friend came over for dinner and pronounced the old table a valuable antique. It was rare, handsome, turn-of-the-century "mission furniture," she said, and worth more than all the furniture we owned combined.

Long ago there were tables in the Temple in Jerusalem, too....

The courts of the Temple in Jerusalem were crowded with tables heaped with gold and silver, the tawdry treasure of the money-changers. The one table of true worth—the huge square central altar on which sacrifices were offered and an eternal flame burned—was forgotten.

Christ was angry as He strode among the tradesmen in the clut-tered Temple. With His muscular carpenter's hands, He overturned the tables, leaving the moneychangers to scramble in the dust after their lost coins.

"It is written that 'My house shall be called the house of prayer,'" He thundered at the astonished crowd. "But you have made it a rob-ber's den!"

He thrust the faithless dove sellers and money changers out of the Temple gates and threw their worthless belongings after them—coins, cages, trinkets...and tables.

Then, His anger spent, Christ ushered in the sick and resumed the true work of the Temple: healing, teaching, prayer. He stayed to honor the treasure the people had overlooked: the one table of worth—the altar—where a believer could offer his richest, truest gifts to God.

Carpenter of Nazareth, sweep the false altars and false idols from my life. Make my heart pure enough to lay at Your table.
—LINDA CHING SLEDGE

DAY THREE—SEEING—AND DOING—IS BELIEVING

29 TUESDAY

And all things you ask in prayer, believing, you shall receive. —MATTHEW 21:22 (NAS)

The ancient elm that leaned over our house died two summers ago, the victim of some mysterious blight. I didn't think it was possible for any tree to die so fast. One week it was full of thick green branches. Then in a month they were gone. I loved it. I called the tree service. But it couldn't be saved.

The fig tree that Christ saw in Jerusalem a few days before His death died an even quicker death than my beloved elm. Hungry from His walk back from Bethany where He had spent the night, Christ spied the fig tree and went up to it. But it offered no fruit for Him to eat.

"May no one eat fruit from you again!" He declared.

Puzzled, the disciples pressed on to Jerusalem. Why curse an insentient tree, they must have wondered.

The next morning, they passed the same tree only to find that its boughs were bare, its trunk shriveled to its roots. Christ's words had come to pass!

The puzzled disciples blurted, "How did it wither at once?"

Jesus' answer was simple, stark, unsentimental: *Believe!* Faith would enable them to do as He had done to the fig tree. Faith would enable them to cast mountains into the sea. By faith, you live, He seemed to imply. To be faithful, you must *do* your faith, to show forth its fruits to the world.

Soon He was to leave them. And He knew that without a strong, active, generous faith to support one another, they would die.

On this third day of Holy Week, repeat to yourself Christ's answer to the disciples at the sight of the withered fig tree: *Believe.* It's the church's unsentimental formula for distinguishing disciple from doubter, those who give from those who withhold, those who will live from those who will die.

Stern Teacher, I choose life in You, over death without You. Give me a faith that moves mountains.   —LINDA CHING SLEDGE

DAY FOUR—THE HIGH COST OF HEAVEN

WEDNESDAY
You fools and blind men: which is more important, the gold, or the temple that sanctified the gold?
—MATTHEW 23:17 (NAS)

One of my credit cards has a hologram in the corner, a white dove set against a silver sky. Tilt the card to catch the proper angle of light and the

dove moves. Flip it back and forth quickly and the dove flaps its wings!

Some marketing wizard had the idea of putting the two symbols together: the credit card, the plastic stand-in for gold, and the dove, the symbol for the Holy Spirit. Money and God? The two don't mix!

So what's the message? I'm confused.

The Pharisees confused their symbols too.

"Should we pay a poll tax to Caesar?" they asked Christ.

It was a trap. A "yes" answer would bring down on Jesus the wrath of the Roman-hating people of Jerusalem. A "no" answer would make Him a traitor in the eyes of their Roman overlords.

Jesus called for a coin. "Whose face is on this coin?" He demanded. "Caesar's," they ventured.

Jesus' reply has come ringing down the centuries: "Render to Caesar the things that are Caesar's and to God the things that are God's."

The Pharisees had nothing to say.

So Christ won this debate with the Pharisees, but the victory would cost Him His life. For now the Jewish leaders, convinced that He threatened their power, began to plot how to seize Jesus by stealth and slay Him.

This fourth day of Holy Week, be guided by Christ's clear-headed answer. Don't confuse your loyalties. Keep the cross above all. Leave coins and credit cards to the world.

What can I render to You, Lord, for the dangers You endured for me? A heart fixed on heaven's treasure—You.

—LINDA CHING SLEDGE

DAY FIVE—THE EXTRAORDINARY PROMISE

31 MAUNDY THURSDAY

Then he took the cup, gave thanks and offered it to them, and they all drank from it. —MARK 14:23 (NIV)

I drink coffee from the same brown mug each morning. It's an ordinary cup, the sturdy glazed sort found in any dimestore. There's a chip on one side, but I'll never give it up. It came as a premium nineteen years ago from a gas station in Oakland, California: "Free mug for a Fill-Up." I was just married then.

Today, I have fancier cups in my corner cupboard. Yet that old mug is the one I always reach for. I drink memories along with my coffee, for my best years are in that cup—two small apartments, first child, first house. It's a memorial of the living covenant I still keep with my husband....

The cup Christ offered His twelve disciples at their last Passover meal together was doubtless one of inexpensive glazed clay. Even the meal itself was an ordinary Passover supper...until the moment Jesus told the disciples that one of them would betray Him.

Consternation followed. "Surely not I?" eleven voices protested...while the one called Judas quietly slipped away. In the uneasy silence, Jesus filled His cup with wine, blessed it and handed it round. The disciples drank, frightened by Christ's grave face and cryptic words. Was He saying that He was leaving them? Impossible!

Much later, when the tragic drama on the cross had been played, they remembered what He had said: "This cup is the new covenant in My blood which is poured out for you."

Now they understood.

That ordinary cup held an extraordinary promise made clear by His death: The wine was His blood, the means by which God guaranteed their salvation. And every time they drank in His memory, they *did* remember. That cup. His blood. The healings. The stories. His love for the small, the weak, the outcast. The promise that He would sup again with them in heaven.

This Maundy Thursday, as you take up the communion cup, remember that ordinary cup that Christ lifted. And in the spirit of discipleship, drink down Christ's healing and forgiveness, the symbol of God's abiding love—the living covenant we keep with Him.

Lord, I would drink from Your cup. Lord, I would see You face to face. In this quiet moment, come close. Be here with me now. —LINDA CHING SLEDGE

Thank-You Notes to God

1

2

3

4

5

6

7

8

9

10

11

12

13

14

15

16

17

18

19

20

21

22

23

24

25

26

27

28

29

30

31

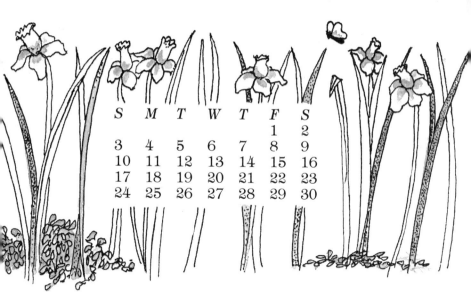

S	M	T	W	T	F	S
					1	2
3	4	5	6	7	8	9
10	11	12	13	14	15	16
17	18	19	20	21	22	23
24	25	26	27	28	29	30

APRIL

BE A FORGIVER
Your Spiritual Pilgrimage

I say not unto thee, Until seven times: but, Until seventy times seven. —*MATTHEW 18:22*

Nobody resents April showers. Six hundred years ago Chaucer was praising them because they ended "the drought of March." It's easy to forgive April for being occasionally damp because we know her showers don't last long and also because the greening earth needs them.

This month, as new life springs up everywhere, why not practice the healing art of forgiveness? Starting today, choose one old, tired grievance and get rid of it. Then another and another, one a day for the next thirty days.

April's golden sun will shine more brightly if you do.

DAY SIX—HOW FIRM A FOUNDATION

GOOD FRIDAY

1

They took Jesus therefore, and He went out, bearing His own cross, to the place called the Place of Skull, which is called in Hebrew, Golgotha. There they crucified Him... — JOHN 19:17–18 (NAS)

In the basement of our house, a wooden cross beam bridges the foundation. The house was built a century ago upon that wooden joint. The previous owner added a sunroom and a downstairs bathroom. We're redesigning the kitchen. But every anticipated addition depends on the strength of that beam.

When the last carpenter came to do some work downstairs, he ran his hands along the ugly, rough-hewn wood. "They sure knew how to build 'em in those days," he said with a shake of his head....

On such a cross beam Jesus died on a dark Friday in early spring. He had carried it Himself at first, as all condemned men were forced to do. But He was so weak from the flogging that the Roman soldiers had given Him, that a passing stranger was made to bear it the rest of the way. At Golgotha, the place called "The Skull," His hands and feet were nailed to the ends of the beams. Slowly, the heavy structure was hoisted upright.

For hours Jesus hung high above the jeering Romans, wracked with thirst, hardly able to breathe or see. Yet He refused the narcotic wine that was offered Him. And even in His agony He asked God to forgive His tormentors, "for they know not what they do."

Finally the end came. Jesus cried out with a loud voice, and then He died. The shadow of the cross fell across the world. Night swallowed up the sky. Rocks hurtled off mountains. Tombs were ripped open. The veil of the Temple was rent from top to bottom.

The cross. The beam which held Christ's broken body. Why do we revere rather than despise it? Why has it come down through the centuries as the last symbol of hope, not despair? Why is this Friday, this day of sorrow, called Good?

Go down into your basement if you have one, and look at the cross beam. Run your hands along its rough surface. Feel its scars and crevices, the marks of hammer and nails. Marvel at the strength that becomes more apparent from year to year. Remember then the cross on which Jesus' frail flesh hung. Those crosspieces of wood did not kill. They lifted up. That wooden cross became the center beam of our faith, the bridge between our world and eternity.

Father, when I survey the wondrous cross on which my Savior died, I remember how His sacrifice lifts me up from the pit of death. And I tremble with awe at the price He paid.

—LINDA CHING SLEDGE

DAY SEVEN—THE COVENANT

2 SATURDAY

And behold, the curtain of the temple was torn in two, from top to bottom; and the earth shook, and the rocks were split.   —MATTHEW 27:51 (RSV)

I've never liked curtains. But our kitchen door is half glass, and I have to put something heavy over it in January to keep in the heat. So I tack up the only thing close to a curtain in the house—a baby quilt with a big, blue bird. It works. The kitchen stays warm all winter—but dark, too dark.

I can't wait to take it down in April. For when I do, I know what I'll see outside. Green shadows and yellow light. Budding branches. The veil drops. And my heart rushes out into the spring....

In the ninth hour, as Christ was dying on the cross, a strange thing occurred; the curtain of the Temple was "torn in two, from top to bottom."

This was the *parokhet*, the veil of scarlet linen that hung between the Sacred Place of the Temple and the Holy of Holies, the small room where the Ark of the Covenant, the golden box holding the two stone tablets of Moses, was hidden.

The parokhet torn open? Impossible! No one was allowed to touch it except the High Priest who lifted it once a year on the Day of Atonement to gaze into the ark. The parokhet enclosed God's covenant with His chosen people; it safeguarded the very place where God had chosen to dwell.

Imagine the terrified laments of the priests as they beheld the torn curtain, the screams of the people on Calvary as the ground shook and rocks fell. The Son of God was dying; and every corner of the earth felt His agony, from the loftiest mountain to the most sacrosanct and private room of the Temple.

Yet something wonderful was happening, too. What had been

99

safeguarded in Jerusalem was now open to all. The covenant binding God to the children of Abraham was now open to every human being.

It took a dreadful sacrifice, Christ's dying, to tear the veil of a former age away. But the reward was immediate and immeasurable: Christ's spirit leaped out of His broken body to dwell with us. Our God. No temple could hold Him. Now He is everywhere.

Savior, tear the veil of sin from my soul; set my spirit free.
—LINDA CHING SLEDGE

DAY EIGHT—THE GLORIOUS TRIUMPH

EASTER SUNDAY

| 3 |

But on the first day of the week, at early dawn, they went to the tomb, taking the spices which they had prepared...but when they went in they did not find the body. —LUKE 24:1,3 (RSV)

There are three of us, Barbara, Lynn and I, who gather in the kitchen each Easter to cook. The kitchen smells of spices—cinnamon and cloves, pepper and sweet ginger—and of lamb, yams and cider simmering on the stove, and the fragrant dough we are twisting into loaves. We chatter. We bustle. We listen to the voices of the men in the parlor arguing about church, money, politics....

After Jesus' death, the men were locked behind closed doors, arguing, no doubt, about their uncertain futures. Luke says that three women—Mary Magdalene, Joanna and Mary, the mother of James—went to the tombs with spices.

I can see them: three slight, veiled figures, leaning together, as women do in sorrow, and brushing away their tears. The long night of mourning had ended. It was left to them, as women, to do the sad work of washing the body and anointing it with spices for burial.

But they found the stone barring the entrance of the tomb had been rolled aside. They went in to look and found the tomb empty. Christ's body was gone! As they stood there in great confusion, two youths suddenly appeared in robes of dazzling brightness.

"He is not here," they said to the women. "He has risen, just as He said. Remember what He told you back in Galilee?"

Then the women remembered what He had told them: that not even the grave would hold Him.

They hastened to tell the men, and on the way, according to Matthew, He whom they thought dead appeared to them on the road. The women fell down and kissed His feet.

"Go tell my brothers," He told them.

But when the women told the disciples, the men did not believe, for in those days women were not counted reliable witnesses. Only impetuous Peter and loyal John ran to the tomb to see for themselves.

And they found that Jesus' body was indeed gone.

Barbara lays the bread upon the festive table, while I pour the amber-colored cider into the goblets Lynn places at each plate. Spicy smells float from the kitchen into the dining room, enveloping us in warmth.

"Come and eat," we women call. The men wander in still talking.

We take our separate chairs, men and women, each of us from different backgrounds, experiences and interests. In some cases holding different values and opinions about worldly, even spiritual matters. Yet as we break bread together, we are one, for in Christ Who loved and saved us all, there is neither east nor west, slave nor king, man nor woman.

The smell of spices rising up off the table reminds us how near to death we walk, and how sweet and special is the life He gave us.

Lamb of God, Who triumphed over the grave, bind us together this glorious Easter day as one heart, one people, one world.
—LINDA CHING SLEDGE

Tandem Power for April

 LEARNING TO HOLD ON LIGHTLY
God is our refuge and strength.... Therefore will not we fear though the earth should change.

—PSALM 46: 1–2 (RSV)

The other day after school, Kendall and I stopped at a department store. Though she's ten years old, she's the baby of the family. As we crossed the parking lot, I instinctively reached down for her hand. Instinctively, she pulled it away.

"I'll hold your hand at home and at church, but not here," she shyly smiled up at me. Her tone was half apologetic, half pleading. The sentence was short but the message was weighty.

All through our shopping, I pondered. Kendall was growing up, and for a while she was going to yo-yo back and forth, sometimes holding on, sometimes pulling away. It was, after all, a necessary and predictable part of God's overall plan for families through the seasons of life. And how would I respond? Would I resist or cooperate? Instinctively, I wanted to resist by reaching down, grabbing her hand and holding on tightly. But I know that is not God's plan. I thought momentarily of Mary. How difficult it must have been for her to accept God's plan for her son Jesus. What if she had resisted and held on tightly instead of lightly?

Always, we face inevitable changes that are part of God's plan for our lives. The children grow up. A best friend moves. The doctor says, "Slow down." Retirement comes. And we have a choice. We can resist and hold on tightly and get stuck wallowing in our grief for what was. Or we can cooperate and hold on lightly, gathering up the blessings from our past and moving forward.

As we live out these days following the reality of the Resurrection, we realize that God has a plan that is bigger than this moment. When we face changes through the seasons of life, we are comforted in knowing He is working out that plan. We have a choice: to resist or cooperate. To hold on tightly—or lightly. Which will you choose?

Lord, the death and Resurrection of Jesus remind us that change is part of Your plan. Please help us to hold on lightly and look forward instead of backward as we face changes.
                                                    —CAROL KUYKENDALL

 TUESDAY
So is it with the resurrection of the dead...it is sown in dishonor, it is raised in glory.
                                    —I CORINTHIANS 15:42–43 (RSV)

When I was growing up, my mother always gave each of us six children a present on Easter Sunday. When we were young, she gave us homemade Easter baskets, cornucopias of candy and toys. When we outgrew the candy stage, we would receive new softballs that gave us hours of pleasure on the ballfield.

Then one year she gave me something that changed my life forever. Mom handed me a set of children's garden tools: a miniature rake, a pint-sized hoe and a small shovel. From my first chop of the hoe, I was hooked on gardening. Nowadays, every spring I'm restless for the frozen earth to thaw. With every seed I sow, my hope grows richer and my spirits brighter. The flowers and vegetables that burst forth from the earth are a kind of spiritual lesson in my own backyard.

Perhaps you have some unfulfilled ideas or dreams that just seem to sit in the back of your mind. Today may be the time to "plant the seeds" so that God can help you realize your dreams. The first step is to write down one or two things that you would like to accomplish in the next few months. Just the act of writing them down is like sowing a seed. Watch carefully in the next few weeks to see what opportunities God brings into your life.

Lord, I realize that sometimes we don't receive because we don't ask. As I sow these seeds today, I know You will bring them to fruition:

1. _____
2. _____
3. _____

—DANIEL SCHANTZ

6	WEDNESDAY

But they that wait upon the Lord shall renew their strength... —ISAIAH 40:31

It used to annoy me to have to wait for people. I'm a punctual person—often five or ten minutes early—so I usually was the one waiting for an interview, a business appointment or a doctor's visit. My wife Ginny, on the other hand, is more easygoing, and when I waited for her I'd stew and fidget, getting angrier by the minute.

Ginny admitted to having a problem "getting her act together," as she put it, and I would sit in the car, beeping the horn, turning the motor off and on, and getting myself worked up.

One day I saw that this problem was not going to go away by itself. I had to *accept* that people are different from me and that I wasn't going to find carbon copies of Sam Justice everywhere I went! In my case, I found the answer in using the waiting time to speak with God, but other people have found that meditating or reading the Bible, writing an overdue letter or balancing their checkbook will help.

The prayer that helped me the most was the famous Serenity Prayer that acknowledges that there are things in this world that we can't change, but we can always do something about changing ourselves.

Do you have an annoyance or irritation that isn't going to change or go away easily? Then why not pray with me:

God, grant me the serenity to accept
the things I cannot change,
courage to change the things I can,
and wisdom to know the difference.
—SAM JUSTICE

7	THURSDAY

...God hath not given us the spirit of fear; but of power, and of love, and of a sound mind. —II TIMOTHY 1:7

Positive Thinking Really Works, Researchers Say.

That headline in my morning newspaper must have been received with chuckles from lots of people who read it. That's because they don't need an exhaustive study to prove what they already know, namely that optimism pays more dividends than pessimism.

Nonetheless, I was interested to see that social scientists have been able to quantify the benefits that accrue to people who think positively. Among them: They are healthier, they are happier, they live longer and they are more successful in their jobs than pessimists.

How would you characterize your outlook: generally positive or negative? Though no one can be optimistic all of the time and still have a grip on reality, it is true that how we choose to see things colors every facet of our lives. Worry and fear trigger negative reactions; hope and faith portend positive ones. The Bible tells us, "As a man thinketh in his heart, so is he." The heart of one who believes in Christ and His promises has every reason to be optimistic. Though this person does not deny life's pain and problems, he or she is confident always that God will prevail over every trial, even death.

Through all our struggles, trials and groping,
Keep us, Father, ever faithful, ever hoping.

—FRED BAUER

8 FRIDAY
...Thou shalt love thy neighbour as thyself...

—*LEVITICUS 19:18*

One day some years ago I was in Montreal having lunch with Dr. Hans Selye, the great Canadian authority on stress. We talked about religion, and how a strong faith tends to relieve stress.

I remember we discussed the great commandment the Bible gives us about loving our neighbor. Dr. Selye admitted that it's hard to obey that rule all the time, "Because," he said ruefully, "there are always people who rub us the wrong way, and it's very difficult to love them as much as we love ourselves. But," he added, "I've discovered another way of approaching the same goal, and it's this: *Try to earn your neighbor's love.* Even if you find him less than attractive, make yourself do little things that will earn his appreciation. If you show interest in him and his welfare, why then *he's* going to begin to love *you.* And when you've earned his love, you'll find it far easier to love him back!"

Not long after that I was at a gathering where a certain high school principal was also present. I had never liked him much; he seemed cold and aloof and opinionated to me. Nevertheless, remembering what Dr. Selye had said, I went up to him and asked a few friendly questions about the school. I said that I thought he was doing a fine job (which he was). If I could ever be of any help, I added, I hoped he'd let me know.

It was amazing how the surprise in his eyes turned to pleasure, and how the cool manner became a warm one. And Dr. Selye was right: I found myself liking him more than I thought possible.

Earn thy neighbor's love. It's not the Golden Rule, perhaps. But I think you might call it a silver one.

Dear Lord, You did everything to earn my love. Accept it—and reflect it back to me, please.

—ARTHUR GORDON

APRIL 1988

9 SATURDAY
Where wast thou when I laid the foundations of the earth? —JOB 38:4

It was one of those glorious early April days when the air is still crisp and the sun brilliant. I was raking the winter debris off the daffodil beds. Mr. Bergman, across the road, was pruning his hedge. At first we could only hear their rhythmic honking. Then the Canada geese appeared in perfect formation, streaking north across the Connecticut sky.

"They're letting us know that spring is coming!" I shouted to Mr. Bergman.

"Maybe *we've* let *them* know!" he shouted back, waving his pruning shears in the air. "Look around you!"

Up and down the road I saw that my neighbors were all out in their yards, raking, digging and pruning. Was Mr. Bergman suggesting that this flurry of human activity was sending a sign of spring to the geese? I had to smile at such a whimsical thought.

But I do know that my heart beats faster and my step is lighter as the sun gets higher and April days approach. So maybe that *is* God's way of urging me to get outside and announce spring's coming to His creation. We humans rake and plow. The daffodils send forth shoots. The geese fly north. It's God's harmony. We—each one of us—are called to play a part.

Dear God, it was You Who laid the foundation of this earth. Thank You for letting me be a part of it.
—MARILYN MOORE JENSEN

10 SUNDAY
...And yet I am not alone, because the Father is with me. —JOHN 16:32

Sometimes I'm uncomfortable when people stand around visiting in small groups, such as at the coffee hour after church. Unless I quickly spot a close friend, sometimes I have left rather than try to work my way into a group that is already conversing.

Recently I mentioned this to my friend Cheri. "I used to feel that way, too," she said, "until I started looking around the outside edges of

106

the little groups, and I found out that there are *always* others in the same predicament! So I've made it my job to go talk to each one of them. Now I have a wonderful time, and my only problem is that the coffee hour never seems quite long enough!"

Cheri's right! It was hard for me, at first, to go up to people I didn't know very well and start a conversation, but I found that most of them were just hoping someone would come and speak to them. If you're a little uneasy in unstructured social situations, realize you're not alone! Then make it your job to go around making *others* feel that they belong.

Today, Lord, help me to make someone feel wanted.
—MARILYN MORGAN HELLEBERG

|11| MONDAY
In every thing give thanks: for this is the will of God in Christ Jesus concerning you. —I THESSALONIANS 5:18

My mother's heart attack was a frightening surprise. She was seventy-eight, but she had seemed immune to the aging process. Characteristically, although her pain began at three A.M., she waited until nine to call her doctor.

"I didn't want to disturb you on a Saturday," was her excuse.

She did poorly right from the start. Her heartbeat was irregular, punctuated by frightening pauses. Her pain was constant. Open heart surgery would be necessary. During the next few days of tests, my prayer was that God would not only spare Mom's life, but also grant her a full, vibrant life as well.

The surgery was finally over and I went into the recovery room to see her. "You look great," I lied. But her puffed and ivory face was almost that of a stranger.

"Good," she struggled to say. "Can I go back to sleep now?"

As I walked away, her faint call drew me back. I leaned close to hear her words.

"Son, did you remember to thank Jesus?"

It was perhaps the moisture from her oxygen mask that made my cheek wet, but I quickly dried it with my handkerchief.

Though drowsy and pain-racked, she had remembered to give thanks. I had not. Standing outside her room, I no longer prayed for her future but offered grateful thanks for her past and a lifetime of example.

Help me to remember, Lord, that my prayer to You needs to begin with thanks...in all things. —SCOTT HARRISON

12 TUESDAY
There were prophets in Jerusalem and Judah...who brought messages from the God of Israel...encouraging them to begin building again! —EZRA 5:1–2 (LB)

Two years ago Milwaukee had so much rain in one week that much of the city and surrounding suburbs became flooded. I drove home from work through riverlike streets to discover my carpeted basement family room was under water.

Desperately I threw beach towels on the floor and spent the next hour sopping and wringing, sopping and wringing. Finally I just sat down on the steps exhausted, defeated and alone.

It was then that I remembered a newspaper article I had read sometime before about a shoe factory in Belgium, Wisconsin, that had burned to the ground shortly after Christmas. The next morning the owner of the company made arrangements to use an empty school in the small town for temporary offices. By noon that day he had already conferred with an architect on plans for another factory on the site. Then, the same day, he made arrangements to keep his employees working at another of his plants in a nearby town.

How inspired I was by his quick, no-nonsense reaction. How to get over a disaster? His actions seemed to say, the only way is to get up, get going, start doing, rebuild...and to stay with the job until it's finished!

I stood up, threw more beach towels on the mess at my feet, pulled the carpet outside for a good scrubbing, finished mopping the floor, and by the next day, I felt my family room would survive the flood—and so would I!

Lord, when disaster strikes, don't let me give up. Help me to get up, get going, start doing and...rebuild, too.

—PATRICIA LORENZ

13 WEDNESDAY
...Ye have received the Spirit of adoption, whereby we cry, Abba, Father. —ROMANS 8:15

Our eight-year-old son Nathan is a lot like me, and it is sometimes difficult to see a carbon copy of myself walking around, making some of the same mistakes I did. In fact, because of this I've probably been harder on Nathan, our middle child, than on his two brothers.

The other night I was making the usual "drink of water, tuck in the blanket, give a kiss" rounds at bedtime. I came to Nathan last and was in a hurry to get back to reading the newspaper. Nathan looked up and asked, "Dad, can't you stay a little while?" I was about to tell him it was time to sleep, but something in his eyes stopped me. I stretched out beside him, and his arm went around my neck and his head onto my chest.

We talked about school and a few silly things. Finally I said, "Nathan, was there some reason you wanted me to stay?"

"No," he answered, "I just wanted to see if you would."

That hit me hard. What could be more important than spending time with a child who wanted to be with me? Not much, because all too soon he'll grow out of that need and I'll be asking *him* to spend a few minutes with his mother and me.

Today I'm going to concentrate on my relationships with loved ones. Perhaps there is someone with whom you, too, would like to spend quality time. With God's help, we can find that time.

Lord, let me slow down and appreciate the people You have brought into my life. Help me find some time for them today.
—ERIC FELLMAN

14 THURSDAY   FIRESIDE FRIEND
Then let us no more pass judgment on one another...
—ROMANS 14:13 (RSV)

When I was a young girl growing up in that part of Oklahoma known as No Man's Land, I *hated* tumbleweeds! The ever-present wind tossed them gleefully prickling against my bare legs, or suddenly in front of me blocking my way, or unexpectedly striking me from behind as I walked along the dusty street to school.

It's hard for me to believe that this treacherous tangle could ever be good for anything more than littering landscapes and attacking hapless victims. But it seems I am wrong. This unwanted nuisance has been successfully turned into a form of firewood known as "tumblelogs," a gainful cash crop for brave desert farmers.

As I have grown older, and walk along other streets, I am sometimes reminded of this audacious weed by other people I have met! My high school English teacher, Mrs. Curry, was a perfect example—always pushing, always demanding, never satisfied. I used to think that she went out of her way to make my life more difficult.

But time has proved I was also wrong about Mrs. Curry. I am now reaping the rewards of the challenge she presented me through her persistence and dedication as a teacher.

Do you know someone who seems determined to make your life more uncomfortable? Think about it—are you misjudging them, as I misjudged the tumbleweeds and Mrs. Curry?

Father, give me victory over my tendency to pass judgment.
                                                    —MARY JANE MEYER

Family Time

15 ADVENTURE AND RISK
Forget the former things; do not dwell on the past. See, I am doing a new thing!   —ISAIAH 43:18–19

The Lord's message to Isaiah is clear. He is saying that the status quo isn't satisfactory. We are to move on from the past, for, "I am doing a new thing."

It was that way with Noah. He wasn't a shipbuilder by trade, but the Lord told him to do something new—build a boat.

It was that way with Abraham. He apparently had a comfortable way of life in the cosmopolitan city of Ur, but he was told to move out to a new place—the land of Canaan. Abraham and his clan migrated north along the Euphrates River and settled for a time in Haran, then in northern Mesopotamia, now southern Turkey. They stayed there until Abraham's father died, and then, even though Abraham was seventy-five years old, God sent them on to another new place, southern

Canaan. From beginning to end, Abraham's life was made up of doing new things.

Centuries later Jesus told His listeners, "A new commandment I give unto you." And the Apostle Paul picked up on this theme when he wrote his friends in Corinth, "Therefore if any man be in Christ, he is a new creature: old things are passed away; behold, all things are become new" (II Corinthians 5:17).

Yes, it is important for us to be enriched by the traditions of our past, to appreciate our roots. But to grow spiritually, as people and as family members, we just can't afford to remain comfortable. Life at every stage and age is risk, movement, adventure. Somewhere we read about the man who boasted that he always drove his car with the emergency brake on. That way, he said, "I'm always ready if there's an emergency." Our tendency so often is to play it safe, to live life with our brakes on and never venture out to do new and untried things.

After our "awakening" in midlife Harriett and I set a goal each New Year's Day to learn to do something new that year we hadn't done before—knitting, playing golf, writing, hooking rugs, photography. At the same time we planned to cultivate at least one new friendship. Then, instead of traveling to the same old places for our vacation, we deliberately ventured out to new places. It was threatening at times, but fun; we became new people. And we even enjoyed each other more.

But vocationally we were still comfortable and secure—until I retired and moved out of a forty-five year routine. I was scared, and my faith was weak. Harriett was confident and strong. She was right. Together as a family of two, we started doing new things. Now, this spirit of risk and adventure is giving our life sizzle. We've discovered, though, that we don't do new things by accident. We have to plan, write down our plans, visualize ourselves doing them. Try it— it works!

Jesus was right. When you "put new wine into new skins...both are preserved" (Matthew 9:17, JBP).

Give us the courage, oh God, to move out in faith into the unknown You've prepared for us.

—FLOYD AND HARRIETT THATCHER

16

SATURDAY
Ask, and it shall be given you; seek, and ye shall find; knock, and it shall be opened unto you.

—MATTHEW 7:7

The city dump.

That's what it was that day in 1904 when a young black woman, Mary McCloud Bethune, saw it. Nevertheless, she and other willing hands built a shack on that desolate place, for she had a dream that, with God's help, she could help other black women learn to read and write. The first desks were wooden packing crates; the ink was blackberry juice.

As I wandered among the collection of tall buildings, classrooms and dormitories that is now Bethune-Cookman College, I stopped at a plain stone that marks the place where Mrs. Bethune's body was laid to rest at the age of seventy-nine. It had taken more than half a century for her dream to become a reality. The words carved on that stone told her whole story:

SHE HAS GIVEN HER BEST SO THAT OTHERS
MIGHT LIVE A MORE ABUNDANT LIFE.

She had not been alone in her long struggle. God had given her encouragement. She began and ended each day with prayer, asking His guidance. And He answered her.

God's help and inspiration are available to all of us. With His guidance men and women have produced electricity, flight and the wonders of electronics, medicine and science. What marvels lie in your future? Seek His help in fulfilling your dreams; He will not fail you.

Lord, I knock at the door of this dream: _____

Help me now to fulfill it. Amen. —WALTER HARTER

17

SUNDAY
Now therefore ye are no more strangers and foreigners, but fellow citizens with the saints, and of the household of God. —EPHESIANS 2:19

Several years ago I attended a church that had many "ministries" for its members. There was a Singles Ministry, a Youth Ministry, Mariners (couples group), Ancient Mariners (retired people) and a Young Couples Ministry. Each had its own Bible study class, prayer meetings, church school, social gatherings, outings, etc. I never found my niche.

Recently, at my little country church's annual meeting, someone asked if we should have a Singles Group. One widowed gentleman was troubled by the idea.

"I'd like to think that at least here, at church, is one place I won't be categorized," he said. We all agreed.

And his words rang true for me. I finally understood my loneliness at the other church. The "ministries" had categorized the congregation and separated us from one another.

It's a thought, but I wonder...maybe we should all try to promote fellowship in our churches by seeking out the strangers—those *not* in our category—and strive for just *one* household, God's.

Father, thank You for Your precious gift of the Church. Let me be a worthy member of Your household.

—MARILYN MOORE JENSEN

18 MONDAY
...It doth not yet appear what we shall be...
—*I JOHN 3:2*

One day I visited a man who was very fond of roses. He told me he was going to give me a prize rosebush, but what he showed me appeared to be a dead stick with some dry strings attached to the bottom. Now, I know what a rose looks like and can recognize its beauty and fragrance, but I did not see these delightful things in this dry stick. But he assured me that if I planted the stick, in due time, God would perform the miracle of producing a thriving plant, covered with lovely, fragrant prize roses. And it was true. In due time, the most beautiful, sweet-smelling roses I had ever seen appeared on the plant.

I was musing about the rosebush as I thought about my life. How some areas of my life seem as unproductive and barren as that prize rosebush. But if God can make something that looks like a dry stick with strings thrive, I thought, then He can make those parts of me thrive, too.

And then an uncomfortable thought came to me: *Yes, God can make anything thrive...but only if I plant it first.*

Father, I know You'll help me grow. But first I have to show my faith by planting my hopes in You. —LEE WEBBER

| 19 | TUESDAY

FIRESIDE FRIEND

...I have loved thee with an everlasting love: therefore with loving-kindness have I drawn thee.

—JEREMIAH 31:3

On a holiday weekend I was frustrated and lonely, wishing for the love and care of faraway friends. Not knowing what else to do, I drove out to a tiny park several towns away from the crowded streets where I live. I was enjoying the azaleas and rhododendrons when I heard a rustling in a pile of last year's leaves. Turning quickly I saw one leaf twitch, then another—and a chipmunk emerged, ears alert, nose sniffing for whatever delicacies might be hidden.

You're a beauty, I thought, *a lovely chipmunk*, all the while standing stock-still. He scuffled a few minutes but soon I noticed his activity slowing down. His head began to sink forward and his whole body became still. Only his eyes remained bright. I turned my eyes away so my gaze wouldn't disturb him, and when I looked back his were completely shut.

My shoe crunching on the gravel startled him awake and he began to scrabble in the leaves. But when I stayed motionless, he relaxed again in the pale warmth of the late afternoon sun. His eyes were drifting shut when he obviously decided to do the job right this time. He curled himself up into a ball, his nose under his front paws. He was safe, he was loved, he could sleep.

This time I moved silently, and left him to the last of his winter slumber.

If you can send your love to a chipmunk so that he can relax enough in your presence to go to sleep, a voice sounded in my mind, *how much more can I send My love to you—My love that always and completely surrounds you. Just open yourself to receive it. I love you.*

I drove back home no longer lonely.

Dear Lord, forgive me for forgetting that You are always with me. Thank You that You will never leave me or forsake me.
—MARY RUTH HOWES

| 20 | WEDNESDAY | **FIRESIDE FRIEND** |

...Lord, teach us to pray... —LUKE 11:1

Every Wednesday afternoon, the neighborhood kids—up to thirty-five of them—would settle themselves in my living room for Bible club. One of the youngest was Charlie, an elfin blond, not quite old enough to go to school. One day I found him on my back steps, trying to talk a friend into coming to club with him. I wondered what features Charlie would use to entice his friend: the catchy songs? exciting games? wonderful stories? maybe the fresh-baked cookies?

Then I heard him say, "You'll really like Bible club, Kevin. The best part is, we even get to talk to God there!"

As I saw the excitement and wonder in that little boy's eyes, I felt an amazement of my own. In my efforts to make club interesting to the kids, I had focused on activities and prizes. How beautifully the Spirit had overridden my clumsy busy-ness and placed His own gentle emphasis—in Charlie's heart at least—right where it belonged! How priceless is the gift of communication with our God!

Renew in me, Father, the wonder of prayer.
—VICKI SCHAD

| 21 | THURSDAY |

...And be ye thankful. —COLOSSIANS 3:15

My friend Fran gave me a prescription for insomnia that might help you, too, if you ever have trouble falling asleep. I seem to be especially wakeful on the night before a trip, or when I've been working on a project that refuses to fall into place, or when I'm worried about one of my children. Here's Fran's prescription: Beginning with *A*, think of something to be thankful for, starting with each letter of the alphabet. For example, "Tonight, Lord, I'm thankful for *A*unt *A*lta, my comfortable *b*ed, *c*hrysanthemums...."

It's amazing how focusing on this kind of thankfulness can take my mind off a problem that's trying to keep me awake, or squelch all of those busybody thoughts that won't seem to quit. Next time you have trouble falling asleep, why not try it? I'd guess that, like me, you'll probably not get past *L* or *M* before you're sound asleep. And what better way to fall asleep than with a thankful heart.

Tonight, Lord, I'm thankful for A _____, B _____, C _____....   —MARILYN MORGAN HELLEBERG

Spirit Lifter

Great occasions for serving God come seldom,
but little ones surround us daily.
          —ST. FRANCIS DE SALES

| 22 | FRIDAY | FIRESIDE FRIEND |

...There is...a time to cast away.

—*ECCLESIASTES 3:1,6*

I've heard it said that when rodeo gets in a cowboy's bloodstream it never leaves. My youth was spent as a bucking horse rider. I traveled this world over until I quit the rodeos because Uncle Sam needed me in World War II. When I returned to the States after a long, bloody siege in Europe, I knew my days as a bronc rider were over. Adolf Hitler seemed to have taken my nerves.

But then I heard that the Wolf Point, Montana, rodeo paid big cash prizes. Though I was forty years old and scared, I decided to enter the bronc-riding contest. I rode a big Canadian bronc. But I had a terrible time with him. And as I held on to the bucking horse, I could see in my mind this pick-up rider coming to get me. He wasn't dressed in cowboy garb. This fellow seemed to have a white sheet over him. His face I could not see. Over his shoulder he seemed to carry a scythe. I knew it was Death who wanted to take me off this bucking horse. In my mind, he sat me on the ground safe but I heard a message: *Don, you are bucking a young man's game. It's time you quit.*

Those words I still hear. They tell me there are some things we older folks shouldn't mess around with as we did when we were young. Sooner or later, there's a time when you've got to let go and say goodbye to outgrown things.

Is there an old habit, an outmoded dream, a stubborn attitude, belief or desire you're clinging to? Think a moment. Could this be *your* time to "cast away"?

Lord, I know You've planned good things for my future. Give me the common sense to give up fool things I'm too old for.
—DON BELL

23 SATURDAY
...Knowing that tribulation worketh patience; And patience, experience; and experience, hope: And hope maketh not ashamed... —ROMANS 5:3-5

It was his first year—when most players are afraid to swing and never hit the ball—and our son Jason was up at bat. It was the last inning of our Little League championship with two outs, score tied, runners on first and second base.

Crack! The ball shot off the bat straight at the first baseman. It got by him, but Jason, so stunned by his success, forgot to run for a couple of seconds. The outfielder's throw beat him to the base by a heartbeat.

Jason burst into tears of frustration. I broke all the rules of parental protocol, jumped the fence and hugged him close. "Jason," I said, "You did fine! You hit a fair ball for the first time! Now just go out and do your best."

Wondering if he'd ever forgive me for signing him up for the team, I returned to my seat. Wouldn't you know that the first batter hit a line shot straight at him? I watched in wonder as he fielded it like a pro and threw the runner out by three strides.

Jason's team eventually lost, but it didn't matter; he'd been a winner. No amount of fatherly lecturing could have taught him more about trying, failing and trying again. If you are anything like me, that is a lesson that bears repeating.

Lord, let me walk away from yesterday's defeats and toward tomorrow's opportunities. —ERIC FELLMAN

117

|24| SUNDAY

Remembering without ceasing your work of faith, and labor of love... —I THESSALONIANS 1:3

Back in the nineteenth century, Robert Louis Stevenson, author of *Treasure Island*, suffered from ill health and couldn't live in England's damp, cool climate. So he and his family moved to a house on a hill on Samoa, a South Pacific island. Below, two villages of Samoans were at war. The problem was that the Samoans thought hurricanes were sent by angry gods who wanted a child sacrifice. Naturally, every time there was a hurricane, each village preferred to sacrifice a child from the *other* village, so they were always fighting.

When Stevenson saw this state of affairs, he worked tirelessly to teach the villagers that hurricanes weren't sent by angry gods, so that they would stop sacrificing children and warring with each other. Eventually, his efforts paid off, but in the meantime, his own health grew worse. It grew difficult for him to take the rough path down the hill. The leaders of the villages, now at peace, noticed this. And together they decided to build a road from their good friend's house down to their villages. They called it "The Road of the Loving Heart," a road they promised each other they'd never let grow muddy or lack repairs.

As the different villagers worked on the road, they were cool toward one another, only cooperating because they felt they were building the road for Stevenson. But as the work progressed, something happened. They began to know one another and to heal broken relationships, cementing the formal truce into deep peace as they worked together out of mutual love for someone. By the time they were done, "The Road of the Loving Heart" not only reached between Robert Louis Stevenson and the villagers, but among the villagers themselves, one that helped them live in peace and friendship always.

Oh Father, remind me that working together out of love can bring healing. Let me walk a path that always leads to love.
—OSCAR GREENE

MONDAY
...Man looks on the outward appearance, but the Lord looks on the heart. —*I SAMUEL 16:7 (RSV)*

You never know what you'll find down the road in rural Alaska. There might be a luxury home with a private plane parked out back or a log cabin with the bathroom out back. Our children attend an elementary school that has up-to-date computers in every classroom, but also has showers for students who are without running water and electricity.

In the suburban neighborhood where we lived before moving to Alaska, I didn't let my kids run around with just anybody. If he or she didn't talk correctly, wear nice clothes and live in a house like mine with a landscaped yard and a brick fireplace, then I was suspicious. Now here we are in Alaska living in a somewhat weatherbeaten mobile home with only a woodstove for heat, and a lawn that looks exactly like what it is—a mother earth original. I wouldn't pass my own social acceptability test!

As for our kids, one once returned from an overnight smelling strongly of ferrets, another received a secondhand present on his birthday inscribed with someone else's name, a third has begun saying "ain't" and our youngest is home with a mild case of flu "borrowed" from a classmate!

Yes, you never know what you'll find in rural Alaska. I discovered I was a rather smug person who believed as long as God loved everybody, I didn't have to. But Jesus, by His own example, taught that following Him means showing God's love to *all people*—no matter how they live or dress or talk.

Dear Father, I'm sure glad Your depth perception is better than mine. Show me how to truly love. —CAROL KNAPP

 TUESDAY
...Open thou my lips; and my mouth shall show forth thy praise. —*PSALM 51:15*

In my first year as a fifth-grade teacher, I had many difficulties with Juan, a problem child. My constant scoldings only increased his misbehavior. Finally, completely discouraged, I sought advice from an older, experienced teacher. "Ignore his misdeeds whenever possible," she suggested. "Find something each day to praise."

I was skeptical—but desperate. The next day Juan, apparently inattentive, was scribbling in his notebook while I was reading aloud Kenneth Grahame's *The Wind in the Willows*. I took the notebook from him. To my surprise he'd made an excellent sketch of Badger, a character in the story.

Great! I thought and held the sketch up for the children to see. They were impressed and suggested that Juan make large drawings of each book character to exhibit in the halls. Immensely pleased, Juan followed their suggestion. As Juan continued to receive recognition for his drawings, he lost his reputation of "tough guy" and became known throughout the school as "the kid who does all those neat drawings."

Gradually Juan's schoolwork and behavior improved. And I learned an invaluable lesson: The person who receives the least praise needs it the most.

Dear Lord, You have given each of us the power to change the lives of those around us. Help us always to emphasize the good. —ALETHA JANE LINDSTROM

 WEDNESDAY
Two are better than one…For if they fall, the one will lift up his fellow… —ECCLESIASTES 4:9, 10

A bird-watching friend says that there are some things we could learn from the fowl that fly in seemingly perfect formation across the sky. One, they take turns at leading; and two, they honk from behind. Any group that wants to reach its destination, he says, needs leaders and honkers. And each member has to do a bit of each.

That's something to think about, isn't it? At my office, in my clubs, at church, even at home, we all have certain assigned roles: president, treasurer, parent, child, officer, clerk, secretary. Yet I've observed that if we want to achieve particular goals it's sometimes necessary to relinquish leading and take up honking, and vice versa.

For instance, when I was working on a complicated annual budget, my secretary was one terrific honker. She encouraged me and gave me practical help. But when an important business reception was to be arranged, I learned to step back—she had the strong organizational skills—and let her do the leading while I did a lot of honking myself.

Today, let's examine ourselves. Do we lead *and* honk from behind? On this Secretary's Day, let's salute our colleagues who do just that!

Thank You, God, for those who lead me and those who encourage me. Help me to be to them what they have been to me.
—MARILYN MOORE JENSEN

 THURSDAY
...It is more blessed to give than to receive.
—*ACTS 20:35*

As a child the day I enjoyed most, even more than Christmas, was May Day. In early April my brothers, neighborhood children and I would gather at one another's houses after school. Equipped with wallpaper sample books, scissors, and flour-and-water paste we'd painstakingly construct small colorful baskets. The last of April we'd scour woods and fields for wild flowers to fill our creations.

Then at dusk on that magical day, we'd tiptoe to a neighbor's porch, hang a basket on the doorknob, knock and scurry away to hide behind bushes. What fun to witness the surprised smiles and exclamations of joy. When all our baskets were distributed we'd return home to find similar offerings by our doors.

Why did we enjoy this so much? Partly, I suppose, because we were welcoming spring. But mostly, I'm sure, because we were discovering the joy that simple gifts, lovingly prepared, can give.

Come to think of it, there are several people I know who would delight in this spirit-lifting surprise—and there are violets and daffodils blooming in my garden. Are there any in yours? Would you like to join me in this old-fashioned welcome to spring? We may both be surprised by the joy we give—and receive.

Lord, help us to remember that a simple gift, lovingly prepared, often brings the most joy.
—ALETHA JANE LINDSTROM

APRIL 1988

 FRIDAY

...Let us practice loving each other, for love comes from God and those who are loving and kind show that they are children of God... —I JOHN 4:7 (LB)

Not long ago I heard someone ask an elderly woman to express the secret of abundant living in the sunset years. I confess I never heard her answer for immediately my mind flashed to Mr. Card.

He was eighty when his first letter arrived at my house. He'd met me, he said, in the pages of *Guideposts.* For six years his letters came once a month without fail. Warm letters about his farm, the Scottish music he loved, the spinning wheels he made in his workshop, his love of poetry and the little country church where he'd taught Sunday school more years than I'd been alive. Not once did he ever ask me to write back (though I often did).

Sometimes little presents arrived mysteriously without a card. A honey drizzle, homemade wooden toys for the children, a worn book, an old album of Scottish music, framed poems written in a familiar shaky scrawl. I always knew exactly where the gifts came from.

One May his letter didn't come and Mr. Card's family notified me of his death. But in June I opened the mailbox to find his familiar handwriting on an envelope. "By the time you read this," Mr. Card wrote, "I shall have gone on to my next great adventure. This last letter is to thank you for letting me love you...."

Today that letter—which he'd requested be mailed to me at his death—is a tender reminder that the secret to abundant living at any age is going through life asking, not how much do you love *me*, but rather, how much can I love *you*?

Lord, don't let me wait any longer or until it's too late; show me how to reach out to others in love now.   —SUE MONK KIDD

 SATURDAY

But whosoever drinketh of the water that I shall give him shall never thirst... —JOHN 4:14

Our cottage at Lake Erie overlooks a vast sweep of shining water. But each spring when we open up, we must carry jugs of water from home. The water table is low, the pump erratic; we know there will be hours of waiting while my husband crawls under the house, inspects gauges and does mysterious things at the tank before even a trickle can be coaxed from the faucets. Meanwhile, every drop must be hoarded: We use as few dishes as possible, recycle the dishwater to flush the toilet; we eagerly set out pans to catch the rain that now seems more precious than gold.

Inconvenient, yes; but distressing? Not really. I always feel a sense of challenge, a testing of ingenuity to meet this sheer primitive need.

Almost every year Clarence, one of our neighbors, strolls down to see how we're doing. "We came last week and got ours going," he says, wearing his usual kindly grin. "Let me give you a hand. Meanwhile, go up to the house and help yourself."

He helps carry our pails to the car. The two men confer while I drive to his house to fill them. His wife Blanche has a pot of coffee going, which we drink as we discuss how to clean windows—with a minimum of water. And how soon the children and grandchildren will be arriving to fish and swim.

This caring and sharing. I think of the women of the Bible chatting as they drew their jugs of water every day from the well. I think of the verse above and Jesus saying, "Drink of this water that I give you and you will never be thirsty again."

I return with full jugs and a full heart.

Dear Father, thank You for the times that really make us appreciate these blessed essentials: Water. And good neighbors.
—MARJORIE HOLMES

Thank-You Notes to God

1 _____

2 _____

3 _____

4 _____

5 _____

6 _____

7 _____

8 _____

9   · _____

10 _____

11	

12	

13	

14	

15	

16	

17	

18	

19	

20	

21	

22

23

24

25

26

27

28

29

30

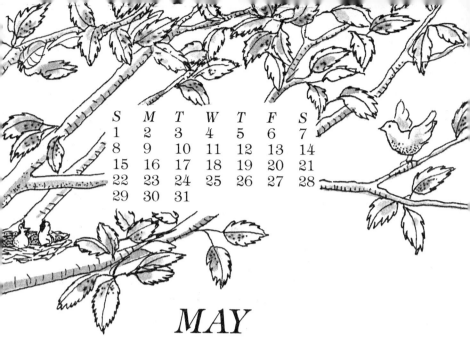

S	M	T	W	T	F	S
1	2	3	4	5	6	7
8	9	10	11	12	13	14
15	16	17	18	19	20	21
22	23	24	25	26	27	28
29	30	31				

MAY

BE A JOY-BRINGER
Your Spiritual Pilgrimage

And thou shalt have joy and gladness... —*LUKE 1:14*

The whole world seems to smile in May. The sun shines confidently, birds sing cheerily, flowers bloom bravely, trees burst into full leaf... no wonder the world seems to be laughing.

Why not make up your mind to smile more often this month? It's a simple step in your pilgrimage, but an important one. Even if you don't feel like it, smile anyway; it's hard to stay gloomy when you do. And when others see you smiling, chances are they'll smile back.

The Bible says, "A merry heart doeth good like a medicine" (Proverbs 17:22). A smile is the best prescription to help make a merry heart.

Tandem Power for May

| 1 | FOCUSING ON OTHERS

For the Holy Spirit, God's gift, does not want you to be afraid of people, but to be wise and strong, and to love them and enjoy being with them. —II TIMOTHY 1:7 (LB)

I have a problem. I forget names. I can look into a perfectly familiar face and draw a total blank. The other day while wheeling my grocery cart down the frozen food section, I recognized a mother whose children go to school with our children. "What is her name?" I asked myself frantically as I faked a search through the frozen vegetables to avoid eye contact with her. It worked. She passed me by.

At that moment, I felt an increasingly familiar nudge between the flesh and the Spirit, between my way and God's way. Rather than swallowing the embarrassment of admitting I'd forgotten her name, I wanted to avoid talking to this woman altogether. That was my way. And I knew God's way: Name or no name, He wants us to reach out to others because reaching out is more important than turning away.

So there I stood, staring at boxes of frozen peas, feeling nudged into an awareness of how God depends upon people like me. We are in the age of the Holy Spirit and God works in our world today through personal relationships. Today we are God's arms and legs, and He reaches other people through us. Yet how many times I resist, responding to my self-centered self-consciousness instead of focusing on others.

With new resolve, I pushed my cart to the next aisle, and sure enough, God gave me another chance to make a choice. Right there in the cereal section, this same woman was studying a handful of coupons. I could scoot by or pause. His way or my way?

"Hi," I said, stopping my cart. And then instantly her name came to me. "How are you, Laura?"

Coincidental? Maybe. But when I stepped out of the paralyzing grasp of self-centered self-consciousness and cooperated with God, I shifted into Tandem Power, and see what happened? During this month, why don't you try stepping out of your self-consciousness by focusing on others and see what happens?

Dear Lord, May is a springtime month when buds are

blossoming all around me. May I blossom into a vessel that You will increasingly use. —CAROL KUYKENDALL

2 | MONDAY
...If I...understand all mysteries and all knowledge...but have not love, I am nothing.
—I CORINTHIANS 13:2 (RSV)

One afternoon while my daughter Ann was doing finger exercises on the piano, I opened Erich Fromm's classic, *The Art of Loving.* In the book I found the remarkable idea that loving is not a pleasant sensation we fall into, or something we do without learning and effort, but that loving is an art.

"If we want to learn how to love," he wrote, "we must proceed in the same way we have to proceed if we want to learn any other art, say music, painting, carpentry, or the art of medicine or engineering." He believed the more you practice, the deeper becomes your capacity and ability to love.

In the background I could hear Ann at the piano, hard at work on her scales. *Why not undertake "heart exercises" each day, the same way Ann undertakes finger exercises?* I thought. I wrote out three exercises to be accomplished during the day. It went like this:

1. Give something without any thought of return.
2. Affirm the gift and the beauty in someone else's life.
3. Listen deeply.

When I seemed to become more proficient in these areas in my life, I made out a new list. Maybe you'd like to begin your own daily heart exercises. For no matter what we attempt to master in life— music, teaching, selling, medicine, mothering or preaching—it is nothing without love. Indeed, love is the art to which Jesus gave His entire life.

Master of Love, make me Your apprentice through these daily heart exercises for today:

1. _____
2. _____
3. _____

—SUE MONK KIDD

TUESDAY
...All things work together for good to them that love God... —ROMANS 8:28

She lives on the island of Hawaii. Her name is Kuulei Pavao and she learned the art of *lauhala* weaving from her mother, who learned from her mother's mother, time out of mind. Long before they settled these islands, Polynesians had perfected the craft of making ornaments from the slender leaves of the *hala* or "walking tree."

The traditional patterns—checkerboards, stripes, zigzags—are passed from one generation to another. The bracelet Kuulei had just completed, though, was like no other I'd seen. I turned the woven circlet in my hands, tracing an intricate sequence of diagonals, complex and beautiful.

"What an unusual design! Is it a family secret?"

Kuulei laughed and shook her head. "Sometimes," she explained in her lilting island English, "my mind is far away when I weave. I make a mistake! But I do not throw the work away. I look to see how I can fit the mistake into the whole. In the end I have a pattern no one has made before."

I'm so grateful, Father, that You don't cast aside Your imperfect creations. In awe I watch You weave my very failures into Your unique design for my life. —ELIZABETH SHERRILL

WEDNESDAY
...Be ye doers of the word, and not hearers only... —JAMES 1:22

We use words so much in our daily communications that we take their ordinary meanings for granted. But don't some words have deeper meanings? Not everyone will agree with the list I've made, but these words speak very strongly to me.

The deepest word is *Soul.*
The longest word is *Eternity.*
The swiftest word is *Time.*
The nearest word is *Now.*
The darkest word is *Sin.*
The meanest word is *Hypocrisy.*

The broadest word is *Truth.*
The strongest word is *Right.*
The truest word is *Love.*
The sweetest word is *Home.*
The dearest word is *Mother.*
The greatest word is *God.*

Can you make a list of your own? Why not try?

Help me, Lord, to find the deeper meaning in the shining symbols we call words. —WALTER HARTER

5 THURSDAY   **FIRESIDE FRIEND**
The grass withers, the flower fades; but the word of our God will stand for ever. —ISAIAH 40:8 (RSV)

They were very special tulips, imported from Holland, with narrow stripes of pale yellow and rose, and when they bloomed one spring about fifteen years ago, I thought that I'd never seen such *huge* flowers. I was gathering a bouquet to take to my husband Walter, who was in the hospital. He'd planted the tulips the previous November, before he had his stroke. He died the following year, never having seen his special flowers bloom in the garden.

I went through the usual period of bereavement, missing my partner of forty-three years; and during the springtime after his death those tulips represented all my feelings of sadness and loneliness. *It's so unfair*, I thought. *He never had a chance to see how beautiful they are.*

In late spring, the tulips faded and died, but my resentment stayed with me. As I thought of the flowers, sorrow would overwhelm me. Summer came, and then a hard winter. The following spring I was doing some cleaning when I started to wonder if the tulips would bloom that year. Or, more specifically, if they would seem as beautiful as they had been. I threw on a sweater and went into the backyard to see if any flowers were up yet.

To my surprise, three tulips were in bloom—and they were as huge, unusual and lovely as the ones I'd taken to the hospital! *Oh, Walter, they are living on—and so are you!* Time *had* worked its healing, and instead of sadness, I felt happy that what my husband had planted would continue to please others. They were a living memorial to the kind of person he had been.

MAY 1988

This year I've made a donation to a group that purchases plots of native prairie in Illinois to make sure that part of our land remains unspoiled. Years from now other people will enjoy what they're doing today.

Lord, let me so live my life that there will be reminders years from now that will bear witness to my faith.
—GAIL BROOK BURKET

 FRIDAY
Peace I leave with you, my peace I give unto you: not as the world giveth… —JOHN 14:27

In first grade I quickly devoured the adventures of Mother, Father, Dick, Jane, Spot and Puff in my reader. They lived in a world where peace prevailed, especially in the family. I couldn't identify with Jane much. My only brother had been stillborn. My own father had died when I was a baby. My mother had to work. A neighbor accidentally ran over my beloved dog. Years later when I married, I secretly longed for the peaceful life I'd read about in my first-grade reader. It began to happen. I was Mother. Jerry was Father. Julie, Jennifer, Jon and Jeremy arrived. Pets joined the family circle.

But slowly, painfully, I discovered that family life was very, very difficult and not peaceful at all. Motherhood wasn't always fun. Dick and Jane had never fought or rebelled in the book I loved. They never left crumbs or unmade beds. Mother and Father agreed on every aspect of life. Spot never had an accident on the new carpet. I had to admit that just as I hadn't been able to be a joyful, polite Jane as a child, neither was I a wise, wonderful Mother.

Finally, I discovered that real peace doesn't come from circumstances or people. For my children rebelled, my husband died much too soon and countless other events changed my pristine world. I learned life is full of hurts and it's sometimes nearly impossible to live at peace with your family. Nevertheless, there is a peace.

His name is Jesus.

Thank You, Father, for keeping us in perfect peace when [our] "mind is stayed on thee" (Isaiah 26:3).
—MARION BOND WEST

7

For where two or three are gathered together in my name, there am I in the midst of them.
—*MATTHEW 18:20*

I leaned against the telephone booth as the tears began to fall and my body was wracked with sobs. I had just learned that I'd lost my dear friend and colleague, Glenn Kittler. Glenn had suffered with a lingering illness that required hospitalization. Then came a fatal heart attack. That Saturday afternoon, while I waited at a Westchester railroad station for a train to take me back to Manhattan, I had called the hospital to inquire about Glenn's condition. That's when I received the sad news.

The train arrived. In a daze I boarded it. As we hurtled along, bound for Grand Central Station, I stared out the window at the sparkling Hudson River. I felt so alone. I wanted desperately to talk to someone who had known Glenn, someone who could comfort me. But this was a sunny spring weekend. Many people were out of town. I didn't expect to see any of Glenn's friends until Monday morning.

Thirty-nine hours, I thought. *Thirty-nine long hours. Oh, dear God, how will I endure them?*

Finally, the train neared Grand Central, so I rose and headed toward the exit doors. As I did, I looked up and gasped. For there, coming toward me from the other end of the car was a colleague who was also a good friend of Glenn!

"Bill!" I practically shouted his name. As we talked, I learned that Bill hadn't heard about Glenn's death. And he "just happened" to be on my train.

"What a coincidence!" I said.

"Maybe not." Bill smiled as he led me to a nearby coffee shop. Together we quietly talked and prayed, remembered and grieved and found comfort in His name.

Dear Lord, thank You for using "happenstance" to fulfill Your promises. —ELEANOR SASS

8 SUNDAY

Honor ...thy mother, as the Lord thy God hath commanded thee... —*DEUTERONOMY 5:16*

Did you know that the idea for Mother's Day was born in a small Methodist church in Grafton, West Virginia?

It was 1876 and the nation still mourned the Civil War dead. While teaching a Memorial Day lesson, Mrs. Anna Reeves Jarvis thought of mothers who had lost their sons. She prayed that one day there could be a "Memorial Day" for mothers. The prayer made a deep impression on one of Mrs. Jarvis's eleven children. Young Anna had seen her mother's efforts to hold the war-split community and church together. As she grew into adulthood, the younger woman kept Mrs. Jarvis's dream in her heart. On the day of her mother's death, Anna was determined to establish a Mother's Day in her honor.

On May 12, 1907, a local observance was held which later spread to Philadelphia. By 1909, Mother's Day was celebrated in forty-five states, Puerto Rico, Hawaii, Canada and Mexico. Elated, Miss Jarvis told a friend, "Where it will end must be left for the future to tell. That it will circle the globe now seems certain."

On May 8, 1914, President Wilson designated the second Sunday in May as Mother's Day "for displaying the American flag and for the public expression of love and reverence for the mothers of the country."

Today let's say a prayer of thanks for Anna Jarvis, who for thirty years kept her mother's dream alive. Then let us turn to the woman who gave us birth, and others whose mother love nurtured us through the years, and find our own special way of expressing heartfelt thanks.

Dear God, on this day, bless mothers everywhere.
—SHIRLEY POPE WAITE

9 MONDAY

Comfort one another... —*I THESSALONIANS 4:18*

We didn't know each other, but we ate at the same coffee shop sometimes, and we might acknowledge each other with a nod. I knew that a few years ago her husband had died. She probably could tell that I was a recent widow, too. One day she spoke up as I passed her table. "Hi, how are you?"

"Fine, just fine," I said quickly, very brightly. I asked the polite question in return, and she assured me that she, too, was fine. During my meal it bothered me that I hadn't told her the truth. I rationalized that "no one really says how they are, especially to strangers...And anyway, people don't care since they have their own troubles." But I longed to tell this almost-stranger that today wasn't a good day at all.

We happened to leave the coffee shop at the same time, so I took a deep breath and said, "Er...actually I'm not so fine today. Today is very hard because yesterday was Mother's Day. You'd think Father's Day would be the difficult holiday, wouldn't you?"

"Oh, I'm not fine, either. Yesterday was so hard for me, too." We parted after agreeing to get in touch. My friend didn't forget. What started as a brief encounter when I shared my honest feelings became the impetus for a support group that she started a few months later— a ministry for women who have lost their husbands. It became a place for me to make new friends and find comfort.

Each of us can reach out in support to a loved one, a friend or stranger who is hurting. Each of us can be a self-appointed "comforter" to another.

Today I will try to share my feelings with a new friend, Lord. Help me to comfort _____ *today.*
(Name)

—MARION BOND WEST

Spirit Lifter

Tenderness and good will are potent factors in promoting the unity and stability of the family.

—A. J. CRONIN

10	TUESDAY

Then the Lord said unto Moses, Behold, I will rain bread from heaven for you... —EXODUS 16:4

"Whirly-gigs" we called them as children. Those little single-winged seeds that come swirling down, hoping to find a spot of earth on which to grow, meanwhile covering walks and cars and porches with their golden clutter.

This morning our balcony was paved with them, glistening with last night's rain. The wooden floor was grimy from winter's neglect; it needed scrubbing anyway, and the storm had given us a hand with the water. My husband suggested we sweep the maple pods to the railing, then scoop them through.

The sun had come out and was beaming as we began. The blackened floor began to yield its dirt, the deep red paint began to show. But as we worked, more of the merry intruders came twisting down, as if trying to see what we were up to. Like children who always come running, getting in the way, eager to help!

As indeed they *were* helping, we both realized. These seedpods gathering under our brooms were the best scouring pads we could have. Each seed was pronged, sharp enough to pierce the soil. Each graceful wing was likewise tough and strong. They were a well-armed heavenly host descending!

Pausing to rest, we picked up a few to admire. What beautiful things! What artistry God uses to fashion even a simple seedpod. Each wing of palest gold was formed by tiny, featherlike fronds branching from the central stem. The little airship was propelled by the single wing, the nose tough and sharp, the compartment for its passenger delicately but strongly protected. Inside this sturdy cabin was its precious cargo—an elliptical seed of vivid green, soft as flesh to the fingers.

All this exquisite artistry and engineering, we marveled, flung into the air in such abundance to land on field or forest—or our balcony. Seeds ready to root and grow—so many that even the few that survive will richly replenish the earth for us!

Dear God, we are awed when we pause to observe the simplest of Your creations. Thank You for sending such treasures onto our very doorstep. —MARJORIE HOLMES

11 WEDNESDAY   FIRESIDE FRIEND

For if a man think himself to be something, when he is nothing, he deceiveth himself. —GALATIANS 6:3

I grew exasperated as the letter I was typing became blotched and untidy. Every time I hit the capital letter *I* either it would not print at all or it came out so dim that it was hardly discernible.

I kept writing in ink over the missing or pale letter until the page grew more and more sloppy.

At last I phoned my friend at the typewriter shop. "Can you tell me what is wrong?" I asked. "All of the letters on my typewriter imprint fine except the capital *I*. I can't get the letter to come out right at all."

My friend laughed. "Maybe it's worn out," he said. "Maybe you're using that capital *I* more than any other letter!"

I felt a pang of guilt. I knew that he was right. That defective key can be replaced easily. The hard part will come when I tackle my own egotism.

Dear God, help me to control the capital I *in my life.*

—FAYE FIELD

12 THURSDAY

Blessed is the man that trusteth in the Lord...for he shall be as a tree planted... —JEREMIAH 17:7–8

Sometimes I think that we New Yorkers have a lot in common with the trees that grow here.

Take our backyard shade-giver, the ailanthus (remember the tree that "grows in Brooklyn"?). Nobody has to bring that fellow in from outside the city; he's rooted here, and he's tough—he'll break through concrete to get where he wants to go.

And so what if we city-dwellers are crowded into a small area? In Central Park there are more than twenty-six thousand trees over six inches in diameter, yet the park people know the name and location of every single one! There are one hundred fifty species of trees, some of which by rights shouldn't flourish there, but they do. (Just like some of us transplanted New Yorkers.)

Recently I went over to see a friend who was having a tree

planted down the block from her apartment house (anyone of us can arrange this through a contribution to our block association or directly through the Parks Department). Mary Ann was just giving the soil a final pat when a ragged woman carrying two junk-filled shopping bags came by and stopped.

"You have the love of God in you, don'cha honey?" she said to Mary Ann, who looked up in embarrassment. The woman put her bags down and studied the young ginkgo. It was as though she could see that tree taking root and growing, its twisted branches shading the way for new passersby for years to come.

"Yes," she said, "anyone who plants a tree loves other people."

You see, trees give us New Yorkers beauty, but they do more than that. They bring out the beauty within us.

Father, keep reminding me that by loving others I am loving You, too. —VAN VARNER

| 13 | FRIDAY |

In God have I put my trust: I will not be afraid…
—PSALM 56:11

I've always loved to dance, and one of my favorite dances is that classic from long ago, the Charleston. I'll never forget the time a friend taught it to me so we could perform in an upcoming variety show.

Bob wanted us to look very professional, so he'd worked out an elaborate costumed routine for us. At one point, I was supposed to sing out, "Boop-boop-a-doop," the nonsense phrase of that era, and fall backward with outstretched arms. He would be there to catch me, he said, just a second before my body touched the floor. Then he'd lift me to my feet again.

Rehearsals began. The "boop-boop-a-doop" part was easy, but I couldn't bring myself to fall back. *What if his timing is off?* I wondered. *What if he doesn't stand close enough? I could crack my skull!* I worried.

Bob sensed my fears. "Ellie," he said, "I won't let you hit the floor. You've just got to trust me." Then he motioned for the piano player to start the music.

Again we went into the routine—knees twisting in and out, heels swinging sharply to the lively music. Finally, the crucial moment came. "Trust me!" Bob yelled. *Trust*, my brain echoed as I fell backward. As he had promised, in one graceful movement, all in time with the music, Bob caught me and lifted me to my feet again. Our dance act was a hit—because trust made it work.

That happened many years ago. Yet, today, at crucial moments when I'm afraid, I remember it. For then I hear God's voice—like Bob's—saying, "Trust Me!" When I do, my fears fade away.

Dear Father, especially when my faith is small, give me the courage to trust You. —ELEANOR SASS

| 14 | SATURDAY | **FIRESIDE FRIEND** |

But the wisdom from above is first pure, then peaceable, gentle, open to reason, full of mercy and good fruits, without uncertainty or insincerity.
—*JAMES 3:17 (RSV)*

I'm no expert on chemical reactions, but I've caused a couple in the kitchen.

When I need buttermilk, I often add a tablespoon of lemon juice or vinegar to a scant cup of milk, wait five minutes and *voilà!* Sour milk.

A tastier concoction is called Friendship Sauce. A friend gave me a "starter" in a gold-colored glass jar. It was a mixture of canned peaches, pineapple and cherries to spoon over ice cream. Every two weeks, I poured in a cup of sugar and some drained fruit and I had Friendship Sauce to share with others.

I visualize my mind as that jar. Sometimes I pour in envy, greed, gossip, resentment, complaints, a judgmental attitude, unrealistic expectations and an obsession with money, and end up with a curdled mess.

Other times I follow the recipe the Holy Spirit gave the believers at Philippi through Paul (Philippians 4:8). When I mix in spiritual fruit—faith, hope, love, generosity, complimentary thoughts about others, joy over others' successes and forgiveness of slights—the Master Chef ferments them into a positive outlook.

How would you like to be? He lets you place your own order.

Lord, I want my deeds and attitudes to reflect Your divine recipe for happiness. —B. J. CONNOR

15 SUNDAY

...He being not a forgetful hearer, but a doer of the work, this man shall be blessed... —*JAMES 1:25*

I received a phone call the other day from a telephone salesperson trying to sell me symphony tickets, and obviously reading the long pitch off a card.

I usually handle telephone-sales calls in one of four ways:

1. Hang up on them mid-sentence.
2. Let them finish their spiel and then politely decline.
3. Buy something I really don't want because I don't know how to say "no."
4. Or I purchase the product joyfully because it's a good idea or a nice value.

It's funny...but sometimes those are the four ways I find myself listening to sermons at church:

1. Some Sundays I find myself "hanging up" on the sermons completely. My mind wanders and I'm thinking of other things.
2. Sometimes I listen, but at the end I decline politely by ignoring the message—and the word of God.
3. Still other times I accept the words and their meaning, but once I get home I never quite figure out what to do with them.
4. Or I am a joyful listener who absorbs the word of God and happily puts it to good use in my daily life.

Today at church, I'm going to try harder to listen more carefully, joyfully and with more acceptance of God's word. And at home this week, I'm going to put those words to good use. Will you join me?

Lord God, teach me to listen...and to act on Your word!

—PATRICIA LORENZ

Family Time

16 GRACIOUS WORDS

All spoke well of him and were amazed at the gracious words that came from his lips. —LUKE 4:22

Yogi Berra was one of the greatest managers in professional baseball. But years ago one of his players made this astute observation, "Yogi knows more about baseball than all the rest of the team. It's too bad he doesn't know how to tell us about it."

What a different reaction from that of Jesus' relatives and neighbors in His hometown who were amazed at His gracious words! Without question, Jesus is a marvelously practical model for us as we attempt to communicate with and relate to our family and friends. When we walk behind Him through the Gospels, we see a Jesus Who could express His feelings and thoughts in open and scintillating fashion. Unlike Yogi Berra, our Lord knew how to "tell us about it."

Jesus' one-on-one conversations with the woman at the well in Sychar and with Nicodemus at night, just to mention two of them, show how sensitive and perceptive Jesus was as a conversationalist. Wherever He went people wanted to talk with Him, and we just have to believe it was because of the openness and caring concern that came through in His conversation.

Several years ago when we were doing research for a book on marriage, we discovered that the inability to really talk to each other on a deep level was the root cause of most fractured relationships. It seems that we have become masters of inane trivia at the expense of being able to express "gracious words." One of the most moving scenes in the musical *Fiddler on the Roof* comes when Tevye, the struggling Jewish peasant, asks his wife if she loves him. She brushes off the question and retorts that she washes his clothes, scrubs the floors, looks after the home and has raised their children. But that doesn't satisfy Tevye. So he asks again, "Do you love me?" only to have her rehearse other things she does for him. Still not satisfied, he asks the question a third time, but she can't and won't say it. Of course she loves him, and he knows it, but he desperately needs to hear her say it.

The Jesus model was "gracious words." We all need to hear them—to be assured that we matter, that our family and friends care. And we know this best if we're able to communicate intimately and on a deep level with each other. Like everything else in life that matters, "gracious" communication doesn't happen by accident. We must work on it every day.

We have happy memories of a friend who used to ask, "Are you fun to live with?" In fact, he even wrote a book with that title. Lee believed that God wanted all of us to be fun to live with. And we believe that the key is caring enough to really talk to each other about our deepest needs and feelings. Learning to do this even a little has put life into our living and loving as a family.

We thank You, Father, for the gracious words of Jesus. Help us to learn to talk to our loved ones and friends.

—HARRIETT AND FLOYD THATCHER

 TUESDAY   **FIRESIDE FRIEND**
Don't you know that you yourselves are God's temple and that God's Spirit lives in you?

—I CORINTHIANS 3:16 (NIV)

The other day I had two visitors at my house: my nephews, ages two and six. It's often interesting to listen to the chatter of children, so I sat and "eavesdropped" as the two of them played. The younger boy grabbed a small blue chair to sit down. "This is *mine*!" he exclaimed. The six-year-old immediately retorted, "No, it isn't! It's mine, 'cause I had it when I was little."

As the argument continued, I found myself remembering the little flea market in Danby, Vermont, where I first spied the tiny chair. I lovingly carried it all the way home to New York. It was truly a favorite possession of *mine*, and in those days I put great emphasis on my ownership, just as my nephews were claiming possession now. I realized that while part of me resented giving up ownership, another part was happy that the boys treasured this chair, too.

There are so many things that God "owns" that I used to think were my possessions: the trees, the birds, my front yard, even myself. Yes, He owns me, too. For a long time I acted as if I owned myself, but now I realize that I haven't been under proper ownership. Jesus holds the deed, and only He knows my true value. Day by day, I'm trying to give myself entirely to Him and let Him renovate my "house." In the same way that my nephews can now use a dear little blue chair much more than I can, I believe my heavenly Father can use my life in a better way than if I held on to it, saying, "But it's mine!"

Lord, forgive me for trying to run my own life. Help me to truly live for You today. —SYBIL LIGHT

18 WEDNESDAY
But Jesus said, "Let the children come to me, and do not hinder them…" —MATTHEW 19:14 (RSV)

This is the story of the Michael Surprise cake.

One afternoon while my children were in school my four-year-old neighbor Michael came to visit. Since he is mostly full of giggles and always full of questions, I didn't expect he'd let the day pass quietly. But I was unprepared when he fastened his lively dark eyes on me and announced, "Let's make a cake."

With a sigh, I set aside my letter-writing and began rummaging in the cupboard for baking supplies. I decided we would make an apple cake. Michael chattered happily as he helped crack eggs and measure flour. When it was time to stir in the chopped apple, he spied his bag of gumdrops on the counter.

"Let's put these in, too," he suggested.

The sensible grown-up in me muttered, "You don't put gumdrops in an apple cake." He stood there looking so pleased with himself I couldn't say no. In went the gumdrops.

"I know," I said, entering his fun, "we'll call this a Michael Surprise cake!" He giggled, and the neglected child in me giggled back. (By the way, the cake was delicious!)

Children take such a fresh approach to life and faith. I need moments that remind me of what it's like to be a child. Otherwise I forget, and go about the business of following recipes exactly as they're written, driving the same roads to and from our house, greeting the same people at church on Sunday mornings. There are no happy surprises in my cakes or my life, and that can make for dull living.

We don't have to be four years old to put adventure and surprise—and joy—into our living. Whatever our age, we can do it now.

Lord, here's a new thing I can try today to experience childlike surprise: _____.

—CAROL KNAPP

MAY 1988

EDITOR'S NOTE TO READER: *If you participated in the daily letter-writing-to-God experiment as suggested in the February 18 devotional, today is the day to review your progress. Go back and read your entries of the last three months and then write us about the results. If you haven't begun, maybe you'd like to start now, then in three months, tell us how you've done. Send letters to: Daily Guideposts Editor, Carmel, New York 10512.*

19	THURSDAY

...But ever follow that which is good, both among your-selves, and to all men. —I THESSALONIANS 5:15

Near our cottage is a leafy glen, where a little waterfall spills over the rocks and a path leads down to the lake. Here the trees soar skyward, some of them almost buried beneath masses of wild grapevines. Among the tall grasses daisies are scattered like stars, and the frail white doilies of Queen Anne's lace.

Unlike the vines in adjacent fields, none of the vines bears fruit. But for a day or two in early September, their leaves seem to come alive with golden wings. For here in this open yet secret dell, the monarch butterflies pause to rest on their way to warmer western climes. It's a lovely sight to see them circling like dancers above the tallest branches before descending to cluster high among the vines. Poised there they are quite still: silent golden visitors, wings closed as if in prayer.

After a few hours, they begin to quiver, then spread their wings and lift, little circles and wheels of them together, flying off toward the sun. By evening most of them are gone.

Yet each year, to our distress, there are always a few who are too tired or get lost along the way. We see them coasting witlessly along the shoreline, often going the wrong direction.

"Hurry!" our hearts cry out to them. "You're late, the others have left, they're already far ahead. You mustn't go back, go forward. Go west—California's that way!"

Others, we know sadly, have already given up and lie still in the glen. If only we could save these errant wanderers, we think. Yet we know it is hopeless. We can no more catch and steer them along the path they should be following than we can our own children, or even ourselves sometimes.

And I sense how God must feel about us, going the wrong direction, insisting on having our own way, even if it leads to destruction. He wants us to land safely, whole and strong, in the wonderful place He has prepared for us.

Dear Lord, thank You for the beauty of butterflies and children. Take care of all of us when we wander, and lead us all to our destination. —MARJORIE HOLMES

 FRIDAY
I will bless the Lord at all times; his praise shall continually be in my mouth...O magnify the Lord with me, and let us exalt his name together! —PSALM 34:1,3

Yesterday a friend who is going through a divorce said, "I have nothing to be thankful for." I thought immediately of the privilege of living in God's incredibly beautiful, wonderful world. I wondered if, perhaps, she was hurting God's feelings.

I was about to count her blessings—but, thank goodness, I stopped in time. We can *never* count another person's blessings. Besides, although I've never *said*, "I have nothing to be thankful for," there are times when I *feel* that way. Perhaps I, too, have hurt God's feelings. So I decided that each morning I'd list three things for which I'm thankful, each one something I hadn't listed before. And I know I'll never run out of new things to add to my list. My list for today:

1. For the wonderful gift of loving and being loved,
2. For beautiful white billowing clouds in a blue sky,
3. For the unfaltering devotion of my faithful collie,
4. For spring rain on the roof, violets in the yard and the fragrance of leaf smoke,
5. For the gift of books—first of all the Bible—to be read and reread before I fall asleep in bed at night.

Could you benefit from a similar list? I'm sure it will increase awareness of how richly we are blessed.

Oh, Lord, I thank You most of all for the gift of living in Your world and for these gifts: _____
_____.

—ALETHA JANE LINDSTROM

Spirit Lifter

If God sends us on stony paths,
He provides strong shoes.
—CORRIE TEN BOOM

---

21 SATURDAY   **FIRESIDE FRIEND**
Watch ye, stand fast in the faith, quit you like men, be strong.   —I CORINTHIANS 16:13

My son is a ninth-grade wrestler. This means his first competition match will occur the winter of 1988-89, assuming the flu decimates the seniors on the team that year. If it doesn't, he's off the mat until the fall of 1989.

Yet he's at practice every day, getting sore muscles and bruised ribs. He suits up for every match, although his main contribution seems to be rolling up the mat when it's all over. He loves it. He's proud of himself. He's totally faithful to his team. I couldn't help wondering why. This is a kid who's made a career out of not sweating, yet there he is, working his heart out every day. For what?

It's all in the coach. This coach has built a *team*—a team that includes ninth graders and considers them as important as the seniors who do the actual wrestling. A team of back slappers who even clap for one another in practice, win or lose. A team that asks a lot, but gives a lot in return. A kid can be very faithful and work extraordinarily hard for that kind of satisfaction.

I've learned a lot from that wrestling coach. Isn't a family the ultimate "team"? If I want my children to grow up close, to stay friends for life, to work hard for their mutual goals, I have to do a lot of daily back slapping and encouraging. A family like that asks a lot of its members, but it gives a lot in return.

Lord, help me to be a good family coach today—building my family members into a strong and supportive team.

—TONI SORTOR

FIRESIDE FRIEND

He hath made every thing beautiful in his time...
—*ECCLESIASTES 3:11*

A few years ago I bought a red flowering crabapple tree and carefully planted it in our yard. But it didn't exactly thrive—in fact, one by one the leaves started dropping off! My husband Jim failed to see the urgency of the situation. "Give it a little time," he murmured.

The next spring it did a little better—it had swelled buds and leaves, but no flowers. "That does it! I'm getting rid of this *flowering* crabapple!" I sputtered.

Jim surveyed the scraggly branches. "Maybe this isn't the flowering kind. Some of 'em never blossom, you know."

"But that tag says: *Flowering Crabapple, Red!*"

The third spring came. Still no red flowers. But this time Jim took me outside and showed me some tiny clusters of red balls nestled in among the leaves. "Blossoms?" I asked, incredulous.

"Blossoms!" he said.

Now, as I watch the little red tree become brilliant with color, it reminds me of how impatient I can be with other things in my life. Dreams, for instance. Instead of nurturing them and giving them time to grow, I get impatient and rip them out.

Starting today, I'm going to try to have some faith, no matter how small and scraggly and unpromising my dreams appear. I'll plant them lovingly, nourish them with work and prayer and give the good Lord time to help them grow.

Father, grant me the faith to trust my dreams to You.
—VICKI SCHAD

Seven Days To Joy
Antidote to Loneliness
More and more people we know are faced with living alone. Empty nests, widowhood, divorce, retirement or just simply the fact of singlehood bring many of us to the realization that solitary homemaking is going to be our lot in life. This week Marilyn Moore Jensen helps us tackle that sometime

companion to life alone—loneliness. Maybe we can find some antidotes to a condition that robs us of joy. Jesus did promise: I will not leave you comfortless (John 14:18). Can we claim that promise? Let's try! —THE EDITORS

GIVE YOURSELF LIGHT THERAPY

23 MONDAY
...Walk as children of light. —EPHESIANS 5:8

I know a young woman who would fall into a numbing depression in the winter months. Some days she couldn't drag herself from bed to get to work. Other days she could barely function. "I thought there was something wrong with my attitude. That it was all in my head. Why couldn't I feel cheerful?"

Then my young friend heard of some experiments in light therapy that were being done at Johns Hopkins University. It seems that scientists are discovering that just as plants need a certain number of lumens (a measurement of light) to thrive, so do people! My friend volunteered for the program. The doctors discovered that her depressions were induced by her light-starved environment, triggered by the shortening of daylight hours in wintertime and further aggravated by her "convalescence" in her dark bedroom. They prescribed for her a "light" lamp for her apartment and several hours of daylight, regardless of the weather.

"It works!" exults my friend. And she is now cheerful and productive, even in darkest December.

Today, let's give ourselves some light therapy. Open the blinds; get out of the house. Take a walk. Go to a brightly lighted mall. Feed your light-starved soul.

God created light and called it "good." Use it.

Father, let Your light shine on me. —MARILYN MOORE JENSEN

GIVING AWAY THE RESULTS

24 TUESDAY
Freely ye have received, freely give. —MATTHEW 10:8

Now that my children don't live at home, I seem to rely on TV dinners or a simple broiled chop and salad. But I miss the kind of cooking that entails having a large pot simmering away on the stove...chopping, slicing, stirring and tasting to make a hearty stew or nourishing soup. I realize now that I didn't care about the *eating* of it. It was the *doing* that nourished me.

I've found a way to satisfy my hunger. I soak salt pork or a ham bone from the butcher with a pound of split dried peas, chopped onions, carrots, celery and a few black peppercorns and then slowly simmer the lot for hours. The aroma is heavenly. Steam frosts my kitchen window. My whole house seems infused with the warmth from the stove and from my heart as I stir...and sniff...and taste. Soon I'll ladle the rich pea soup into coffee cans I've been saving and then pop the cans into the freezer.

Next week the cans will be distributed: one for my secretary, one for a neighbor, some for the family down the road. They love split pea soup but don't know how to make it.

How foolishly we sometimes abandon our gifts because we've lost the primary recipients of them!

Today, do something you enjoyed doing for a lost loved one. Savor every moment of the activity. Then give the results away with this silent prayer:

Dear God, thank You for the talents You have given me. Let me use them. —MARILYN MOORE JENSEN

SHOWING YOU CARE

25 WEDNESDAY
...There is a friend who sticks closer than a brother.
—*PROVERBS 18:24 (RSV)*

One problem with living alone is that there's often no one at home to answer the telephone. Single people don't necessarily keep the predictable schedules that families do. We eat out more often, work longer hours, go to a movie or make spontaneous dates. You see, we don't have anyone we have to go home to. But we often miss important greetings and invitations.

When I realized that people were getting frustrated at not being able to reach me, I bought a telephone answering machine. Some friends were angry. "I hate talking into that machine!" they bellowed. Then I explained....

When I come home at night to a dark and empty house, I feel so very welcomed by the little red light that is flashing on my answering machine. *Someone wants to talk to you*, it says. *Someone cares about you.* I turn on the tape and am warmed by the voice of that someone. And then I call. A connection is made.

My answering machine can't replace the real, live person on the other end of the telephone, I know. But it does serve to maintain a connection between me and far-flung friends and family. I'm grateful for that. And grateful for all who care enough for me to talk to it.

Today, Lord, I will make a connection with someone who could use some good news. Let my voice or presence say to them, "See, someone cares!" —MARILYN MOORE JENSEN

PURSUE YOUR INTERESTS

| 26 | THURSDAY |

...I was afraid, and went and hid thy talent in the earth... —MATTHEW 25:25

"I don't know," the woman sighed. "I go to the singles groups and newcomers meetings and mixers but I don't seem to make any friends."

"What are you interested in?" I asked her.

"Well, I want to make friends," she replied.

"But what are you interested in?" I persisted.

She thought a long time and then confessed, shyly, that she'd always thought she had a talent for mathematics. "But who cares about that?" she shrugged.

I encouraged her to sign up for a calculus course at a nearby college. Now she is immersed in her homework, socializing with like-minded people she's met at school and preparing for high school teacher certification. She isn't lonely.

What's the lesson? I think it's that when we pursue friendship it often eludes us; when we pursue our interests, friendships follow.

Jesus said that if we will be faithful over the few things the Lord has given us we can enter into His joy. Isn't that the best antidote to loneliness?

Dear God, cast out my fear. Help me to use my talent as Your good and faithful servant. —MARILYN MOORE JENSEN

THIS DAY IS GOOD

27 FRIDAY
…Behold, now is the day of salvation.
—*II CORINTHIANS 6:2*

I have a friend who seems to take pleasure in the simplest things; budding trees, trinkets, a chat with the checkout girl at the super-market. Yet I know that her life has had unhappiness. Early widow-hood, financial problems, disappointing children.

"How do you manage to be so cheerful?" I asked her.

"I use to wait for someday," was her reply. "You know, *someday* I would take a trip, *someday* I'd have more money, *someday* a new love would come my way…

"But someday never came. Now I say to myself, *This day is as good as any may ever be. I will live it to its fullest.*"

Someday. It's a word that can draw us into playing a waiting game. It's a word that allows us to put off effort for today. What if this day IS as good as any will ever be? Let's live it!

Do you want to take a trip someday? Take a walk today. Have finances got you down? It won't break your bank to treat yourself to a pair of earrings, a tie clip or a new wall calendar. And let's get some loving by giving some away—to the store clerk or the neighbor we pass on the road. This day, let's toss out all our *somedays* and pray in the words of the psalmist:

This is the day the Lord has made. I will rejoice and be glad in it.   —MARILYN MOORE JENSEN

TAKING INVENTORY

28 SATURDAY
…Ye are of more value than many sparrows.
—*MATTHEW 10:31*

Once a year at the company where I work we take inventory. By tally-ing up the actual products (finished goods) in the warehouse, the materials in the plants (goods in process) and the value of the land, buildings and equipment (capital assets) we can determine the true value of our company.

Taking inventory is a good exercise for today. Through this week you may have begun to notice that feelings of loneliness are connected with negative feelings of self-worth. And that the more you value yourself the more you can enjoy being with yourself—alone or in the company of others. So, get a pad and pencil. Let's take inventory!

Finished goods: Well, there are those grown children who are off living productive lives...a beloved parent who is now gone...the friend or colleague to whom you gave a fresh start in life...

Goods in process: What about that relationship that still needs your attention?...the not-yet-completed project on your kitchen counter or desk or in your dreams...your prayer life, Bible study and spiritual growth...

Capital Assets: Consider your earthly home...the gift of life itself...the precious value of God's unlimited and everlasting love for you....

Now, write down your personal inventory and tape it to the refrigerator door. Then pray this prayer:

Dear God, help me to remember that I am precious to You. Teach me my true value. —MARILYN MOORE JENSEN

WE ARE FAMILY

29 SUNDAY
Who is my mother? and who are my brethren?
—*MATTHEW 12:48*

Florence's grown children make their homes in faraway cities. Education and career opportunities drew them from rural Wisconsin. Florence encouraged them to develop their potential. But she misses her children's presence.

Evelyn's brothers and sisters all married and moved from the family home. Then her mom and dad sold the large homestead and bought a condo. Evelyn had her own apartment in the city where she worked. But when her family's home was gone, she felt cut off...isolated...on her own.

These scenarios can ring painfully true for many of us. The loss of a natural family proximity comes to most of us at some time or another. And if our family has been our defense against loneliness, that loss can be devastating.

Jesus understood that. In a dramatic gesture to all lonely people of His world and ours, He stretched out His hand to His disciples and said, "Behold my mother and my brethren!" Can you imagine the stir He caused?

"We are family?" they must have muttered as they sized one another up.

But it's true, isn't it? When we follow Christ we join His family.

Today in church think about that: The old gent up front is your brother...That woman who sings so loud is your sister...And might you be mother, too, to those fidgety youngsters across the aisle?

"Family" life can never be more fulfilling than when we can stretch forth our hands to one another and say: *These* are my parents, my sisters and my brothers."

Dear God, may loneliness serve as Your call to meet my brothers and sisters. Thank You for this family that will never let me go. —MARILYN MOORE JENSEN

 MONDAY
...Let the peace of Christ rule in your hearts...
—*COLOSSIANS 3:15 (RSV)*

Last spring as my thoughts turned to planting a garden, a friend sent me an unusual package of seeds in the mail. "Peace seeds," it said on the outside. Inside were six different colored pods along with the following instructions:

To grow a peaceful world, sow these seeds:
White—*Forgiveness* for someone who's wronged you.
Red—*Prayer* for someone you dislike.
Green—*Hospitality* to a stranger.
Yellow—*Acceptance* of someone who sees things differently.
Blue—*Kindness* in the face of rudeness.
Pink—*Generosity* toward someone less fortunate.

Today on Memorial Day I find myself wondering if perhaps the best way to commemorate wars of the past and all those who have fought—and died—is by sowing peace seeds for the future. Maybe you'd like to join me in planting some seeds today. Just think what bright blooms of love our world-garden might grow!

Let Your peace blossom forth in our world, Lord, and may it begin in me. —SUE MONK KIDD

| 31 | TUESDAY
...Thy people shall be my people, and thy God my God.
—RUTH 1:16

As a child growing up in California, I often visited the family plot at the cemetery with my grandparents. At the foot of the mountains, graced with live oaks and royal palms, Pasadena's cemetery was a friendly place, the perfect spot for a picnic. I liked reading the names on the granite stones and studying the dates of the tablets on the lawn. When we came to our family plot, we would prune the rosebush and trim the grass. My grandparents would tell us who was who and how we were related to them. This was our corner of the graveyard.

One day a year, though, our corner looked a lot like the rest of the cemetery. Each Memorial Day, Grandfather and his fellow members of the local American Legion planted small American flags next to the gravestones of every former soldier. Veterans of the Civil War, the Spanish-American War, the World Wars and Korea all wore the Stars and Stripes. As far as the eye could see, the grass was covered with flags. And at the end of the day we helped my grandfather—and the American Legion—pick them up.

On that day I think I started to learn what it means to be part of a community, and part of a nation. Big ornate monuments with angels and scrolls, simple stone crosses, marble slabs with only a name, the graves commemorated all kinds of Americans. But all the people there had served the same cause; they all carried the flag. Their flag was my flag; their cause was mine. I'll tell you how it made me feel: proud.

Lord, make Your people our people, and Your cause ours.
—RICK HAMLIN

154

Thank-You Notes to God

1.

2.

3.

4.

5.

6.

7.

8.

9.

10.

11.

12.

13.

14.

15.

16

17

18

19

20

21

22

23

24

25

26

27

28

29

30

31

S	M	T	W	T	F	S
			1	2	3	4
5	6	7	8	9	10	11
12	13	14	15	16	17	18
19	20	21	22	23	24	25
26	27	28	29	30		

JUNE

BE AN ON-GOER
Your Spiritual Pilgrimage

I press toward the mark for the prize of the high calling of God in Christ Jesus. —PHILIPPIANS 3:14

Now comes June with her long calm days and scented nights. This is a look-forward month, really. Brides and grooms promising to love and cherish forever. High school graduates moving on to college or jobs. College graduates ready at last to face the challenging world.

This month try to be an on-goer. Look forward, not back. The past is gone; let it go. The present is a springboard to the future. St. Paul said it well: "Forgetting those things which are behind, and reaching forth unto those things which are before" (Philippians 3:13).

Press on!

Tandem Power for June

1 HOPE AND OPPORTUNITY
I the Lord have called thee in righteousness, and will hold thine hand, and will keep thee, and give thee for a covenant of the people... —ISAIAH 42:6

Seated in Kathy's living room at precisely 7:30 P.M., we look over the agenda for our Women's Ministry meeting. As usual, the first item is a short devotional aimed at inspiring us for the tasks ahead. "During this meeting," Kathy proposes simply, "why don't we use the word *opportunity* instead of *problem* and see what happens?" The idea catches on slowly as we begin our agenda.

I am one of the first. "We have this...*opportunity.* We need to recruit more members." The discussion that follows is filled with suggestions about building new relationships within our large church membership. Then there is the *opportunity* of chairing the mother-daughter banquet and the *opportunity* of clarifying our goals by rewriting our organizational guidelines.

The last item is the resignation of one of our members. She begins with a wobbly voice. "Many of you don't know yet, but—" she pauses and takes a deep breath—"I recently found out that I have cancer. And with this new...*opportunity*...in my life, I am getting involved with two different cancer support groups that are filled with hurting people. The Lord is helping me not to ask *why?* but instead, *what?* What is it that He wants me to do? I think He wants to use me in these groups, so that is where I'm spending more time now." By the end of her last sentence, her voice has grown strong and steady in a room of hushed silence.

As I drive home, I keep seeing an image of my friend with cancer reaching up and taking God's hand and turning her fear into hope as they face this new challenge together. With Tandem Power, in partnership with God, she is transforming her stumbling block into a stepping stone. Her *problem* is becoming her *opportunity*.

How about spending the whole month of June practicing this same suggestion? Maybe it begins with the way we choose to look at our problems. What are your problems today? A deadline? A phone call? A broken relationship? Loneliness? Reach for God's helping hand, seeing it as an *opportunity* rather than a *problem*.

Lord, let us accept Your helping hand each day this month— and together let us turn our problems into opportunities, and find hope instead of despair. —CAROL KUYKENDALL

| 2 | THURSDAY |

Praying always with all prayer and supplication in the Spirit... —EPHESIANS 6:18

Not long ago I was complaining to a friend that, for me, it was impossible to have both morning prayer and morning exercise. "If I spend a half hour in the swimming pool," I said, "then I must dry and set my hair, eat breakfast, prepare to go to the office. There's no time for praying."

"There's a way to do both," my friend answered. "For instance, I like to jog four mornings a week. As I run, I mentally recite the Psalms. The beautiful rhythm of these words of worship blend well with the movement of my body. Try it while you swim. You'll see."

So the next time I got ready to dive into the pool, I paused and sent up a prayer, asking God to bless my body, to keep it healthy for His service. Then as I stroked through the water, I prayed for people I knew, people with problems, people who were ill. And by the time I'd completed thirty laps, I'd also accomplished quite a lot of praying!

Do your soul and body need rejuvenating? Try prayer along with exercise. After all, God has promised to hear us, no matter where we are.

Dear Father, help me to keep fit—all of me.
—ELEANOR SASS

| 3 | FRIDAY |

And I will give thee the treasures of darkness, and hidden riches of secret places... —ISAIAH 45:3

Years ago, when we bought our place in the country, we were advised to cut down the poplars. The yard was full of these ordinary, taken-for-granted trees, with their trunks of pilgrim gray and their pleasant rectangular leaves. "But they're only poplars," the agent said. "Not much good for firewood or lumber. Cut them down.

One of the neighbors was already attacking his. The children stood at a safe distance watching as the trees came crashing down, bearing with them a veritable treasury of unsuspected blooms.

"Look, look at all the beautiful flowers!" Gathering as many as they could carry, the youngsters came running home. "Tulips, big fat tulips, from the top of Mr. Urman's tree!"

We trained the field glasses on the tops of our own trees—and behold! A vast sky-garden, tossing its mass of green-golden petals to the sun. Birds were flitting happily about, chirping and singing among these lovely cups of color unknown to most of us below.

All of a sudden the humble poplars had attained new grace and loveliness. We regarded them with an astonished new respect. And though some of them had to go, we cherished those we could save, knowing that at their tops, where we couldn't see it, existed all this beauty.

Like people, I have often thought. Like some people who go through life modest, taken-for-granted, hiding their talents—or merely not flaunting them. Then suddenly you discover a quality unsuspected. Like our mailman—I finally learned his limp was due to a war injury; he'd been decorated for bravery and now works with handicapped boys. That woman who delivered our eggs—she also painted eggshells, fragile works of art that took my breath away, when at last I bothered to go see them. My son's history teacher—a colorless man I always thought, until I read his poetry.

Why didn't I realize this before? Each time I wonder. And then I remember the poplars. The flowers were there all the time. I just didn't look high enough.

Dear Father: Sometimes a tree has to fall at our feet before we can see its beauty. Don't let me wait to find the wonder and joy in simple, everyday people. —MARJORIE HOLMES

4 SATURDAY

...And what doth the Lord require of thee, but to do justly, and to love mercy, and to walk humbly with thy God?
—MICAH 6:8

The parade is coming down the street. The police escort has passed, motorcycle sirens whining. The flag has brought to attention the crowd lining both sides of Main Street, and here comes the high school band. How smart the members look in their blue and white uniforms! Every foot is in step, marching in time with the music they play.

And there is their director, Mr. Bennett, walking along beside the band. Strange, I have never really noticed him before, and yet I can't remember a parade when Mr. Bennett wasn't there. He just seemed a part of the background. Through the years, young musicians have marched and played and been applauded and gone on to bigger things. But Mr. Bennett has just stayed, growing older and walking quietly beside the band, keeping the members in step, ready with aid if any got too tired along the route. Just there to help, no praise, no glory for him.

My heart surges with thanksgiving for Mr. Bennett and for people like him, those faithfuls in the background, doing what needs to be done and letting others get the praise. I'm going to write some notes when I get home, and Mr. Bennett will get the first one. He will know that he is noticed and appreciated. And as the parade goes by, I'm making a mental note of others to whom I'll write.

Don't you have a list to start, too?

Lord, help me to learn to serve You and my fellowman humbly and without desire of praise or recognition. Amen.
—DRUE DUKE

5 SUNDAY

...Speak, Lord; for thy servant heareth.
—I SAMUEL 3:9

Whenever our travels take Norman and me to Spain, I'm always impressed by the friendliness of the Spanish people. They seem to like American visitors. They always try to make us feel welcome.

161

The telephone operators in the hotel where we stay in Madrid have a pleasant way of answering if you lift the receiver in your room. They say, *"Dígame,"* pronounced "Dee-gah-may," which in Spanish means, "Say to me" or "Tell me." "Tell me what you wish," they are saying in their gentle Castilian accent. "Tell me what you need. Tell me what you want me to do."

I think sometimes that simple Spanish word would make an eloquent and effective prayer. *"Dígame,* Lord. Tell me what You want me to do. Tell me what I should do. Tell me what I can do today that will be pleasing in Your sight."

And what is the telephone wire between the Lord and me? It's the invisible thing called prayer.

Dígame, Lord! —RUTH STAFFORD PEALE

| 6 | MONDAY | FIRESIDE FRIEND |

I can do all things through Christ which strengtheneth me. —PHILIPPIANS 4:13

Every day had been filled with "worthy" causes. Monday, the United Way; Tuesday, a meeting; Wednesday, a church report...and on it went. I wrestled with the question: Have I overextended myself? And believing that to be the case, I prayed that God would take some of my responsibilities away from me.

Not long after that I came across a quotation from the American clergyman Phillips Brooks. He said, "Do not pray for easy lives. Pray to be stronger men! Do not pray for tasks equal to your powers. Pray for powers equal to your tasks."

Those words made me realize something. I was praying all wrong. To be sure, there are times when I need to say "no" and not crowd my life unnecessarily. But when the problem is not one of too much to do, but of attitude (or lack thereof), then instead of asking God for a smaller crop, why not ask Him to help me carry a bigger basket?

Lord, help me not to forget...though I am weak, You are strong. —TERRY HELWIG

7	TUESDAY

Every good gift... is from above, and cometh down from the Father... —JAMES 1:17

I had driven the carpool that day and my nine-year-old grandson had left graded homework on the back seat. A sheet of drawing paper graded with an A at the top caught my eye. On it, in evenly ruled spaces, Bogart had printed boldly:

I help others	I'm caring	I'm not a tattletale
I'm kind	I'm talented	I'm smart
I'm polite	I share	I'm fast
I'm friendly	I'm brave	I'm loyal

Hm-m-m, he has a very high opinion of himself, I thought a little sadly. It bothered me enough that I approached his fourth-grade teacher about it.

"An excellent paper," she said. "Bo has a fine self-image."

"Isn't it a little conceited?" I asked. "What of those virtues of modesty, humility, meekness?"

"The assignment was to list things for which to give thanks. Most of the other children listed material possessions. Bo had a different idea." She smiled, turning the paper over.

On the back he had written: "Thank You, Lord, for me and my talents. I love You dearly. Amen." It was signed with a red heart trailing a rainbow tail.

Father, in times of self-doubt and small confidence I will praise Thee for these talents and graces I know I have received from You:

1. _____
2. _____
3. _____.

—ELAINE ST. JOHNS

8	WEDNESDAY

Husbands, love your wives... —EPHESIANS 5:25

When I was a boy and read the newspaper for its Tarzan cartoons each day, I ran across this little poem in the Lifestyle section. It's not great poetry and I have no idea who wrote it, but it's stuck in my mind all my life:

> Two lovers walking down the street.
> She trips, he murmurs, "Careful, Sweet."
> Now wed they tread the selfsame street;
> She trips, he growls, "Pick up your feet."

It's the same street, and the same woman, but somehow the growling husband has forgotten what the lover once knew: how to cherish the woman he loves. What a loss!

Forgetting to cherish...it can be so easy, and so dangerous. I've done it, and maybe you have too. So today I'm making a list of things about my wife: What she likes. What she dislikes. What she's good at. What she dreams of. What makes her special. I'll bet I'll find a lot of things I have forgotten to cherish about her.

You could try it, too—with your spouse, or a child, or a dear friend, or anyone you've been taking for granted lately. God gave us a wonderful gift when He gave us our families and friends, and only asks in return the simple, essential Christian commandment: *to love them.*

Father, today I will especially cherish _____,
(Name)
for these reasons:
1. _____,
2. _____,
3. _____.

—LEE WEBBER

9	THURSDAY

...Lay up his words in thine heart. —JOB 22:22

I enjoy those quizzes in newspapers and magazines. I never get a hundred percent—I rarely even get a passing grade. But trying is fun. So I thought *I'd* make up a quiz today. I was noticing that people I admire are busy, but that somehow they seem to find time in each day to nurture and improve themselves and others, so I thought I'd make up my quiz from people I admire. Are you ready?

- Do you try to walk at least fifteen minutes a day—both to exercise your body and clear your mind?

- Do you try to do at least one kind thing a day—run an errand, pay a compliment, smile at the harried bank teller or salesclerk?
- Do you spend "quiet time" with God every day?
- Do you spend time listening to your loved ones—*really listening?*
- Do you read books? According to one recent statistic, the average American adult reads less than one book a year. Do you do better than that?
- Do you praise God by what you do as well as by what you say?

Well, I can't say I'd get a hundred on that quiz. But I've been trying to stretch myself a little bit more each day. Would you like to join me?

God, You've given us such potential. I'm going to try to pack more of it into each day and make the most of Your gift of life.
—OSCAR GREENE

Spirit Lifter
A PRAYER FOR MARRIAGE
*May God send you
enough joy
to keep your hearts singing,
enough sorrow
to make you understanding,
enough trials
to keep you strong,
enough leisure
to refresh your spirits,
and enough love
to make the world seem beautiful.*
—AUTHOR UNKNOWN

10 FRIDAY

And if God cares so wonderfully for flowers that are here today and gone tomorrow, won't he more surely care for you? —MATTHEW 6:30 (LB)

I'd been feeling like an overloaded circuit recently. As a single parent with four children and three part-time jobs, I had absolutely no time for myself.

One busy day I looked out our dining room window at the barn-sized willow tree with a thousand branches hanging to the ground, forming a geodesic dome, and impulsively I found myself inviting six-year-old Andrew to have lunch with me under it. We spread a blanket, ate, read stories and tree-gazed.

The next day while running errands with a car full of kids, I happened to see a family of woodchucks popping their heads up and down in a cabbage field. I stopped the car and we all watched the antics of these little wild creatures. That little reprieve from our rush-rush routine brought out a flurry of comments, questions and later an encyclopedia session.

The kids learned about woodchucks, but I learned how important it is to take time from my busy days to enjoy the little things in life. That picnic under the willow tree and the furry creatures in the field had somehow eased the stress and worry in my life.

Today, why don't you find something small, maybe even incidental, in your life and just plain enjoy it. You might be surprised to find that a little bit of pleasure can help dispel a mountain of troubles.

Open my eyes, Lord, to the little things around me that can calm me down. —PATRICIA LORENZ

11 SATURDAY

...He hath sent me to bind up the brokenhearted, to proclaim liberty to the captives... —ISAIAH 61:1

I came across the statue in the central plaza of Agua de Dios ("Water of God"), a hot, tropical town about a three-hour drive down the mountain from Bogotá, Colombia. George, an old schoolmate, had left me to wander while he made a business call. "It's an unusual town," he'd told me, though he didn't say why. I myself found it rather typical: dusty streets, brick and adobe houses, a large church dominating the town's center. Then, in the plaza, this peculiar, life-sized statue of a man playing a piano.

It was a hybrid work of art—the piano made of stone, the man sculpted in metal—yet there was something compelling about its innocence. The pianist's fingers fluttered happily over the keyboard, his face aglow. He was obviously enjoying himself. I couldn't recall ever having seen a smiling statue before.

"That's Luis A. Calvo," George explained later. "Wrote some of Colombia's favorite songs. Beautiful music. They're very proud of him here."

"Is that why the town is 'unusual'?"

"No," he said, frowning. The reason was a darker one, for until recent times Agua de Dios had been a leper colony, its large population despised and feared. In the days when leprosy was still thought to be contagious, anyone found to have "the sickness," adult or child, was snatched up and sent here to remain behind barbed wire, forever cut off from family and friends. At last, in the late fifties, the government let down the barriers, but a great number of the sick continued on in the town.

"And Calvo?" I said. "Did he have the sickness?"

"Oh, yes. He died here."

We were driving out of town now, past the checkpoint stations no longer in use. I thought back to the statue in the plaza, its smile a simple memorial to the transcendent power of the human spirit. Beautiful music from pain and humiliation. Beauty for ashes....

Yes, Lord, You have taught me that I, too, can overcome the world. —VAN VARNER

 SUNDAY   **FIRESIDE FRIEND**
If we follow on to know the Lord...he shall come unto us as the rain... —HOSEA 6:3

As the tour bus wound through the narrow streets of St. Thomas, our guide pointed out government buildings, luxury hotels and breathtaking vistas. Everywhere beauty bloomed in a profusion of bright flowers. Row after row of white houses lined the streets, their red roofs glistening in the afternoon sun. Someone asked the guide about springs and rivers on the island. "We have none," he replied simply. "All our water comes from rain."

"What do you do when it doesn't rain?" I asked.

Our guide smiled. "I'll show you." We stopped in front of a typical house. "See," he said, pointing at the corrugated tin, "the roof has little tunnels in it. Rain runs down these into gutters. From the gutters it goes into a cistern." I looked and, sure enough, the gutter pipe disappeared into the basement of the house, where the cistern waited to be filled. "So this is how we have plenty of water for cooking and drinking and washing," he finished.

"But if it doesn't rain..." I persisted.

He waved the idea aside with his hand. "It always rains. Sometimes it takes longer for the drops to fall. But, in time, it always rains."

I think about those houses now, when my spirit seems lifeless and dry, when the refreshing rain of God's presence seems far away. That's when I dip into my "cistern" of past blessings and kept promises: my husband's safe tour of duty overseas; my speedy recovery from pneumonia; the deep peace that eventually enfolded me after a friend's suicide; the birth of our two healthy children. Then, encouraged, I wait for fresh outpourings. And in time—God's time—they always come.

Today, Father, I will remember Your past goodness to me:
1. _____
2. _____
3. _____

—MARY LOU CARNEY

| 13 | MONDAY
Lord, thou hast been favourable unto thy land.
—PSALM 85:1

When I was a youngster, I would gaze in awe at the huge flag on the J. L. Hudson department store in Detroit. For decades this flag, which measured 170 by 90 feet, was the largest in the world. Today a larger flag flies on the Verrazano-Narrows Bridge in New York. It measures 410 by 210 feet—even bigger than a football field!

But the flag I remember best stood in the corner of our schoolroom. I can close my eyes and still hear the cadence of youthful voices rising and falling as we recited in unison Henry Holcomb Bennett's poem "The Flag Goes By":

> Hats off!
> Along the street there comes
> A blare of bugles, a ruffle of drums,
> A flash of color beneath the sky.
> Hats off!
> The flag is passing by.

I admit to a lump in my throat whenever I see a flag being raised. Maybe it's because it reminds me of my solemn and joyful responsibilities as an American. Because when I see the Stars and Stripes waving above me in the breeze, it reminds me that whatever I do as an American, I do "under God" and His watchful eyes.

Father, under You, let me do my part to make being an American something to be proud of. —SHIRLEY POPE WAITE

14 TUESDAY
Behold, how good and how pleasant it is for brethren to dwell together in unity! —PSALM 133:1

At the school across the street from our house, a flagpole towers over the schoolyard. Today is Flag Day and the little ones are outside saluting. I watch the children standing straight and proud under the flag, part of a ceremony they barely understand. These small Americans, preparing to take our places, to become the next generation that makes their mark on the world. I imagine telling them something about the flag they're saluting....

On June 14, 1777, our first Flag Day, George Washington said, "We take the stars from the heaven, and the red from the Mother Country, separating it by the white stripes, thus showing we are separated from her, and the white stripes shall go down to posterity representing liberty."

I imagine telling them about the homemade flag that flew over Fort McHenry on that September 14 back in 1814, outlined against the rockets' red glare. Telling them it was fifty feet long, with fifteen stars and fifteen stripes—two more than needed. Would they be thrilled to hear of Lieutenant Colonel Theodore Roosevelt and his Rough Riders storming San Juan Hill and planting our flag ninety years ago? Would they be proud of the six United States Marines raising our flag on Iwo Jima, during World War II?

The children return to their classrooms. The flag whips in the breeze. It has been planted in many places. But perhaps no better place than in a schoolyard, for children to learn their first stumbling lessons in what it means to be an American. With its red for courage, white for liberty and blue for loyalty, the flag stands for a heritage we've been given, and a future we're making.

Father, a new generation looks to us to see what it means to be an American. Let our actions show them it is a good and proud thing. —OSCAR GREENE

| 15 | WEDNESDAY |

The Lord bless thee, and keep thee. —NUMBERS 6:24

Yesterday was my daughter's birthday. Karen has been such a blessing to me that I wanted to find a tangible way to express my love and prayers for her. Since I'm praying for special blessings on her marriage, for serenity amid the rush of her busy life and for all the treasures of spiritual growth, I chose some ingredients that symbolized these blessings, put them together with my love and made Karen a Blessing Pie. I'm going to deliver it with a card that reads:

BLESSING PIE
Hidden in its ingredients are my prayers for you:
A spicy crust, signifying the many treasures of a giving and receiving relationship (1 Kings 10:10 and 10:13).
A cool green filling, symbol of serenity (Psalm 23:2).
Pineapple, coconut and almonds, to represent the fruits of the spirit (Galatians 5:22).
Serve with a generous helping from the blessing passage in Deuteronomy 28:2–6.

If you'd like to make a Blessing Pie for someone you love, here's the recipe: Pat into a 9-inch pie pan 22 ginger snaps (crushed), 5 T melted butter or margarine (*not* diet). Bake 10 minutes at 300°F. Mix 1 8-oz. tub whipped topping; 1 small package pistachio instant pudding mix; 1 8-oz. can crushed pineapple (drained). Pour into cooled crust. Top with ½ C slivered almonds and ¾ C flaked coconut. Wrap in your love and deliver with a blessing card.

Today, Lord, bless my friend, _____.

—MARILYN MORGAN HELLEBERG

Family Time

| 16 | LEARNING TO LISTEN

The Lord came and stood there, calling as at the other times, "Samuel! Samuel!" Then Samuel said, "Speak, for your servant is listening." —I SAMUEL 3:10

Three times young Samuel heard a voice in the dark call his name, and three times he ran to Eli saying, "Here I am; you called me." And each time the old prophet assured the boy he hadn't called. The third time Eli suspected something unusual was occurring, so he told Samuel to go back to bed and listen. Once again the voice called, "Samuel!" This time the boy didn't move, but instead he said, "Speak, for your servant is listening."

Three times Samuel heard the voice. But the fourth time he really and actively listened, and there was a difference. This time he got the message!

"I know you can hear me, but you aren't listening!" Sound familiar? We've said it to each other more than once.

Someone has said that most Americans make good talkers but lousy listeners. And Dietrich Bonhoeffer, the German Christian martyr of World War II, said, "Most Christians are talking when they should be listening." At the same time a lot of us are just *hearing* when we should be *listening*. We're much like Dennis the Menace in the marvelous Hank Ketcham strip when he said to his friend, "Sure I was listening; I just wasn't paying attention."

Jesus understood the importance of listening. At one point He "called the crowd to him and said, 'Listen and understand'" (Matthew 15:10, NIV). The idea here is that if we listen attentively, actively, with open minds, we will understand. Picking up on Dr. J. B. Phillips' idea: When we listen like that, we allow God's Word to find a home in our hearts (John 6:38, JBP).

This same kind of listening can revolutionize our family relationships. When Harriett and I are really communicating with each other, we are listening carefully and are concentrating on what is being said. Our heads are tilted toward each other, and our eyes are locked together. Each of us is seriously trying to be responsible for our half of the transaction. We are listening because we care. This is what we believe theologian Paul Tillich meant when he said, "The first duty of love is to listen."

In our instant gratification culture, really listening doesn't just happen. We try, we practice, we concentrate. When we're careless, we may fail, but we don't want to. So we work at it again, and succeed. The rewards of listening to each other are great, for listening is a way to understanding and growth and healthy relationships in the day-to-day give-and-take of family life.

Samuel listened and he was never the same again. The Old Testament writer put it this way, "The Lord was with Samuel as he grew up" (I Samuel 3:19, NIV).

Lord, give us the wisdom to talk less and listen more.
—FLOYD AND HARRIETT THATCHER

| 17 | FRIDAY | FIRESIDE FRIEND |

But the fruit of the Spirit is…faithfulness.
—*GALATIANS 5:22 (RSV)*

Years ago, Mom's pride and joy was a small two-foot-high dogwood that my older brother Stanley had planted at the back of our yard. She loved dogwoods but had found them impossible to grow. This one, about two years old, looked as if it were going to make it, and Mom was thrilled.

That year I took over the mowing job from Stanley, who strongly cautioned me to be careful of the tree. Not paying much heed, I tried to cut the grass as close to the dogwood as possible so that I wouldn't have to trim by hand. One day I crashed the lawn mower into the fragile little tree. The tree was bent double. If left unattended, it would have slowly died under the hot June sun.

I've got to do something, I remember thinking. I rushed to the house and grabbed a big roll of masking tape and raced out to the backyard. There, I wound the tape around the tree again and again until, although somewhat crooked, it was together again.

In my innocence, I never doubted that the tree would heal. When my mother found out about the accident, I could tell she was disappointed, but she just said, "Well, David, you'd better not count on saving it. Dogwoods are so delicate."

Today, I can walk out to see that same dogwood tree standing ten feet high. It's covered with buds, but if you look closely at the base of the trunk, you'll see a small curving scar, a gentle reminder of the innocence of a little boy who wouldn't lose faith.

God, when I am tempted to give up, help me to hold on and do what I can. Then, with the faith of a child, leave my problem in Your hands. —DAVID CORNELIUS

| 18 | SATURDAY
...*None of us liveth to himself, and no man dieth to himself.* —ROMANS 14:7

One Saturday afternoon I strolled over to the convenience store for a newspaper. When I stepped inside, the store was dark and quiet.

"Are you open?" I asked.

The clerk shrugged. "We're open, but I can't sell anything because the register is out. Some car hit a power pole on the edge of town."

As I browsed, hoping the power would return, I couldn't help pondering the far-reaching effect one person can have on countless others. One customer needed change to buy postage for an urgent letter. The letter would be late. A gasoline customer had to drive away on a nearly empty tank. Many other customers entered the store and promptly left. Sales would be down. And with the equipment malfunctioning, the clerk would have to stay late and check on it. All this was happening in just one of several stores and houses affected by the power outage.

Then I wondered about the effect I have on others. What do my students lose when I don't teach well? How is my family affected when I am rude or impatient? What about strangers or people in service jobs, when I am unfriendly or curt?

On the other hand, who can measure the long arm of kindness or the electric effect of cheerfulness? Today and every day, I've learned I have the power to brighten my world and make it hum if I choose to. What kind of far-reaching effect can you generate today through kindness or love, peace or joy? Try it, now.

Father, help me to remember that all my acts, big and small, will affect others, sometimes in ways unknown to me. So let me always act for good. —DANIEL SCHANTZ

| 19 | SUNDAY |

A fool despises his father's instruction, but he who heeds admonition is prudent. —PROVERBS 15:5 (RSV)

My father's frown can melt granite—which is why he made a terrific high school principal. He rarely lectured or scolded. It was not his way. And because his standards of behavior were so high, a simple scowl was punishment enough. Boy, did his disapproval hurt. I know.

Once in the tenth grade, I left an important paper to the last day. The deadline was firm. My teacher was strict. No paper? F! And still I procrastinated.

At eleven the night before the paper was due, I was furiously writing behind a huge wall of library books. My father peeked into my room. "I'm going to bed," he announced. And frowned. His disapproval added to my shame. He didn't have to say more. My aching fingers and head told me what a stupid mistake I had made.

At three A.M. I had finished the rough draft and was typing the final copy. With only a few pages left, my fingers gave out. Tearful and exhausted, I rolled onto the bed. There was nothing to do but face the teacher the next day, explain my situation. And accept the F.

My father poked his head in the door. "Get some sleep," he said. And typed the last six pages of my paper.

When I awoke, my paper lay on my desk in a neat pile with a paper clip at the upper edge. And Dad? He was out in the kitchen frying eggs for our breakfast.

Now that I am grown, I know the disguises fathers wear. I know their fear and heartbreak as they yearn for their children's success. I have learned to look for the care disguised by the frown in my father's face. The love entangled in the disapproval. The laugh wrinkles etched in the corners of the watchful eyes.

On this Father's Day, we thank You, God, for fathers every-where who exhort us sternly to soar, yet bear us up gently so we will not fail. —LINDA CHING SLEDGE

| 20 | MONDAY

I have taught thee in the way of wisdom; I have led thee in right paths. —PROVERBS 4:11

Many years ago my stepfather gave me a gift I have treasured all my life: a love for words and the way to use them. He did it without even realizing it. He simply shared his own enthusiasm for language with me.

In our family, in the days before television, we read after dinner. My dad always had his nose in a book about words, stuffy-sounding things like grammar, syntax and sentence structure. Except that he didn't think they were stuffy, and you could tell that by the look on his face: intense, concentrated, half-smiling.

When I asked my dad what he was reading, he always put the book down and told me about it. About how important it is to use the correct word to describe what you want to say. There was, he said, only one correct word, and the important thing was to find it. How many apples were in that bowl on the table? A few, a couple, or sev-eral? When I looked, it was as if I were seeing the bowl for the first time—it made me think. And it was fun.

My dad also showed me that a dictionary is a friend with answers to lots of questions. Going through its pages, we felt like explorers tracking down the way a word is spelled, what it means and how to use it. Gradually words began to unlock thoughts and feelings that had been inside me—and that *is* exciting!

Taking the time to share our interests with a child is a gift that will last a lifetime. Thanks, Dad!

Bless fathers everywhere today, Lord. And make us grateful for their many spoken and silent gifts that enrich us all our lives. —PHYLLIS HOBE

21	TUESDAY

Come and dine... —*JOHN 21:12*

"Summer," someone said, "is when we take time off from making a living in order to do some living." Certainly from a family standpoint some of our most memorable times together have come during summer.

One of the kids recently reminded me of such a moment that occurred on a family hiking trip several years ago. It was a hot day, our canteens were empty and our mouths dry when we came down a mountain into a lush valley parted by a dirt road. Several cars had parked nearby, the occupants of which were gathered up the way at the face of a rocky wall. Coming closer we saw that they were filling containers with water, which bubbled cold and clear from the stone. We licked our lips at the prospect and when it came our turn the mountain's gift did not disappoint. We buried our heads under the flow and took long, satisfying drafts like workhorses at a trough. "Water never tasted any better," my son reflected.

Memories of times spent with friends and loved ones at play are some of the most lasting, and like scrapbooks by the fireplace on cold winter nights, they have a way of thawing frozen hearts. Maybe it's the slower pace of Junes, Julys and Augusts that make the atmosphere more conducive to conversation and caring. These languid days offer a great opportunity for reaching out to people. "Come join us for a cookout," "How 'bout a picnic?" or "Meet us at the beach" are all icebreakers for overdue reunions. When on a trip, take time to visit old friends along the way. Fifty miles or a couple of hours may seem a lot, but in retrospect those get-togethers will make nicer memories than a few missed museums and monuments. Summers in particular are a good time for putting people ahead of things.

Teach us the value of things present, Lord, so in the future we won't regret the past. —FRED BAUER

22	WEDNESDAY

...Ask, and it shall be given you; seek, and ye shall find... —*LUKE 11:9*

One day on our Florida vacation we were settled on a secluded stretch of beach when we spied a large fishing craft in the distance.

"They're probably fishing for marlin," my husband said. "Do you have the field glasses? Let's have a look."

"Oh, dear, no, I thought you brought them," I wailed. And all afternoon we had a sense of something missing. When a flock of strange birds flew over, they were beautiful, yes, but without the glasses we couldn't tell. And not far behind them a huge jet with a foreign insignia. *Lufthansa*, we believed, like the one we'd flown to Germany. Frustrated, we gazed at the sky.

At last I began gathering up gear and, opening the beach bag, gave a little cry. For there they were, in plain sight at the bottom. "Our field glasses have been here all the time. Oh, if only I'd looked!"

Over and over such things happen. For instance, the time I thought I had lost my favorite pin. I'd gone back to the library to look for it, searched the car, combed the house, and finally, grieving, given up. Until one day, reaching into the back of the closet, my fingers touched something. And there it was, this tiny treasure sparkling in my hand. It had been waiting quietly in the one place I hadn't thought to look.

Isn't it that way with our problems, too? Oh, the hours I've wasted fretting, worrying, searching for answers from family, close friends, even lawyers and counselors. Looking, desperately looking, but seldom in the right places. Then when all else fails, and at last I turn to the Bible—what a joyful surprise. The solution was right there all the time. If only I'd thought to look!

Dear Jesus, You promised "Seek, and you shall find." When next I search in vain, help me to remember where to look.
—MARJORIE HOLMES

23	THURSDAY

They helped every one his neighbour; and every one said to his brother, Be of good courage.   —ISAIAH 41:6

In an attempt to "bring back the bluebird," my husband and I maintain fifty nesting boxes near our Lake Michigan cottage. This past summer we were delighted when a pair of these lovely, endearing birds settled into a box in our backyard.

Then one morning, shortly after five babies hatched, I found the male dead by the roadside, apparently struck while fluttering down for insects to feed his young. Heartsick, I picked up the small, limp, still-warm body. The loss of even one of these endangered birds is a tragedy. Surely this was a double tragedy, for the mother alone could never feed her hungry brood.

That evening the unbelievable happened. A pair of bluebirds from a nearby field and their five nearly grown fledglings appeared on the back fence. Daily from dawn till dusk they helped the widowed mother feed her nestlings. They stayed even after the babies were out of the box to assist in training them to become self-sufficient. At summer's end they migrated together.

Love thy neighbor? These gentle, unassuming birds *lived* their love—a lesson I badly need in this fast-paced age. And it's one lesson I want to practice every chance I get.

Dear God, I've so often turned aside when a neighbor needed help or comfort. Thank You for a poignant reminder.
—ALETHA JANE LINDSTROM

---

24 FRIDAY
...They shall obtain joy and gladness, and sorrow and sighing shall flee away. —ISAIAH 35:10

During the drive to my mother-in-law's house my mood turned glum. In the back seat Bob and Ann bickered constantly.

"Mama, he crossed the line," Ann cried.

"You touched my side first!" Bob said.

Five miles back, after a fight over who was taking up the most space, I'd divided the back seat down the middle with an imaginary line. Now they were fighting over the line. I glared at them, then turned to the window with a sigh. Not only were the children fighting, but the dog had gotten carsick on the seat and the coolant in the air conditioner had given out. "It will take me all weekend to recover from this trip," I muttered to my husband. The rest of the way I frowned in silence.

At last we turned into my mother-in-law's driveway. But instead of driving up, Sandy braked the car. For there in the middle of the concrete driveway, growing from a peephole crack in the cement, was a pink periwinkle nearly a foot high. We got out and gathered around it. And standing there marveling how a flower could bloom out of concrete, the thought came: *God's joy is like that periwinkle.* Even when life becomes "cemented" with frustrations—when the children bicker, the dog gets sick and things break down—His joy can spring up. It can bloom through any sort of barrier. It only needs a tiny opening....

I looked at my family. A small "peephole" of a smile was breaking across my face.

Father, despite all the circumstances, big and small, keep Your invincible joy blooming in me.   —SUE MONK KIDD

25 SATURDAY
Do not judge by appearances, but judge with right judgment.   —JOHN 7:24 (RSV)

My new friend and I sat on her front porch getting acquainted. I liked her and her home, an old southern house with a big front porch, rocking chairs and lovely hanging baskets. All the baskets were alive with radiant blooms...except one. It was obviously dead, ugly, an eyesore. My friend offered no explanation as we admired the blooms, so I didn't ask the question forming in my mind.

Then she had to go in to answer the phone. Curious I tiptoed over to the dead plant, pulled apart the brown leaves, thinking I might somehow find an answer as to why she allowed it to hang on her porch. Suddenly I was looking right into three pairs of bright little eyes. Startled, the baby birds began chirping. I quickly sat back down in my rocker. Instantly their calls brought their mother from under the eaves. Ignoring me, she nestled down inside the ugly lifeless plant with her babies, all of them totally hidden. Still looking at the unattractive plant I thought, *Don't be too quick to judge by appearances. What appears ugly can be beautiful, when it gives shelter and guards love.*

Lord, let me look closely, beneath the surface, to find Your beauty, before I dismiss something or someone as useless.
          —MARION BOND WEST

179

26 SUNDAY

A good name is rather to be chosen than great riches...
—*PROVERBS 22:1*

When I was a boy, my father rarely spanked, but he had a method of correction I feared far worse than a sore backside. He would set me down, quietly telling me what a disappointment I'd been. The feeling of failing all the Fellmans since my great-grandfather took the ship from Sweden was enough to set me straight.

Later, as I headed off to college, my dad gave me a plaque with our family name inscribed at the top and these lines below:

You got it from your father, it was all he had to give.
So it's yours to use and cherish for as long as you may live.
If you lose the watch he gave you, it can always be replaced,
But a black mark on your name, Son, can never be erased.
It was clean the day you took it, and a worthy name to bear.
When he got it from his father, there was no dishonor there.
So be sure to guard it wisely, after all is said and done;
You'll be glad the name is spotless when you give it to your son.

Looking at that plaque as it hangs in my office, I'm reminded of the other name I've received from my heavenly father: Christian, meaning "Christ's one." In humble thanks to Him for my earthly father's example, I hope always to bring honor and never shame to both my names.

Maybe you are facing a decision today that is tugging at your integrity. At times like that I always remember that a good name can be sold, but it cannot be bought.

Father, thank You for both my names. Grant me the courage to bear each one gracefully, showing by example the kind of fathers I have. —ERIC FELLMAN

Spirit Lifter

Give ten percent, save ten percent, and spend the rest with thanksgiving and praise.
—CHARLIE W. SHEDD

27 MONDAY

Welcome him in the Lord with great joy, and show your appreciation. —PHILIPPIANS 2:29 (LB)

I can see the house from my front porch. It's only two doors up Colbert Street, a cottage that the young couple moved into as newlyweds. I knew then that I should go up and meet them, welcome them to the neighborhood. *But there is such an age barrier,* I thought. *They wouldn't be interested in meeting someone my age.*

I didn't even go when the big pink bow on the front door announced, "It's a girl."

Then a friend told me that the couple was being transferred to Macon, Georgia, my birthplace, and knew nothing about the city. Would I please visit them and give them some information about their future home? I agreed to go, a bit apprehensively. How would they accept my long overdue visit?

They received me warmly. They were grateful for the answers to their many questions about a strange city. And when I stumblingly apologized for ignoring them, they brushed my words aside. "You are here when we need you," they said. "That's what neighbors are for."

But as my mind went over their words, I wondered how many times I could have helped them in the past. I faithfully support my church's overseas missionaries, remembering that people the world over are my "neighbors." Yet I had not offered so much as a smile to those within my shadow!

That couple has gone to Macon. But shortly thereafter, as the moving van deposited the possessions of another young couple, I hurried up Colbert Street to be the first to welcome them. No age barrier held me back this time; none will again.

We are neighbors.

Lord, I have not always kept Thy commandment, "Love thy neighbor." Forgive me and help me to do so in the future. Amen. —DRUE DUKE

28 TUESDAY — FIRESIDE FRIEND

Be of good courage, and he shall strengthen your heart, all ye that hope in the Lord. —PSALM 31:24

Always, no matter what I am doing, when I hear Hungarian-born Franz Lehár's composition, "The Merry Widow Waltz," I want to stop, sit down and just listen.

This well-known Viennese operetta was doomed for certain failure with its used props, shabby costumes and lack of backing. Yet, the story goes, the appeal of Lehár's light-hearted melodies was so great that within two years, "The Merry Widow" was being played in Buenos Aires in five theaters simultaneously! All because Lehár had enough faith in his God-given talent to keep trying.

Does it sometimes seem that what you are trying to accomplish is foiled time and time again—and you wonder why you keep trying? Well, it may not be all wasted effort, after all. If Lehár had given up easily, there would have been no "Merry Widow." Every time I experience the warmth and charm of this lovely waltz, and reflect on Lehár's personal sacrifice and struggle to share his talent with the world, I am filled with a new determination. It's true, my talent may never measure up to that of a Franz Lehár, but I know this: Every time I feel the urge to give up, I am going to try, like Franz Lehár...and try...and try.

I hope you will, too!

Dear God, give me the will to keep on trying—to become all that I can be. —MARY JANE MEYER

29 WEDNESDAY

You will seek me and find me; when you seek me with all your heart. —JEREMIAH 29:13 (RSV)

I have an eleven-year-old son who is a fishing fanatic. Phil would drop a line in the bathtub if he thought he could hook a trout!

He was only eight the summer we came to Alaska. It didn't take him long to discover Fish Creek down the road. Every day he would bike to the bridge, fishing rod swaying in the breeze and tackle box swinging from his handlebars like a gigantic orange butterfly. He spent hours patiently casting and reeling. Sometimes a flash of silver trailed in with his line, sometimes not. He fished for the sheer delight of luring those wily creatures from their underwater hideout.

I remember one particular day when Phil began fishing about noon, stopping only to ride with us to our cousins' lake home for an evening barbecue. After wolfing down his dinner he floated a raft to the middle of the lake and continued fishing happily, unaware of time passing or pesky mosquitoes. Finally, close to midnight, we called him in. There he stood on that raft, silhouetted in Alaska's long summer twilight—a little boy dangling a line in the water. From across the lake his still-enthusiastic voice carried to us, "I can't stop now. There's a twenty-four-incher in here!"

The next time I reflect on God's promise to His people as recorded in Jeremiah—"You will seek me and find me; when you seek me with all your heart"—I'm going to remember Phil and his fishing. And no matter how difficult or impossible my situation appears—I will have faith and be patient. In due time I know He will come, with His answers, with His comfort.

Father, thank You that, unlike an elusive trout, You are waiting to be found. —CAROL KNAPP

| 30 | THURSDAY
Thou crownest the year with thy goodness; and thy paths drop fatness. —PSALM 65:11

Sometimes I feel sorry for myself. I seem to focus on all that's wrong in my world. Not having enough time—that always leads the list. How can I get done all that's expected of me? I start the day at the hospital, then hear patients' concerns all day long. They're hurting or frightened or lonely. They need so much of my precious time. Then home to a family with needs, to hear all that is going on in four other lives. *What about my life?*

After just such a day recently, I walked to an abandoned orchard near our home. A gnarled old pear tree as ancient as Methuselah is the patriarch of those still standing. It hasn't been pruned in this century.

As I leaned against its twisted trunk, a pear dropped at my foot, then another. The musty smell of pears was sweet, rising from the mounds of fruit littering the ground. Some were still fresh and ready to eat; others were rotting, good only for worms. No one came to care for the tree or pick the pears, yet it made no difference to the tree. Each season it blossomed, producing fruit that bent its branches to overflowing with a bounty that went unused.

But today I took something from the tree. It became a tiny reflection of God's bounty to me. As I stopped to think of all God's good gifts to me, the unstinting generosity of the tree made me a bit ashamed of my earlier self-pity.

I would sink my roots deep into the love of God, as this old tree had done, trusting Him to supply my needs. I would continue to meet the needs of those who depended on me. And I would open my eyes to all of God's good gifts in my life.

Dear Lord, You give us so much, yet we often don't pick up the fruit You shower upon us. I ask for one more gift—a sense of gratitude. —SCOTT HARRISON

Thank-You Notes to God

1

2

3

4

5

6

7

8

9

10

11

12

13

14

15

| 16 |
| 17 |
| 18 |
| 19 |
| 20 |
| 21 |
| 22 |
| 23 |
| 24 |
| 25 |
| 26 |
| 27 |
| 28 |
| 29 |
| 30 |

S	M	T	W	T	F	S
					1	2
3	4	5	6	7	8	9
10	11	12	13	14	15	16
17	18	19	20	21	22	23
24	25	26	27	28	29	30
31						

JULY

BE AN ENCOURAGER
Your Spiritual Pilgrimage

Say to them that are of a fearful heart, Be strong, fear not...
—ISAIAH 35:4

It's July; the lazy, hazy days of summer are here. Sunshine pours down like golden rain—blessing the ripening corn, soothing sunbathers, welcoming vacationers, encouraging every sort of holiday activity.

How good an encourager are you, by the way? Do people feel unaccountably cheered when you are around? Do you give disheartened souls a lift with a smile, or a pat on the shoulder, a murmured word of reassurance, perhaps an unexpected compliment?

The world is full of people starved for encouragement. This month, try to supply that need.

Tandem Power for July

TAKING ACTION

For God is at work within you, helping you want to obey him, and then helping you do what he wants.

—PHILIPPIANS 2:13 (LB)

"I can't do it!" I cried in frustration as I stood beside our horse trailer in a crowded parking lot at the county fairgrounds that hot July afternoon. When I arrived early that morning with my daughters Lindsay and Kendall and their two horses, I did what I always do at 4-H horse shows. I positioned the car and trailer widely across two lanes, assuring myself of a straight-ahead path to exit because in three years of hauling horses, I have never learned to back our trailer. The plan always worked—until today. While I was in the arena watching the girls, the parking lot filled up and someone started a new row in front of me. Now I was boxed in with nothing to do but back out or hope the people in front of us would return before we wanted to leave. I felt helpless, so I prayed and put the problem in the Lord's hands.

"You know I can't back up this horse trailer," I complained, "and I'm embarrassed to admit I need help. So please clear my path before we have to leave." Thinking I had done all I could do, I started back into the arena where I worried my way through the afternoon.

When the girls finished their events, we returned to the parking lot to discover we were still boxed in. "I'll get Mrs. Greenlee," Lindsay said. "She's not afraid of backing trailers." I winced, but within a few minutes our problem was solved, thanks to perky Mrs. Greenlee.

Yet my embarrassment sparked some clear thinking as we drove home. God doesn't want us merely to put our problems in His hands. Sure, He wants our prayers but He also wants to use us in the answers to those prayers. He wants us to *do* something. That's Tandem Power. "I pray as if it depended upon God," Mother Teresa once said. "But I work as if it depended upon me." I thought of other nagging worries that I could do something about. I worry about finances because I don't know enough about budgeting. About entertaining because I haven't cultivated some no-fail "company" dinners. About driving alone in the big city because I don't know my way around.

How about you? Do you have a worry caused by something you can learn? Why don't you whittle away at that worry this month by taking a single step of action: Sign up for a class or polish a rusty skill. As for me, every time we hitch up our horse trailer this month, I vow to back it once around our circular driveway. With God's help.

Lord, as I put my problems in Your hands, help me identify my responsibility in solving them. —CAROL KUYKENDALL

| 2 | SATURDAY |

Deal courageously, and the Lord shall be with the good.
—II CHRONICLES 19:11

Richard E. Byrd dreamed of exploring places far away. But in college he broke his foot and crushed his ankle. He was commissioned in the U.S. Navy, but at twenty-eight was retired as being physically unfit. Later he re-entered the Navy through another door by becoming an aviator. Soon, he was a full-fledged pilot and a specialist in lighter-than-air aircraft. Then things went wrong.

He planned an expedition on the dirigible *Shenandoah*. It crashed. He sought to command other test flights and was refused. He offered to pilot one of the planes explorer Roald Amundsen was leading across the Arctic ice. He was turned down. Then, because of his lameness, he was discharged from the Navy a second time. No one wanted his services.

Byrd then begged funds for unofficial expeditions. In 1927, exactly sixty-one years ago yesterday, he successfully flew from New York to France. Later, he planted the American flag at the North and South Poles. He returned home to a hero's welcome and a commission as an admiral. His courage had triumphed.

Lameness touches our lives when we feel crippled by educational limitations, the color of our skin, our sex or events beyond our control. Admiral Byrd's lameness never vanished. Yet he walked toward his goals in faith. Time, patience, confidence and persistence helped him to reach out, and God was there. He is there for us, too.

Lord, help me to persevere when things go wrong. In confidence and trust, I will place my hand in Yours.
—OSCAR GREENE

3 SUNDAY
…Holy, holy, holy, is the Lord of hosts: the whole earth is full of his glory. —ISAIAH 6:3

My Aunt Florence had a favorite saying: "Glory be!" Whenever she was pleased or excited about something, she would fling her ample arms in a vast gesture of joy and exclaim, "Glory be!"

That half-forgotten phrase soared into my mind this morning as I ran out for a sunrise swim. The grasses were dew-bangled, rosy banners claimed the sky, birds were ringing their little bells in the trees, as if to celebrate. "Glory be!" the words sprang unbidden from my lips. And in the sparkling water, the words came again. "How glorious…glory be!"

Then another phrase came singing: "the power and the glory…" For a second I couldn't place it. Then of course—the Lord's Prayer. The very last phrase. Not until that moment had the word *glory* come to me in this sense, as the last attribute of God. *The power and the glory.* The joyous exultation. The magnificence!

All day, making potato salad for our annual picnic, unfolding the flag to be raised, I thought about this word, which we don't hear often any more. How we used to call the flag *Old Glory* and carry it proudly in parades. Oh, those Fourth of July parades! The feeling of sheer exultation that is glory—there is no other word for it.

But this feeling of glory need not wait for parades. We live in a great and glorious country, a place of such privilege and bounty we are the envy of the world. People give up all they have, dig tunnels, swim rivers, risk their very lives in the hope of sharing what we take for granted: life, liberty and the pursuit of happiness.

Just to live here is to be gloriously blessed. Each day can be a day of celebration if we just pause to enjoy life's wonders, large or small. Planting a garden. Pushing an overflowing grocery cart. Bundling up children to play in the snow. Teaching a class, driving a car, working and playing, going to church with our family and friends.

Let's feel it, oh, let's feel it—that sense of radiance, awe and reverence mixed with joy that creates a true sense of glory. Like Aunt Florence, let's raise grateful arms toward the sky and shout, "Glory be!"
God, thank You. Yours is the power and the glory. Ours is the glorious gift of life in this promised land!

—MARJORIE HOLMES

4 MONDAY
And Paul said, But I was free born. —*ACTS 22:28*

Independence Day was my father-in-law's favorite holiday. He celebrated it with great festivity and joy, because freedom was among his highest values. Dad Helleberg came to this country from Denmark at the age of eighteen with fifty dollars in his pocket and only a few words of English in his vocabulary. "But if you have your freedom," he often said, "you have everything."

He had a long and successful career as an architect, but during his final years, he became confined to a wheelchair and finally to bed. It seemed to me that he had lost the thing he valued most—his freedom. Then one evening in late June, I sat by his hospital bed holding his frail white hand. "The Fourth of July will soon be here," I said, trying to make conversation.

"Oh, *yes!*" he replied. Then, squeezing my hand ever so slightly, he said, "You know, there's one freedom no one can ever take from you. You always have the freedom to choose what your *attitude* will be!" My father-in-law died a free man, despite his very restricting circumstances.

This year, as you're celebrating America's freedom by hanging out the flag, or watching a parade or fireworks display, take a few moments to remind yourself that no matter what the outer events of your life are, you always have that most precious of all freedoms—the freedom to choose your own *attitude!*

Let freedom ring, Lord, in my country and in my heart.
—MARILYN MORGAN HELLEBERG

5 TUESDAY
An intelligent mind acquires knowledge, and the ear of the wise seeks knowledge. —*PROVERBS 18:15 (RSV)*

A man sitting in the chair next to my desk at work suddenly slumped over to the floor. I jumped up, tried to take his pulse, then put my ear to his mouth. He wasn't breathing!

I'd taken a course in cardiopulmonary resuscitation a few years earlier, but now I was terrified: a man was dying in front of me! Muttering a quick prayer for help, I began a steady rhythm of heart massage and instructed an office worker to hold the man's nose and breathe into his mouth each time I said, "Now!" Before the ambulance arrived the man started breathing. I was still shaking when I thought about what would have happened to him if I hadn't taken that CPR course years before.

Come to think of it, I've taken plenty of courses: a baby-sitting class when I was a teenager; first aid; swimming classes; senior life-saving; childbirth classes; even a home safety class. I know that if we have faith in the Lord He'll take care of us. But I also believe that He depends on us to master the worldly problems by being prepared.

This year I'd like to take a basic auto mechanics class in case my car ever breaks down on the highway. How about you? Are your swimming skills up to par? Ever had CPR? Perhaps a refresher first-aid course....

Lord, help me to be prepared for whatever test comes my way. And here's one area that I can learn more about: _____
_____.   —PATRICIA LORENZ

WEDNESDAY
...My grace is sufficient for you...
—*II CORINTHIANS 12:9 (RSV)*

My son was eight years old when he went to summer camp for the first time. He seemed excited when he left. Then came his first letter home.

> Dear mama and daddy,
> I hate this place. I got stung by 4 bees. The food stinks. Get me out of here!   Love, Bob
> P.S. Hurry.

When I read his appeal in big third-grade print, I could feel my heart tear a little inside. I wanted to rush to this "wretched" place and break him out! But I didn't. I left him there. But I also wrote him back:

> Dear Bob,
> I'm sorry about the bee stings. And I'm sure the food will taste better soon. I can't get you, but I'm right there pulling for you. I believe in your ability to hang in there.
>   I love you, Mama.

That experience reminds me of those times when I find my own self in a mess and call out for God to get me out. But God doesn't always rescue you and me. Sometimes He leaves us there and lets us grow and learn from our circumstances. Yet He is always near pulling for us, believing in us, loving us.

Turning down my child's SOS was one of the hardest things I've had to do as a parent. But somehow I think God knows just how I felt.

Father, thank You for encouraging me in my troubles.

—SUE MONK KIDD

7 THURSDAY — FIRESIDE FRIEND
...Mine ears hast thou opened... —PSALM 40:6

I've come to feel sorry for the many people I pass on the street or ride with on the subway who have earphones plugging their ears. What bothers me is that not only are they possibly making themselves deaf, but they are missing the incredible sounds around them in this big city.

For instance, yesterday I opened my office window and the pulsating noises of the city entered—traffic, sirens, jackhammers, horns—all the rush and energy of a city at work. But above and through it all came the cheerful whistling of a small bird, singing away in all this din. It was so incredibly beautiful I stopped for a full minute to listen. Yes, it definitely was a bird, but not a sparrow, which only chirps.

Then at noon I was crossing the street at the corner of our building and I heard the trilling again, just over my head. I looked up and there was a small dark finch in the very young tree planted in the all-brick sidewalk. He warbled his song again, then flew up to the side of the building and managed to squirm into a tiny space, where I suspect he and his mate are building a nest to raise a family.

When my ears are open to the world around me there's no telling what I may hear—perhaps even the voice of God.

Dear Lord, help me always to keep my ears open to hear Your voice both in the world around me and in my heart.

—MARY RUTH HOWES

8 FRIDAY
I have shown thee...hidden things... —ISAIAH 48:6

When my friend Fran Horton came back from Germany she brought

193

me a tiny crystal butterfly. I took it from its foam-lined box and held it to the lamplight the night she came over, marveling at the intricate facets. "Put it in a window where the sun will hit it," she advised.

Before going to bed I set it on a high sill in my study. Next morning, stepping into the room, I almost dropped my coffee cup.

The room pulsed with color.

A score of rainbows shimmered on walls, ceiling, desktop. The paper in the typewriter glowed green and lilac. The cup in my hand, my hands themselves, held pools of color.

It was the same sunlight that streams into my study every morning. A prism of crystal was simply revealing what is always there.

Words can do that too...help us see the glory in ordinary things. A smile can do it. A kindness. A prayer.

Thank You, Lord, for the crystals in my life that show me You.
—ELIZABETH SHERRILL

 SATURDAY
That was the true Light... —JOHN 1:9

Some of my friends call me "Ellie the turtler." That's because I've tagged green turtles in Costa Rica, counted eggs of leatherbacks in Mexico, monitored loggerhead hatchlings (baby turtles) in Georgia. It was on this last trip to Wassaw Island, off the Georgia coast, that the turtles taught me a biblical truth.

Up until then I had never seen a real, live hatchling. So when we discovered a mass of eighty-five newly hatched on the beach one moonless night, I became ecstatic. My teammates Kitty, Tania and Dennis had done it all before, so they instructed me on procedures. Since the nest was set back in the vegetation and since there was no moon to guide them, some of the hatchlings had become confused. They were moving in the wrong direction. "We gather them up and put them in this pail," Kitty said. Enthusiastically, I went to work.

When all of the hatchlings were accounted for, we trooped to a spot a few feet from the tide line. Dennis held the pail, ready to release the hatchlings. Tania and I stood on either side of him. Kitty waded knee-deep into the surf and flicked on her bright flashlight to attract the hatchlings to the water. I wanted to see better, so I flicked on my flashlight, too. "Turn off that light!" the three of them screamed at me.

Later, after we had watched all the hatchlings follow Kitty's light safely to the sea, she explained the importance of just *one* light. To the turtles, her light was like the moon shining on the water. It guided them in the right way. My light would have misdirected them.

Often I think about the fact that we have so many lights calling for our attention. But, as Christians, only the one true Light—Jesus Christ—can guide us safely to the direction of fulfillment and happiness.

Lord, may I always be guided by the one true Light.

—ELEANOR SASS

10 SUNDAY
...Hold fast the profession of our faith without wavering.
—HEBREWS 10:23

My neighbor Ross has played golf with enormous enthusiasm and considerable skill for most of his eighty years. And because he has found so much enjoyment in the game, he gets great satisfaction out of helping others learn to play it better. So when he heard me complain about my hook, he volunteered to go with me to the practice range. There he worked with my stance, my grip, my turn and in particular my backswing, which he politely described as tenuous.

"Don't be afraid of taking the club back farther," he counseled. "In order to hit the ball with authority, you've got to put something in the bank." I laughed at the analogy because it was so obvious. If I wanted better results at the end of my swing, I had to put more into the beginning of it.

A spiritual application came a short time later when I heard a minister admonish people for waiting until trouble came into their lives to pray and read the Bible. "That's foxhole religion," he said. "What we need is to build up our spiritual reserves during sunny days so we can draw upon those resources during life's storms." Or as Ross advised me: *Put something in the bank.*

Teach us that we need You every hour, Lord, not just in crunch times. —FRED BAUER

11 MONDAY
For the moment all discipline seems painful rather than pleasant; later it yields the peaceful fruit of righteousness... —HEBREWS 12:11 (RSV)

I'll never forget the day I got a knock in the teeth from my mother—

verbally, that is. She got so exasperated with me her tongue slipped, and...wham!

It happened during one of our long-distance phone conversations. I had interrupted her three times. She snapped, "Will you be quiet! You know, your brother couldn't slide a word in the last time you called him. He said to me, 'Carol is so rude. She always interrupts and never lets anyone else talk.'"

Ooh, that smarted. Hanging up the phone in a daze, I thought, *I'm not like that...am I?* I took a closer look. Wasn't I nicknamed "Mighty Mouth" in junior high? Didn't my high school English teacher often quote "Silence is golden" to me? Doesn't my husband fondly call me "Jaws"?

My mother and brother were right. I was cruising through conversations on a green light. It was time someone stopped me. I reached for the phone to make a couple of thank-you calls...long-distance.

Sometimes it's hard to be honest with ourselves. We secretly think we don't really need to change. Jesus offers us a choice. We can keep following the same dead end or we can turn around and follow Him—Who can turn our dead ends into new beginnings.

Father, perhaps You can help me make a new beginning with this long-held bad habit of mine: _____.

—CAROL KNAPP

12 TUESDAY
Judge not according to the appearance, but judge righteous judgment. —JOHN 7:24

Backpacking into wilderness areas has become an avocation for the youth in my native California. I hear marvelous tales of the spiritual uplift they draw from the solitude, the forests, lakes, smogless skies. But one young man told a different story:

He had bedded down on a moonless night when he heard loud crashing sounds at the edge of his isolated camp. Slowly the sounds circled, unknown, menacing. Instantly he had visions of TV news clips showing mangled hikers attacked by hungry bears and airlifted to hospitals. The sounds continued and his heart raced. He saw himself dying, helpless, in the middle of nowhere.

"I didn't pause to think, evaluate, pray," he said. "I went on automatic fear. After an hour of shaking terror, the sounds receded and I half-slept through the rest of the night."

At daybreak he examined the area. He was on his hands and knees looking for tracks when he sensed he was being watched. Turning slowly, he found himself face-to-face with a mother deer and two lovely spotted fawns. As they saw him the fawns began to make a familiar loud crashing sound as they bounded around their mother.

"These were my ferocious midnight visitors," the young man said. "It was a lesson to me on how ill-founded fear can be."

It was a lesson to me, too. Instead of going on automatic fear, I can always take a second and ask, "Lord, is it a bear? Or a fawn?" Into that second comes a flash of calm and the ability to respond appropriately.

Lord, in the moments when I need clear judgment, be Thou my guide. —ELAINE ST. JOHNS

13	WEDNESDAY

...He hath sent me...to give unto them beauty for ashes... —ISAIAH 61:1,3

Ugly! The recent lava flow was a black scar two miles wide and fifteen feet deep across the green Hawaiian landscape.

My husband John stopped the car where lava covered the road. Only the charred tops of trees poked out from the sullen wasteland before us. Twenty-one homes were buried in the past two months as the sluggish flow inched down the East Rift zone of Kilauea Volcano. Where there had been family gardens, an orchid farm, papaya groves, now there was nothing but this desolation. Final as death.

Silently John turned the car around. It wasn't until hibiscus shrubs lined the road again that a lifeless weight seemed to lift from our own spirits. How bright Hawaii's flowers were, how lush the landscape!

"It's hard to believe," John said, "that all this beauty once looked as it does back there."

He was right, of course! I thought of the slide lecture at the hotel the previous evening: Every inch of these lovely Hawaiian Islands had been built by just such catastrophic eruptions. Kilauea was simply continuing the process, adding land that one day would be as green and fertile as the banana groves we were passing now.

Dead? Yes, for the moment. Final? Of course not.

Thank You, Father, that in You death is only the ground for more abundant life. —ELIZABETH SHERRILL

| 14 | THURSDAY
...Because there was no room for them in the inn.
—LUKE 2:7

It had been a great vacation, but going home late in the car through long stretches of mountain passes had left the four of us tired and grouchy. And then, when we finally decided to look for a motel room, there were none to be had.

After an hour of frantic searching, we found a rundown cluster of cabins languishing under a broken neon sign. V CANCY, it flashed halfheartedly. And when we saw the room, we knew why no one wanted it. It was clean, but old. The toilet clanked after each flush. The beds were lumpy. The walls were bare except for a faded picture of a tropical beach tacked to the paneling.

With sinking hearts, the four of us climbed into our beds.

What a dump, I muttered to myself.

Echoing my thoughts, six-year-old Geoffrey whispered, "This place is spooky."

"Spook stories! That's an idea!" my husband said into the silence.

In seconds, he was deep into a hair-raising story, which left all of us giggling under the thin sheets. Then came my turn to tell a scary tale. And after that, thirteen-year-old Tim improvised a song about our comic adventures on the road. The "No Vacancy Blues," he called it. Each of us added a verse and everybody joined in on the raucous chorus.

Many silly verses later, even as my flesh groaned against the sharp mattress springs, I remembered our Savior's family Who, like us, found no inn to take them in. The image of the stable rose in my head. A dump? No, I thought sleepily. Love had transformed it into a palace of joy.

Dear Jesus, teach us this day the lesson of the stable: that we are not products of our surroundings, no matter how squalid, but that we can by Love transform them—even the whole world. —LINDA CHING SLEDGE

Family Time

15	AUTHENTIC LOVING

*I give you a new commandment: love one another; as I
have loved you, so you are to love one another.*

—*JOHN 13:34*

When Mother Teresa of Calcutta was awarded the Nobel Peace Prize
someone asked her what we can do to promote world peace. Her
answer was deceptively simple but very much to the point, "Go home
and love your family."

Unfortunately, the word *love* has gotten some poor press in recent years, and, as a result, it doesn't have the bite and the meaning
Jesus was talking about when He gave us His "new commandment."
All too often we hear comments like, "I just *love* your new dress." Or, "I
just *love* the sauce Bill uses when he barbecues chicken." Or, "Don't
you just *love* the lines on Hazel's new car?"

But Jesus' new commandment and Mother Teresa's formula for
world peace is a much hardier and more tenacious love than shows
up in casual conversation and in television commercials. Indeed,
Jesus' new commandment is not something we feel; it is something
we do. Authentic love, the kind that binds us together as families, is
not a euphoric emotion that sneaks up on our blind side. Rather, it is
learned and relearned again and again.

We think Antoine de Saint Exupery, the French author and aviator, captured an important slant on love when he said, "Love does
not consist in gazing at each other but in looking outward together in
the same direction." It is looking outward toward common goals and
desires that enriches the love between a wife and husband, that allows
each member of the family to grow and mature as uniquely different
individuals, yet bonded together.

Now, after many years of marriage, we find it very surprising that
some people seem to choke over saying, "I love you." But then when I
stop to think about it, I have to admit, "I have a good memory; it is just
short." For during the earlier years of our marriage I found it hard to
say, "I love you" to Harriett. It came much easier for her. Then I remembered that when she said it, I felt good all over. And so I began to
learn to say, "I love you." The more I said it, the more I meant it and the
easier it came. It wasn't mechanical; it was real.

Something else about Jesus' rugged kind of love was beautifully expressed by Paul when he wrote, "Love believes all things" (1 Corinthians 13:7, RSV). But that phrase might better be translated, "Love is always eager to believe the best." There's the model for us in our relationships—every day believe and expect the best in each other.

As Mother Teresa implied—as we express our love within the family circle through words and touch and loving actions, we will experience a peace and joy that "surpasses human understanding" (Philippians 4:7, JBP). World missionary Dr. Frank Laubach summed up the whole idea of Jesus' new commandment in these words: "When iron is rubbed against a magnet, it becomes magnetic. Just so, love is caught, not taught. One heart burning with love sets another on fire."

Father in heaven, help us to love as Jesus loved.

—FLOYD AND HARRIETT THATCHER

| 16 | SATURDAY |

...He that is of a merry heart hath a continual feast.

—PROVERBS 15:15

One summer when I was a small girl of eight or ten my family took a vacation on a quiet and beautiful Canadian lake. Our rustic cabin, set amid pine trees, was a short distance from the dock where a flat-bottomed boat was tied up. On our second morning there my father, who loved fishing, announced that he'd go out before breakfast and try to catch a few fish. I'd never gone fishing before. The thought of catching fish and having Mother cook them for breakfast excited me. It was so different from our familiar routine at home. So I begged Daddy to take me along. He agreed, and off we went in the boat.

But our luck was not good. We sat out on the lake for a couple of hours without a nibble. Finally, Daddy said we'd better go back. As my father started to row toward the shore, I began to cry. I was bitterly disappointed that we wouldn't have any fish for breakfast.

"Stop your crying, Eleanor," Daddy said as he handed me his handkerchief. "Our not catching any fish today is a good lesson in learning how to take disappointments cheerfully. Life has a way of rewarding those who do, you know."

I wiped my eyes and blew my nose. Just then, a fifteen-inch Northern Pike jumped out of the lake and landed in the bottom of the boat where it flip-flopped wildly at my feet!

Now to you, dear reader, this probably sounds like an incredible fish story, but it did happen. And I like to think that it was the Good Lord Who arranged this minor miracle, just so that a little girl would remember her father's words always.

Lord, help me to look for Your special lesson in each disappointment that comes my way. —ELEANOR SASS

Spirit Lifter

It's what the weather is in your mind that determines the climate of the day.
—AUTHOR UNKNOWN

17	SUNDAY

...And the breath of the Almighty hath given me life.
—JOB 33:4

Most of my life I've been a poor breather. You may ask, "Isn't breathing simply *breathing*?" No, like most people, I've always breathed from the top of my chest, only filling about one-seventh of my lungs with air. This pint of air is sufficient for ordinary functioning, but I read that people who breathe deeply from their diaphragms (at the floor of the chest cavity) fill their lungs with about four *quarts* of air. The article said that these breathers are healthier, feel better and sleep more soundly.

I tried it by consciously lifting my rib cage to get air down to my diaphragm, but when I got busy I'd forget and lapse into shallow breathing again. I had better results at night. I'd lie quietly in bed, trying to erase all thoughts and inhale air down to my diaphragm. It worked so well that I usually fell asleep in minutes.

One day at the gym, our instructor was demonstrating leg exercises. I blurted out, "Are you breathing from your diaphragm?"

She smiled. "Guilty. Why do you ask?"

"I try to breathe deeply, but I keep forgetting."

"It takes practice," she said, "but it's worth it. I think it filters poisons from the air more completely, helps digestion and makes me stand up straight."

I kept at it after that, and it did get easier. One benefit I didn't expect was a spiritual one. As my voice deepened, it became more resonant for singing hymns, so I sing out enthusiastically each Sunday morning. I found in this case that what was healthy for my body was healthy for my spirit as well!

Lord, today may I breathe deeply of Your bountiful blessings, both spiritually and physically. —SAM JUSTICE

18 MONDAY
...Write in a book all the words that I have spoken to you. —JEREMIAH 30:2 (RSV)

"Hey, Mom," thirteen-year-old Lindsay burst breathlessly through the front door after school. "I have to draw a Time Line of my life with thirteen events that make me who I am today. It's due tomorrow and I need your help!"

What a cinch, I thought, remembering the hours of math and Spanish homework we'd struggled through. After all, I was the expert in knowing what made this child special. "This will be fun!" I told her.

It wasn't. As we sat down with pencil and blank paper, I suddenly realized some thirteen years of childhood memories blurred together into one fuzzy ball. What happened her third year of life? Who dumped the cats into the toilet because they needed a bath? Was that Lindsay or her younger sister Kendall?

We dug out her baby book, but after those first eighteen months, I had no written record of the memories I thought I'd never forget. Slowly we labored through the project, and when we finished, I had the sad feeling I'd lost some precious everyday experiences because I hadn't written them down.

When I got up early the next morning, I realized I faced the same loss in my prayer life. Sure, I remember some answered prayers through the years, but the everyday ways God has worked in my life are a hazy memory because I haven't written them down. So right then I decided to start a new habit and I invite you to join me, turning this very book of devotionals into a written record of God's everyday blessings. At the end of each month are spaces to write daily "Thank-You Notes to God." It's the perfect place to jot down a "thank You" for the ways God works in your life.

Don't wait till the memory fades—why not begin your Time Line of precious moments today?

Lord, please help me be a memory keeper, because Your faithfulness in my past gives me a precious promise for my future. —CAROL KUYKENDALL

19 TUESDAY   **FIRESIDE FRIEND**
...I will lift up mine eyes unto the hills, from whence cometh my help. My help cometh from the Lord...
—*PSALM 121:1,2*

Someone once asked me where I was the happiest, and I blurted out what was probably the truth: "In a stationery store." Sounds pretty shallow, doesn't it?

Actually, I gave away a very personal part of myself with that answer. You see, stationery stores are my *secret* love; the place I go alone when I'm down in the dumps. I love the mysterious odor of graphite pencils, the crispness of new paper, the precision of empty forms. I'm enthralled by pads of green accounting paper. Full boxes of paper clips make me smile when I shake them (but rubber bands are boring). And real pens!

I hesitate to call stationery stores my prayer closet (see Matthew 6:6), but that's really what they are to me. Don't you have a place like that? The psalmist found his place looking on the hills around Jerusalem. Maybe yours is a rocky beach...a kitchen filled with the aroma of homebaked bread...the luxury of a steamy bubble bath. It doesn't matter what it is physically; it's where you go to find peace and private pleasure and the person that is you. Hang onto it. Use it with joy, for it's a gift of God.

Dear Lord, if I should find myself "down" today, remind me that there's nothing wrong with taking time to be by myself, wherever I may be happiest, to rejuvenate my body, soul or mind. —TONI SORTOR

20 WEDNESDAY
Hold up my goings in thy paths, that my footsteps slip not. —*PSALM 17:5*

Every summer I try to spend some days in Stone Harbor along the

JULY 1988

New Jersey shore. It's quiet there, a family place. My favorite time is early morning, when the sun is low on the horizon and the breeze is cool. As I slosh along in the waves washing up on the sand, a few other early risers pass me and we always smile shyly or murmur hello. We're strangers to each other, yet I think we feel as if we have something in common: We are adventurers embarking on a new day. None of us knows what this day will bring in terms of happiness or difficulties, pleasure or demands.

This morning I saw a little boy and his father coming toward me hand in hand, laughing as the waves broke around their feet. Suddenly a rambunctious wave, bigger than the rest, came toward them and the boy slowed, his face struck by fear. Then he looked up at his father, who smiled and held the boy's hand tighter. The two of them went on walking right through the big wave, which broke and foamed around their legs. As they passed me the boy was laughing again.

While it's true that none of us knows what this day will bring, as long as we walk with God we can go anywhere and not be afraid. Life really *is* an adventure—if we share it with Christ.

As this day begins, Father, I reach for Your hand, confident that You will guide me safely through the turbulence as You accompany me in the calms. —PHYLLIS HOBE

| 21 | THURSDAY |

And he shall turn the heart of the fathers to the children... —MALACHI 4:6

I had been a father for three years, but like many young fathers I was more interested in my career or in buying a new car. "Child care is *your* job," I said to my wife Sharon.

One afternoon I was waxing our new car, which was parked at the top of our steep driveway. I was working on the passenger side, and I could see our three-year-old Teresa happily jumping up and down on the front seat, playing with the steering wheel.

Suddenly the car began to move backward down the hill toward the concrete retaining wall. I spun around to the front of the car with a desperate prayer, wrenched open the door, and with my right hand, dived for the brake pedal. The wheels clawed at the loose gravel, and the car wallowed to a halt just inches from the concrete wall. Teresa began to cry, and I was barely able to breathe as I took her into my arms.

That was the day I became a daddy. No longer was Teresa something "under my feet." She was something infinitely precious; she was someone to protect and cherish. Someone who might at any moment need a father's strength and watchful eye.

I thought of that long-ago incident the other day when my daughter, now grown, called me from the university. "I'm lonely," she said. "And I just wanted to talk." I guess the job of fatherhood is never over, and I'm glad. Being a daddy has brought me far more joy than my career or all the cars I've ever owned. And it's taught me to value the people around me whom God has placed in my care, to love and cherish—and enjoy.

Father, keep me aware and ever mindful of the priceless value of the special relationships around me. Help me to know it, and show it, too.   —DANIEL SCHANTZ

| 22 | FRIDAY |

Then Joshua built on Mount Ebal an altar to the Lord, the God of Israel, as Moses the servant of the Lord had commanded...   —JOSHUA 8:30 (NIV)

Two summers ago, my wife Shirley and I participated in a fascinating archaeological dig in Israel. On Mt. Ebal near Shechem, archaeologists have discovered what is believed to be Joshua's altar and for several years now have been excavating the site. The long-sought ceremonial altar was found by Dr. Adam Zertal of the University of Haifa and his co-workers in 1980.

"Why were you successful," I asked Dr. Zertal, "when so many others were not?"

"The main reason," he told me, "was that we had no preconception as to where the altar lay. Most thought it would be found directly across from Mt. Gerizim and at Mt. Ebal's very top, and that's where previous searchers concentrated. We didn't limit ourselves to any one location, surveying the entire mountain." They found the altar not on the top of the mountain, but on a lower ridge and not facing Mt. Gerizim, but on the unlikely northeast side.

Dr. Zertal's experience set me to wondering how many times in life I have botched opportunities and missed the brass ring because I have limited God to preconceived conditions. Like the salesman who begins a presentation by saying, "I don't suppose you would be interested in this product," we often plant the seeds of our own defeats by making negative statements or entertaining doubts. Christ's advice in all life decisions, big or small, is for us to relinquish them to God and pray, "Thy will be done." When we come to the Lord's altar open to His leading and attentive to His agenda, our success is guaranteed.

> *Guide me, O Thou great Jehovah, Pilgrim through this barren land;*
> *I am weak, but Thou art mighty—Hold me with Thy powerful hand.*   —William Williams
> —FRED BAUER

| 23 | SATURDAY | FIRESIDE FRIEND |

I will both lay me down in peace, and sleep: for thou, Lord, only makest me dwell in safety.   —PSALM 4:8

Monday through Friday, I rush madly back and forth in a frenzied effort to accomplish all the daily tasks required of me, but not on Saturdays. Saturdays are mine!

Eagerly I roll out of bed so I will be ready when the world awakens to a new day. Summer Saturdays will find me rocking quietly to and fro in my swing on the porch, awaiting the moment when Mother Nature awakens and her breath blows sweet and clean.

Swinging with me this summer morning, glistening just out of reach, was a small brown spider, clinging tenaciously in the center of an intricate gossamer of silk. Woven round like spokes in a wheel with crossbars, the web hung from a single filament, creating a bridge between two branches of the lilac bush. As I watched, fascinated by the diligence of God's little creature, I was amazed at his perseverance as he faced each new gust of Oklahoma air; and I was struck by the thought: *No matter how hard he works, or how careful he is, without the support of that single silver thread, all is lost.*

I, too, must have something to cling to when the winds of life blow strong and cold. So, each morning, upon awakening, I mentally attach my lifeline to God and His promises; secure in the knowledge that, as long as I hold fast, I will not fall.

And you know what? The best part is that God didn't make His promises to me alone—He made them to you, too.

Father, today as I go to meet life's challenges, I accept the promise of Your ever-present strength, which is made perfect in my weakness.   —MARY JANE MEYER

24 SUNDAY
Ye are my friends...   *— JOHN 15:14*

The other day as I was giving my plants a drink of warm water instead of cold, it wandered through my consciousness: *Why, I learned this from Bett!* "Plants are like people," she told me. "They wince at the shock of cold water."

She'd even given me this pitcher, an antique we'd found while we were prowling a dusty store. Swift on the heels of this memory came others of this precious friend now living far away. Her exquisite taste. Her knowledge of books—how many of her favorites became my favorites too. Her shoulder to cry on. Her encouragement. And, oh, the people I had met through her; wonderful people who also became my friends.

I let my mind fasten on first one friend, then another, tallying up the blessings that were mine because of them. Shortcuts, recipes— for a special dish or simply living; ideas, attitudes, philosophy.

It became a fascinating game.

I thought especially of Hope, a born-again Christian, who rescued me when my faith was dim and then went on to inspire my daughter so profoundly that when Melanie went away to college she in turn became a powerful influence on *her* friends.

Then I began to wonder what lasting effect my friendship might have had on others. Was someone right now using a gift I had given her, actual or of the spirit? Had knowing me helped a little bit along the way?

It's impossible for any of us to know. But this we do know: True friends teach us, influence us, make a lasting imprint on our lives. It's good to think that somewhere right now another person may be using a pitcher you gave her. And that whatever plants she is raising will live longer and bloom more beautifully because of you.

Dear Father, help me to give to my friends as generously as they have given to me.   —MARJORIE HOLMES

25 MONDAY
As we have therefore opportunity, let us do good unto all men... —GALATIANS 6:10

It was a blazing hot day in 1904 at the Louisiana Purchase Exposition in Saint Louis, Missouri—a celebration marking the one-hundredth anniversary of the purchase of the Louisiana Territory from France. Charles Menches was there at his ice-cream stand. Like other ice-cream vendors, he sold his treat in dishes. But he was so busy that by mid-morning all his dishes were gone. Customers were turning away and his ice cream was melting.

Charles glanced around. Nearby, Ernest Hamwi from Syria was selling a Middle Eastern delicacy called *zalabia*, a crisp, pastrylike delight eaten with syrup.

"Quick," cried Menches, "give me some zalabia!" He curled the zalabia, scooped in the ice cream and handed each to a customer. They looked startled, tasted, then smiled. The ice cream was saved, and thus the ice-cream cone was born!

What's the moral of this little story? To me it's a reminder that problems and setbacks come to all of us. But God also gave us the qualities of imagination, originality and inventiveness. And who knows—perhaps He sometimes sends a challenging little setback just to make sure those qualities don't atrophy.

Lord, when setbacks come, let me be a problem-solver, using my gifts to turn challenges into opportunities.
—OSCAR GREENE

26 TUESDAY
Yes, be bold and strong! Banish fear and doubt! For remember, the Lord your God is with you wherever you go.
—JOSHUA 1:9 (LB)

Every summer when I was a child, Grandma Kobbeman presided over our annual family reunion at Sinissippi Park in northern Illinois surrounded by her five children, their spouses and her twenty-four grandchildren.

One year, when Grandma was well into her seventies, she decided to ride her grandson's motorized go-cart. We held our breath when she squeezed into the seat, pressed the accelerator to the floor with her heavy brown oxfords and threw the little engine into World Cup competition. She flew across the track and down into the baseball field, barely missing the popcorn stand. As she headed for a row of poplars at the edge of Rock River, she released her foot from the accelerator and came to an abrupt halt at the edge of the water.

For a woman who had watched our country change from horse-and-buggy to men-on-the-moon, Grandma had adapted with a remarkable sense of adventure.

I later asked Grandma, "Why aren't you afraid to try new things?"

She just smiled and said, "Faith in the Lord is all you need, honey."

I'll always be grateful for Grandma's example—and the faith that never fails to inspire me when I feel afraid or am filled with doubt. Last year I soared down a steep water slide with my children, rode on top of an elephant and took my first helicopter ride.

Isn't there something you've always wanted to try but were afraid? Do what Grandma did. Depend on your faith in the Lord and plop down on that go-cart!

Lord, with Your help I'll keep a spirit of adventure alongside my "go-cart of faith." —PATRICIA LORENZ

27 WEDNESDAY
And all the days of Methuselah were nine hundred sixty and nine years... —GENESIS 5:27

Today is my seventy-fifth birthday, an unyielding chronological fact that I regard with considerable amazement. How did this venerable milestone come over the horizon so soon? Seventy-five! There must be a mistake somewhere. But there isn't.

Well, never mind, I don't *feel* all that ancient. Perhaps this is because of an idea I borrowed from a friend some years ago. When I asked him to define old age, he said cheerfully, "Oh, that's easy. Old age is always fifteen years older than the age you're at. When you're forty-five, it's sixty. When you're sixty, it's seventy-five. When you get to seventy-five, it's ninety. That way you *never* reach old age, because it's always receding before you!"

Not a bad idea, you know. Not bad at all. If you can't reach old age you're going to stay young, aren't you? Well, sort of, anyway.

Why not give it a thought now and then when you're not feeling as spry as you might wish? Sometimes a little shift in attitude can work wonders.

For all the good days behind, and for all the good ones yet to come, thank You, generous Lord. —ARTHUR GORDON

| 28 | THURSDAY |

...Forgetting those things which are behind...

—*PHILIPPIANS 3:13*

If a poor memory is a sign of old age, then I've been old all my life. Sometimes I'm almost as absent-minded as the fabled "Professor Brunch, who ate his wife and divorced his lunch." For example, I recently drove down to the library and got so absorbed in my research that when I finally left the building, I couldn't remember if I had walked or driven. It's a small incident, really, but these things can add up—like losing car keys, forgetting to turn out the porch light or misplacing an important phone message.

For years I berated myself about my memory. Then one day my wife said to me, "You know, I almost envy your bad memory."

I looked surprised. "Oh? How so?"

"Well, I wish I could forget hurts and insults as easily as you. And if I could forget my failures I would have more courage for the future."

As I thought about her words, I saw that she was right. At times a poor memory can be a gift; the ability to forget can be a blessing when it comes to escaping the long tentacles of past hurt, failure and disappointment. Perhaps each of us could benefit, at the right times, from poor memory, and promptly discard into a large wastebasket old ideas and painful remembrances.

Maybe we should begin today:

Lord, teach me to forget this mistake, hurt or failure: _____

_____

and remember this achievement: _____

_____.

—DANIEL SCHANTZ

| 29 | FRIDAY |

...If any man thirst, let him come unto me, and drink.

—*JOHN 7:37*

Back in the days of sailing ships, all vessels were at the mercy of the winds. Sometimes the winds were so strong that the ships were destroyed; other times, the winds were completely calm and ships were unable to move for days or even weeks. This could prove disastrous when supplies ran low, especially the supply of fresh water. It would then be, "Water, water everywhere, nor any drop to drink."

One time, a ship was becalmed off the coast of South America, and unless help came soon, it was certain the crew would all die of thirst. Finally, in the distance they saw a ship and frantically signaled, "Water! Water!" To their amazement, the ship signaled back, "Let down your buckets." You see, although they couldn't see land, they were near the mouth of the mighty Amazon River, which pours fresh water into the ocean for hundreds of miles.

Fresh water in the ocean? Impossible. So why should the sailors have bothered to try? Because in spite of the fact there was no way it could be true, it *was*!

Giving the impossible a chance—isn't that what's called *faith*?

Father, You can do anything. Don't let me rule out any possibility. Let me give the impossible a chance. —LEE WEBBER

| 30 | SATURDAY |

For I, the Lord your God...say to you, "Fear not, I will help you." —ISAIAH 41:13 (RSV)

When my close friend Betty was hospitalized with cancer, she called me one morning to say she'd had a vivid dream. She was drowning in a vast body of water when a dolphin swam toward her and pulled her to shore. It was the first real hope I'd heard in her voice.

Feeling a sudden inspiration, I called all over town searching for a helium-filled dolphin balloon to tie on her bed. Believe it or not, I found one. Throughout her hospitalization it floated over her bed, a smiling sign of hope. "I pray one day God sends you a dolphin when you need one," she said, hugging me.

A year went by and Betty recovered, despite an uncertain prognosis. That summer I walked along a lonely stretch of beach on Harbor Island, South Carolina, unable to shake a mild feeling of depression. Numerous problems awaited me back home and they seemed to be looming larger and larger in my mind. I waded into the ocean and stood where the sand dropped off sharply and curved into

Helena Sound. Suddenly I was startled by a smiling bottle-nose dolphin, which splashed out of the water twenty yards away. He dived and surfaced before me in a shining, spinning spray of joy. I began to laugh, feeling an exhilarating wonder. And somehow in those moments, my problems found their way back into perspective and the depression dissolved.

Perhaps it's silly, but I can't help but wonder if God answered Betty's prayer and sent me that dolphin. It's so like Him, isn't it, to send us help when we need it? To send balloons and dolphins and friends to meet the needs His children feel.

Father, today I will watch for the wondrous and surprising ways in which You surface in my life.   —SUE MONK KIDD

31 SUNDAY
Who is like unto the Lord our God, who dwelleth on high.   —PSALM 113:5

Last summer my husband Bob and I made an overnight stop in our camper at a state park near Kingsport, Tennessee. While we were having our dinner, a park ranger knocked on our camper door. On his left wrist he wore a heavy band on which was perched an owl. As we had never seen an owl so closely, we asked many questions about it. We learned that the rangers had found him wounded when he was very young and nursed him back to health. They had to secure a special permit to keep him because state law prohibits domestication of a wild creature.

"He is entirely dependent on us," the ranger told us. "If we were to release him, he could not survive on his own."

As we talked, the bird's round yellow eyes darted toward each speaker. When I remarked about it, the ranger said, "Oh, yes, he is quite interested in us. He's been entirely with humans for as long as he can remember. So he thinks he is one of us."

That was amusing at first, but as I thought about it later, I realized that we humans also tend to become more and more like the one with whom we are most closely affiliated.

What a wonderful reason for staying very close to Jesus!

Lord, this day I do not want to stray from You. I want to be near, learning to become more and more like You. Amen.
—DRUE DUKE

Thank-You Notes to God

1

2

3

4

5

6

7

8

9

10

11

12

13

14

15

16

17

18

19

20

21

22

23

24

25

26

27

28

29

30

31

S	M	T	W	T	F	S
	1	2	3	4	5	6
7	8	9	10	11	12	13
14	15	16	17	18	19	20
21	22	23	24	25	26	27
28	29	30	31			

AUGUST

BE A WARMTH-SHARER
Your Spiritual Pilgrimage

The Lord is gracious and full of compassion. —PSALM 111:4

If months could be said to have colors, surely August would be yellow. Day after day the sun pours down a flood of radiance, gilding the oceans, ripening the fields, making the city sidewalks shimmer, bathing the whole world with warmth.

How warm a person are you? Do you radiate concern and caring? Are you compassionate with those less fortunate? Do you offer shelter to those chilled by the troubles of this world?

This month try to be a miniature sun shedding your own special radiance over God's green earth. Be a warmth-sharer. Some of that warmth will be reflected back to you.

Tandem Power for August

| 1 | SILENCE |

Set a watch, O Lord, before my mouth; keep the door of my lips. —PSALM 141:3

Has this ever happened to you?

• On your way to church, you glance over at your teenager and notice he pulled his shirt from the dirty-clothes hamper instead of his closet. How could he, you wonder, but you know that nothing can be done at this moment. You have a choice: to criticize his appearance or remain silent.

• A friend purchases yet another new outfit, which pushes your "envy button." When someone comments on how nice she looks, you have a choice: make a remark about money spent on clothing or agree with a silent nod.

• The carpool driver forgets to pick up your child and leaves her stranded alone at school and does not call to apologize. Do you tell others about the oversight—or not?

I confess these incidents happened to me within the last twenty-four hours, and I don't know about you, but the Spirit seems to nudge me the loudest when He wants me to remain silent. My choice is to resist His nudge and say what I want, which is *my* way, or choose to remain silent, which is *His* way. Three quick personal proverbs help me pause more often before speaking:

1. Don't criticize something that can't be changed.
2. What I say about others says more about me than it does about them.
3. Never say anything about another person I wouldn't say if that person was standing beside me.

These guidelines don't guarantee that I'll always make the right choice, but thinking about them slows down my responses and gives me a chance to cooperate with God and use Tandem Power. August is a long, hot summer month suited to delayed responses. When the Spirit nudges you toward silence this month, why not pause before speaking and consider your choices?

Dear God, help us remember that sometimes silence is more powerful than words. —CAROL KUYKENDALL

| 2 | TUESDAY

A merry heart maketh a cheerful countenance...

—PROVERBS 15:13

It's National Smile Week and time to get that "cheerful countenance" in place!

There wasn't much to smile about when I was a youngster during the Depression. However, Mother would recite a ditty that I memorized (based on the familiar poem, "Solitude," by Ella Wheeler Wilcox):

> Smile and the world smiles with you,
> Kick and you kick alone,
> For the cheerful grin will let you in
> Where the kicker is never known.

I don't think this means we should grin unconcernedly when real sorrows and heartache beset us. In fact, it is important to be honest with our friends and to *allow them* to help us in times of trouble. We've all had acquaintances who smile and say, "I'm just fine," when we know they are hurting. The ditty doesn't recommend dishonesty.

What the poem *does* say is to look for the silver lining in dark clouds, to be grateful for God's blessings and to smile about the basics of life. It works! When we maintain a cheerful attitude, our hearts can be glad and thankful, even in the midst of hardship.

Lord, in midst of any trouble, You are my sustaining Power. Your constant presence is always cause for quiet joy or resounding cheer. —SHIRLEY POPE WAITE

| 3 | WEDNESDAY

And after he had dismissed the crowds, he went up on the mountain by himself... —MATTHEW 14:23 (RSV)

My grandfather was a busy man, a judge who sat on the bench fifty years, an active churchman and community worker. But I also remember him fishing on the pond at his farm. At times he sat so long, he seemed to become one of those old mossy stumps along the bank. He would cast out the line on his cane pole, then lean back into the quietness. One evening as the sun sank, I said, "Why don't you quit, Grandaddy. You haven't caught a fish all afternoon."

AUGUST 1988

Grandaddy looked at the purple shadows creeping over the pond and said, "It isn't the fish I'm after, it's the fishing."

Some days when I find myself rushing around, more intent on producing results than I am on the glorious experience of being alive in the moment, I can hear his words floating on an old country breeze in my childhood. That's when I pause. I put the fuss and work aside. I simply drop my line into the deep pool of the present moment and lean back into the quietness. For as my Grandaddy knew, "doing" is fine, as long as it's balanced with taking time to "be."

Lord, may my drive for "fish" never remove my joy of "fishing."
—SUE MONK KIDD

 THURSDAY
Behold, how good and how pleasant it is for brethren to dwell together in unity! —PSALM 133:1

When I heard that Tom and Jean, young friends of ours, had become engaged, I told them that before they tied the knot they should take my bicycle test. Shirley and I have a bicycle-built-for-two and my joke is that riding it together will reveal prospects for a fifty-fifty marriage.

Find a steep hill, I tell young couples, and try to pedal up it together. Unless you work as a team, however, you won't make it. If the cyclist in front tires and quits pedaling, the person on the seat behind will inherit the full load and have to push the dead weight ahead. If the person behind lets up, the bicycler in front will have double work. Tandem riders succeed or fail together.

If I were to apply the bicycle analogy to our marriage (thirty-seven years this month) I would have to admit that there were times when Shirley did eighty percent of the pedaling, e.g., when the kids were young and she did the lion's share of child-raising while I chased business rainbows. Still, I don't recall her complaining. But because she was able to endure my deficiencies, we rode on together.

My prayer for every young groom is a wife as loving and as understanding as Shirley. Such a companion will not only pull her share of the load when pedaling life's difficult hills, she will make the climb twice as much fun.

True love overlooks and understands. Lord, help us to do both.
—FRED BAUER

218

5 FRIDAY
Each of us should please his neighbor for his good, to build him up. —ROMANS 15:2 (NIV)

On the day I moved out to the country, I began to get cold feet. As my stepfather and I guided the movers out to my new home, I began to wonder whether I had made a mistake. I had never lived in the country, I didn't know anyone there and I would be quite far from my nearest friends. Would I like it? Would I make new friends?

Once we arrived at the house I didn't have time for my doubts. I was too busy unpacking boxes, arranging furniture and getting used to my new space. But the next afternoon my stepfather went home and I was alone with my dog Kate and Mr. Jones, my cat.

I was about to make my dinner when the doorbell rang. It was a young, attractive woman very much out of breath. "Hi, I'm Ginny Johnson, your neighbor in back," she said hurriedly. "Gee, I'm sorry I didn't get these here yesterday, but we had to take our son to a soccer game as soon as I got home from work!" With a big smile she handed me a foil-covered pan of sweet-smelling honey buns, fresh out of the oven and still warm.

I almost cried. I didn't think people did such things anymore. I felt welcome, known and at home—and I knew I was going to like living in the country. Every bite of Ginny's honey buns told me she was glad to have me for a neighbor. And a few days later, when I returned her pan with some of my apricot bread in it, I told her how happy I was to be a neighbor, too.

Is there a good, old-fashioned way you can say to a friend or loved one or stranger, "Welcome, I'm glad you're here!"?

Dear Lord, let me show hospitality in an old-fashioned way—and make someone feel remembered today.

—PHYLLIS HOBE

6 SATURDAY
...The Lord thy God hath chosen thee to be a special people unto himself... —DEUTERONOMY 7:6

Have you ever yearned to look like someone else? Have you ever been convinced that if you did, everything would be changed for the better?

AUGUST 1988

There was a time, during my high school years, when I fervently wished I could look like Loretta Young, the beautiful and popular screen star of that period. One day I read a movie-magazine article that stated that Miss Young gave her hair a weekly massage with cornmeal. *Hurrah!* I thought. *Here is my key to a new, exciting life!*

So I rushed out, bought a box of the miracle stuff, then came home to lock myself in the bathroom. Hours later I emerged, looking like...no, *not* Loretta Young. Since the dry cornmeal had quickly filtered through my hair to the floor, I decided that perhaps it might be more effective if it were wet. The result, of course, was mush! My mother gasped at the mess I'd made of the bathroom. My father nearly fell off his chair laughing at the mess I'd made of myself.

Later, in telling my Aunt Billie about the episode, I bemoaned the fact that I couldn't look like Loretta Young. Aunt Billie was a wise lady. "Eleanor," she said, "you don't need to look like Loretta Young, or anyone else for that matter. God made you. You are special to Him. Just enhance what He has made—both physically and spiritually. Then you'll be beautiful."

My Aunt Billie was right. When I stopped yearning to be someone else and started concentrating on being myself, I began to see the beauty God had put in my life.

And isn't that what God has in mind for each one of us—His special people?

Dear Father, keep reminding us that we are special in Your sight.   —ELEANOR SASS

 SUNDAY   **FIRESIDE FRIEND**
Let us therefore follow after the things which make for peace, and things wherewith one may edify another.
—ROMANS 14:19

I'll never forget the day the Great Peace March for Global Nuclear Disarmament filed past my house in the summer of 1986. The colorful caravan of hundreds of walkers had started in Los Angeles, and despite strife and hardships, reached its goal and arrived in our nation's capital eight months later.

The first two men in the procession carried a parade banner proclaiming: ONE PLANET—ONE PEACE. Bearded men waving flags, girls wearing tie-dyed skirts, middle-aged couples holding hands—

each smiling and giving the peace sign to us spectators. As I watched them, I was impressed with their dedication, awed that they had left homes, jobs, families, comforts to make this trek, to issue this statement for world nuclear disarmament. And suddenly, as I stood there in my backyard hanging up wet work shirts, I felt very unimportant. *What could I do for world peace compared with their grand efforts?* I wondered.

Then I saw him. He walked with measured tread as he held the arm of the man next to him. As I looked into his face, I realized he was blind. *Blind!* I could only imagine the courage it must have taken for him to walk mile after mile on unknown roads, camping each night in unfamiliar surroundings. How he must have trusted his guide!

The caravan wound out of sight, but its message lingered. *Trust.* That's the real foundation of peace. And it's a foundation I can help lay wherever I am: *my home,* when my daughter Amy Jo and I disagree over curfew; *my church,* while I roll bandages for our faraway missionaries; *my community,* as I become involved in our local school board election....

It's a foundation *you* can build on, too.

Help me, O God, as today I work for world peace in these ways:

    in my home _____

    in my church _____

    in my community _____

—MARY LOU CARNEY

---

8 MONDAY

How beautiful...are the feet of those who bring the happy news of peace and salvation...

                                   —*ISAIAH 52:7 (LB)*

No one thinks they have nice feet. Do you? No...they are either too big, too flat, too wide or too narrow. Everyone laments, "My feet are ugly!"

Naturally, as an orthopedic surgeon, I am very aware of feet. Before patients present their feet for examination, they always apologize for their appearance. I keep waiting to hear the feet protest, "Hey, I'm just doing my job. It comes with the territory. What do you expect?

Putting me in old shoes and walking me over filthy sidewalks—of course I'm dirty."

I have a secret feeling that feet put up with all this because they know how special they are. Because when Jesus waited on His disciples, it was their feet that He washed. He told them, "If I then, your Lord and Master, have washed your feet; ye also ought to wash one another's feet" (John 13:14). What a grand honor they received!

So the next time your feet begin aching, let that remind you that they were singled out for divine attention. And perhaps when we see someone who is also doing a tough, ugly job, we might imagine that they too will be so honored by special treatment from Christ. And so at all times let us honor the least—whether ourselves or others—as highly valued in God's eyes.

Lord, let me never aspire to be the greatest, for You have taught us how important the least are. Then, as You washed the disciples' feet, cleanse me as well. —SCOTT HARRISON

| 9 | TUESDAY
...I was a stranger and you invited me in.
—MATTHEW 25:35 (NIV)

Recently I watched a fence being built around an old home that was easily over a hundred years old. It was a white picket, with a gate that swung open and a matching rose trellis. And it was being painted white to match the old home place.

I wanted so much to venture beyond the nostalgic fence that one day I stopped my car and walked through the inviting open gate and strolled around as though I belonged there. At the back of the house a woman wiped her hands on her apron and said, "Hey, honey."

I felt as though I had always known her. "I...I came to see your fence," I confessed. We sat on her front porch for a long time, rocking and talking and drinking iced tea.

"There used to be a fence here a hundred twenty-five years ago when my great-grandparents built this house. I found a picture of it recently and decided to rebuild the fence. Oh, not for me. I live here alone. For the passersby. So many look at it, slow down, wave, and some like you, even stop and visit." *How wonderful*, I thought, *a fence designed to coax in, not keep out!* As I left, this kind woman called out, "Leave the gate open, hon."

Now I pass the fence several times a day—it's just up the road on Five-Forks-Trickum. Daily I am reminded that each of us has some sort of emotional environment surrounding us. I've been asking God to show me how to leave the gate to the "fence" around me ajar. I want to make new friends.

Lord, in a world full of locks, chains, keys and "No Trespass-ing" signs, thank You for people who have gates that swing open wide. —MARION BOND WEST

| 10 | WEDNESDAY
...Put off all of these; anger, wrath, malice...
—COLOSSIANS 3:8

I read recently that every time you're angry and don't express it, se-cretions build up in your body that can eventually make you sick. The article suggested that when you have to squelch your anger (for fear of losing your job, for example), you do some physical exercise to dissipate the body's "fight or flight" preparations.

I often take walks when something upsets me, but that's not al-ways possible. Lately, I've been using the extra energy generated by negative emotions by vigorously contracting the muscles of some part of my body that I want to firm up, such as my stomach or thighs, holding the tightness long enough to say, in my mind, "Take this anger, Lord." Then I let go, repeating the exercise as many times as I need to, until the painful feelings are gone.

And I've begun to notice (well, not a lot yet, but a tiny bit) of firming in those areas where I need it most. Next time you have some anger to get rid of, decide what part of your body needs firming and try this way of "putting off anger." It's good exercise—for both body and spirit.

Transform my anger, Lord. I let it go now.
—MARILYN MORGAN HELLEBERG

11 THURSDAY
…*The Lord upholdeth him with his hand.*
—*PSALM 37:24*

I remember very well one of my first flying lessons a few years ago. The sky was choppy that day, and I was struggling to keep the small blue airplane level.

"Take it easy," my instructor kept yelling, but I only fought harder to hold the plane steady. He glared at me and commanded, "Take your hands off the yoke!" I glanced at him, then slowly relaxed my white-knuckled grip. For several moments, the plane bobbed and dipped, staggered and lurched, but then it flew steadily forward with no hands on the controls.

"This plane is *built* to fly," the teacher explained. "It *wants* to fly, if you will just stop tinkering with it. Now, try using just one hand." Sure enough, I discovered the aircraft only needed my light, one-handed touch to fly smoothly.

If you are worried today about some problem you're trying to control with all your energy, forgetting to ask for God's touch, try praying with me:

Father, I am going to let go of this problem: _____
and trust it to Your hands. —DANIEL SCHANTZ

12 FRIDAY
…*Ye shall abide in my love…* —*JOHN 15:10*

I'm one of those people who just can't manage time. Each morning I am filled with enthusiasm for all the things I plan to do. I try to set priorities—baking bread for my family, writing letters, walking the dogs, exercising, taking a simple lunch to a shut-in, keeping the house reasonably livable. So many things seem to be priorities!

Too often I just "hit the high spots," especially when it comes to keeping house. I look at God's beautiful, orderly universe and feel ashamed of my cluttered rooms, unfinished projects and dusty floors. And I wonder if God isn't ashamed of me.

Then not long ago I read about "unfinished rainbows." So I started noticing and, sure enough, I found bits of rainbows every-where—in the morning dewdrops, a pool of oil, my sunny kitchen floor. One, the loveliest of all but still unfinished, spread from a vapor trail against the evening sky.

So I wondered...perhaps God isn't a perfectionist after all. I'm glad because I find it hard to relate to a perfectionist. Or was it just His way of telling me He loved me in spite of my haphazard ways?

If you are having trouble completing daily tasks, why not start looking for "unfinished rainbows"? You'll find it reassuring.

Dear Lord, thank You for loving us just the way we are.
—ALETHA JANE LINDSTROM

13 SATURDAY
The Lord is...slow to anger, and of great mercy.
—PSALM 145:8

"I'm going to clobber you," my daughter yelled. Her brother, who was washing the car, had just turned the hose on her. She was drenched. But that didn't keep her from overheating.

"Take a deep breath and count to ten," I told her.

She took a deep breath, counted to ten and *then* she clobbered him. That was the day I revised the old counting-to-ten technique, adding a Bible verse beside each number. We keep the list on the refrigerator—required reading for anyone in danger of losing their temper. It goes like this:

One—A fool gives full vent to his anger, but a wise man quietly holds it back. Proverbs 29:11 (RSV)

Two—Be angry but do not sin. Ephesians 4:26 (RSV)

Three—Let every man be quick to hear, slow to speak, slow to anger. James 1:19 (RSV)

Four—A hot-tempered man stirs up strife. Proverbs 15:18 (RSV)

Five—Love is patient and kind. I Corinthians 13:4 (RSV)

Six—Do not return evil for evil. I Peter 3:9 (RSV)

Seven—Every one who is angry with his brother shall be liable to judgment. Matthew 5:22 (RSV)

Eight—A soft answer turneth away wrath. Proverbs 15:1 (KJV)

Nine—Blessed are the peacemakers. Matthew 5:9 (KJV)

Ten—Love one another. John 15:17 (KJV)

It's almost impossible to read the list without one's angry reaction evaporating. Maybe you'd like to keep it handy, too, for those times when you're in danger of overheating.

Help me control my temper, Lord, by reaching for Your Word.
                                                    —SUE MONK KIDD

14 SUNDAY   FIRESIDE FRIEND
...He went out, and departed into a solitary place, and there prayed.   —MARK 1:35

It had been a while since I last packed a lunch, picked up a pole and took off to the nearest fishing hole! Knowing I had waited much too long, I closed up shop one Saturday afternoon and spent all day fishing with my family and friends.

Now, I will admit to you, I am too squeamish to put the worm on the hook, or take the fish off the hook, or clean the fish. I just like to hold the pole and pull the fish in. One of my friends noticed my strange way of fishing after he had spent his afternoon baiting my hook and cleaning my fish. He finally asked, "Denise, just what is it that you like so much about fishing?!"

Smiling, I responded quickly, "Relationship." He looked puzzled as I turned back to my fishing and began daydreaming back to my childhood when my dad and I fished all day and hardly caught a thing. And when my grandfather and I went fishing, brought back a feast of fish and had a fish-fry for the whole family. And the many times I sat by the water alone, enjoying a cool breeze and talking with God.

For the rest of the afternoon, I sat holding my pole, pulling in the fish, and smiling inside, more than content to keep my secret. For I had always known that the fishing was the least important part of fishing. Fishing was merely an excuse to sit by the still water's edge, quiet and at peace, thinking, dreaming, praying, being...heart-to-heart with my father, with my grandfather and with my God.

I hope today you, too, have your own fishing hole.

Lord, for the fishing holes of life, we thank You. Help us to search them out, and go to them often.   —DENISE GEORGE

Family Time

COMMITMENT-LOVE

Love knows no limit to its endurance...it can outlast anything. Love never fails...Make love your aim...
—*I CORINTHIANS 13:7–8; & 14:1*

Love isn't just a feeling. It is something that is planned for, worked for; it is a way of life that is fought for by people who care deeply about each other. It is commitment.

A friend wrote about a conversation she had with John McCormack, for many years Speaker of the House of Representatives and one of the most charismatic politicians of the twentieth century. When Mr. McCormack was first elected to public office he determined that "Harriet and I are going to be together every night." No political or social involvement was to separate them. That was a commitment he kept for fifty-two years. She was always by his side at public functions. And whenever he had the opportunity to counsel newlyweds, his advice was simple: "Always be sweethearts...being sweethearts is a state of mind."

Speaker McCormack's love for his wife and family had no limits to its endurance; it outlasted everything. Yes, it was a powerful feeling that carried through more than fifty years of married life. But like being sweethearts, *it was a state of mind*—a commitment. The Speaker *made love his aim*.

After giving us that marvelous description of love in I Corinthians, we believe Paul's instructions to make "love your aim" refer to the commitment that is so necessary if love is to last. This year we will celebrate fifty years of marriage. There have been times during those years when we haven't felt loving or very much in love. It hasn't all been a picnic, but never once has our commitment to each other faltered.

Then, too, as with all parents, there were times, especially during the teenage years, when "feelings" of love between our daughter and ourselves were strained because of the normal parent-child differences. But our commitment to each other held steady. And today the bond of love among all of us has never been stronger as we've grown together.

Each of us in our own unique way knows that our love-commitment requires constant maintenance. Regular and repeated affirmation of each other within the family relationship is a crucial part of making love your aim. Commitment-love for God and each other is something we work at and do for each other every day as we strive with the Lord's help to be patient, kind and not boastful. Above all, it is a love that isn't conceited or rude or selfish, and it "keeps no score of wrongs" (NEB).

With Your help, Lord, we will make love our aim.
—HARRIETT AND FLOYD THATCHER

Spirit Lifter

Criticism of others nails them to the past. Prayer for them releases them onto the future.
—FRANK LAUBACH

---

16 TUESDAY
...He maketh his sun to rise on the evil and on the good, and sendeth rain on the just and on the unjust.
—MATTHEW 5:45

We've all been told to count our blessings, but sometimes we overlook the most important ones because we take them for granted. Rain, for instance.

After several rainless weeks last summer, the beautiful, big reservoir I can see from my house was shrinking into a puddle. My well was in no danger, but I was tired of lugging my hose halfway around the house every day to water some new shrubs I had put in.

One afternoon I stopped to buy some vegetables at a nearby farm stand. I noticed that the tomatoes were small and the peppers limp and wrinkled. "It's the drought," Mrs. Thompson said. "We've got an irrigation system, but it's not the same as God's good rain." She looked tired, worried.

Two men in overalls seated at the counter in back weren't even touching their coffee or Mrs. Thompson's homemade cherry pie. "It's bad," one of them said. The other nodded wearily.

Then we all looked up. Were we right? Was it thunder we heard? It was, and soon the sky was zig-zagged with lightning. The rain came down, gently at first and then in a downpour. I looked at Mrs. Thompson and she was crying. So were the men as they ran outside, their faces turned up at the sky. "Oh, thank You, Lord!" Mrs. Thompson prayed.

I had taken rain for granted. The lack of it was an inconvenience. But I learned something from three people whose livelihood depends upon the weather. They know rain is a blessing. And so do I—now.

We thank You, Father, for the rain that sustains life on this earth—and for the downpour of Your mercy that fills our lives with love. —PHYLLIS HOBE

| 17 | WEDNESDAY
Whoso offereth praise glorifieth me… —PSALM 50:23

Six-year-old Jeremy telephoned from New Hampshire. His wee voice said, "Grampa, thank you for visiting and bringing Nannie. Thank you for bringing ice cream." His favorite.

His thoughtfulness warmed me. I was even more touched when my daughter-in-law Marie got on the line and said, "This was his idea, Dad. Jeremy suggested calling you." Now nine, Jeremy still calls up just to say thanks, and it still warms me.

As I was thinking of this wonderful habit of Jeremy's the other day, I wondered what would happen if I actually made an effort to *tell* others that I appreciated them. Opportunity came quickly when another car and mine collided that afternoon. I thanked God that neither one of us was injured. After repairs, I returned to the auto shop and said, "My friends thought this was a new car!" The mechanic beamed. When Ruby returned from her mother's funeral in San Francisco, pleased with the flight accommodations, I called the travel agency and shared her compliments. They were so pleased to hear from a satisfied customer. Soon I found that the more pleasure others got from my comments, the more things I could find to be thankful about, and the happier I got!

Why hadn't I done this before? Saying thank you—out loud. It's made all the difference to me.

Father, remind me: Don't just THINK thank you. SAY IT!
—OSCAR GREENE

18 THURSDAY

The Lord is my strength and my shield; my heart trusted in him, and I am helped… —PSALM 28:7

Revered devotional writer Lettie Cowman tells this story in *Springs in the Valley*, sequel to her better known *Springs in the Desert*:

> In the deep jungles of Africa, a traveler was making a long trek. Porters had been engaged from a tribe to carry the loads. The first day they marched rapidly and went far. The travelers had high hopes of a speedy journey. But the second morning these jungle tribesmen refused to move. For some strange reason they just sat and rested. On inquiry as to the reason for this behavior, the traveler was informed that they had gone too fast the first day, and that they were now waiting for their souls to catch up with their bodies.

I was reminded of that story when I rolled out of bed this morning, limp as a weeping willow. For the last week I had been on an exhausting business trip and today, finally, I was back home. I had more catching up to do than energy to do it. So before plunging into the papers that covered my desk I poured myself a second cup of tea and opened my Bible to the Book of Psalms…and immersed myself in God's word, His forever promises for forgetful pilgrims such as I. In a few moments I felt the first stirrings of restoration, and before I knew it my fragmented mind and weary bones seemed whole again. My soul, I guess you could say, had caught up with my body.

When we try to put too many tasks into too few hours, Lord, slow us down so we can hear Your voice and draw upon Your strength. —FRED BAUER

19 FRIDAY

Let them praise his name with dancing…

—PSALM 149:3 (RSV)

I love to dance. But my husband Gary has two left feet, and as much grace as a potato.

It's the one thing—the only thing—in our twenty-year marriage that I regret. He can't dance! So when a group of couples from church invited us to take a dance class at the local high school, I jumped. It took days of pleading to get Gary to go. But he did, knowing how much it meant to me. Visions began to rise in my head: Gary and I twirling, dipping, gracefully stepping around the dance floor, a 1980s "Ginger and Fred."

My aching feet soon told me we had made a big mistake. No matter what step we learned, Gary couldn't do it. Not the waltz. Not the lindy. Not the tango. And definitely not the samba! Our teacher was stumped. "I've never seen anything like it!" he told Gary, who had managed to step on the foot of the woman—and the man—behind us.

For eight weeks, Gary and I struggled on, while the other couples danced rings around us. The last night we were to learn the hustle. "I saved the hardest for last," our teacher warned, eyeing Gary sadly. Gary insisted that we try. He hadn't given up on himself, even though everyone else had.

The last class began like the others. With our friends gliding easily into the review steps, and Gary and I clomping along in our corner, two beats behind everybody else. Then the teacher lined us up in rows and taught us the hustle. After a few laborious tries, everyone groaned! No one could manage the complicated steps. No one, that is...

Except Gary! Everyone stood amazed as he stepped alone again and again to the tricky rhythms. With a brilliant grin, he reached for my hand, and pulled me expertly into a turn, and suddenly we were dancing! Really dancing! Just like Ginger and Fred!

Lord, sometimes I cannot move to the rhythms of the rest of the world. Give me the grace and confidence to master the rhythm You have set aside for me alone.

—LINDA CHING SLEDGE

 SATURDAY

...No man, having put his hand to the plow, and looking back, is fit for the kingdom of God. —LUKE 9:62

There is a moment in late summer that I want to go on forever. The grass is knee-high where it hasn't been cut, the sky slate blue and the hammock the perfect place for a Sunday afternoon nap. School hasn't started yet, you can still buy watermelon at the supermarket and the teenage girls at church are still comparing their summer tans. But then someone will notice a few leaves turning prematurely red and break my reverie, saying, "I think autumn's in the air."

For a while I resist it. I refuse to hear the cicadas cackling at dusk or read the advertisements for back-to-school sales. But then the season catches up with me. Soon I'm mentally tallying up the woolens in storage and wondering if any storm windows need replacing or if I should put a new coat of paint on the windowsill that gets all the winter rain. The lure of hot tea on a cold day, the maple trees on fire and the World Series has got me. I'm looking forward to fall.

As sure as day follows night, as inevitable as a sunset, change is part of God's world. I might resist it, as I resist a new challenge at work or a change in my routine or someone waking me up from my summer afternoon nap. But then, if I watch closely, I notice that God always hints at new pleasures to come—the crisp autumn day promised in a late summer breeze.

Lord, as surely as I adjust to the arrival of a new season, help me to accept change in my life and the new rich possibilities You bring. —RICK HAMLIN

JOURNEY TO AFRICA
A Doctor's Loving Service

He didn't know why…but Dr. Scott Harrison, an orthopedic surgeon from Mechanicsburg, Pennsylvania, felt compelled to answer the Biblical command "…By love serve one another" (Galatians 5:13). He read about the needs of the poor and suffering people in the small African country of Malawi and went forth to offer his gifts and talents as a surgeon.

In the week that follows Dr. Harrison shares the valuable lessons the people taught him and the one big faith lesson he learned while abroad: complete dependence upon God.

It is a lesson he humbly shares with you…in love and service. —THE EDITORS

Day One—The Mission

21 SUNDAY

For we are his workmanship, created in Christ Jesus unto good works, which God hath before ordained that we should walk in them. —*EPHESIANS 2:10*

Malawi...I'd never even heard of this small country in southeastern Africa until a few months ago. But several magazine articles I'd read recently described an epidemic of polio in this little nation and their need for medical help. After writing to the only orthopedic surgeon in this country of seven million people, about the size of my own state of Pennsylvania, I had decided to lend a hand, or in my case, my abilities as a surgeon. The pastor of our local Evangelical Free Church had asked me to speak Sunday morning about why I was taking time from my orthopedic practice here in Harrisburg and going to such a primitive country. Simple enough, but it was Saturday afternoon and I was still uncertain of what to say.

I turned to my wife Sally. "It's just dawned on me that I don't really know why I'm going," I said. "It sounds sort of smug to say that I'm going to help poor, suffering people in Africa, or to bring them Western technology. I realize that we won't make much of a dent in their problems."

Sally laughed. "Well, at least I know why I'm going," she said. "It's because you're going and God sees us as one!"

That was her answer, but I kept groping for mine. Sick people are there, I told myself, and I am a physician. After all, Jesus didn't talk about blindness, He restored sight. He didn't analyze the paralyzed, He caused them to walk. He didn't discuss the philosophy of disease, He wiped away the scales of the leper.

So if you have been hesitating to do something, why not just follow Christ's example...and *do.*

Obedience...it still may not be out of date.

Lord, help us to be not only hearers and thinkers about Your word, but doers as well. —SCOTT HARRISON

Day Two—Living by God's Clock

22 MONDAY

I will also leave in the midst of thee an afflicted and

> *poor people, and they shall trust in the name of the*
> *Lord.*
> —*ZEPHANIAH 3:12*

It took us four planes and forty-eight hours to reach Malawi. The next morning I was too tired to think as my first clinic began. A seemingly endless parade of black faces began passing in front of me. Serene faces of young mothers with hungry infants at their breasts; old men, their skin deeply etched by the equatorial sun; and children, so many children, attacked by infections long forgotten in our Western world. They slowly slid along the bench from the waiting hall. Then, presenting soiled index cards with their life's medical history on it, they awaited what might be done for them.

Scribbled on a typical card: "Fell from a tree three days ago, arm deformed, needs correction." This patient had walked twenty miles to that first medical outpost where the splint was applied. It was another couple of days before he finally got here to the main hospital. Like so many of them, he had endured a long delay before treatment. But he showed no anger at the long wait.

How different all this seemed from the frantic life at home. My rigid time schedule, my frustration at being late for an appointment or, worse yet, having someone be five minutes late for one with me...all that seemed so senseless now. Almost unreal.

These people have something special, I said to myself. A kind of serenity. An acceptance of things as they are. They live close to God's earth and are part of His seasons. They live by His clock...and it doesn't seem to have a minute or second hand.

Father, I rush about, always looking at my watch. Let me learn to keep my eyes on Your timepiece, and know the peace that comes from living by it. —SCOTT HARRISON

DAY THREE—BECOMING A STUDENT OF HIS KINGDOM

23 TUESDAY

In the law it is written, With men of other tongues and other lips will I speak unto this people...
—*I CORINTHIANS 14:21*

"*Muli bwangi,*" the black man in tattered shorts nodded his greeting.

"*Ndaswera bwino, zikomo kwambiri,*" came his friend's reply. I didn't understand a word except the "hello," *Muli bwangi.* I was taking a Sunday walk in the park among unfamiliar banana and baobab trees. A group of boys were listening to a speaker. *"Kuti tisaope; dalitsani mtsogoleri nd'ife..."* his voice trailed off as I walked on, even more mystified by what was being said.

I was eight thousand miles from home, the language was different, the landscape strange, even the color of my skin looked out of place. I didn't fit in and I knew it. I'd be more comfortable, I realized, if I had learned the language and customs of Malawi before I arrived.

Later that evening in church, the minister's lesson was from Hebrews. "They were strangers and pilgrims on the earth," he read from the eleventh chapter. "We are to strive to be in the world but not of it," he continued. "If we live in Christ's world, we should feel a little like strangers here on earth. We belong in the world, but not of it."

This had always been a difficult concept for me to understand but now I sensed his meaning. I need to begin now to prepare for my trip to God's kingdom by learning His language, one of meaningful prayer. I will also have to study more about His world, using His Word as my guide. And, as I try to become more like the image of His Son, I might even find, that like Him, I will feel at home in both worlds.

Lord, nudge me to feel just a little strange here in my temporary home. Let me begin classes in citizenship for Your kingdom. —SCOTT HARRISON

DAY FOUR—THE PRAYER OF PEACE

| 24 | WEDNESDAY |

Fear thou not; for I am with thee: be not dismayed; for I am thy God... —ISAIAH 41:10

"Have scalpel, will travel" became my motto. This morning as we headed into the bush to help at a mission hospital, I felt as if I were traveling back in time. Things had changed little in the ninety years since this hospital was founded. Elephants still came up from the valley when the season was especially dry. And only a few years before it had been necessary to kill a lion that had terrorized the small village near the mission.

The hospital's operating room, lined in gleaming tile, was surprisingly modern. A stainless steel scrub sink added a false sense of twentieth-century sterility. The sign over the operating room door caught my eye. It was in Chichewa; I couldn't understand any of the words except the last, "YES 41:10."

"It's from *Yesiah*...in the Bible," the mission doctor said in answer to my question. "But I think you call it Isaiah."

"I knew it wasn't the 'Do Not Enter' sign on my operating room door in the States," I laughed.

My patient, a terrified elderly farmer, lay quivering on the table. He grimaced from the throbbing in his crooked arm, crusted with blood from the bites of a wild boar. These surroundings, so different from his thatched hut, heightened his fear. There was no preoperative sedation available to ease his apprehension. The missionary doctor placed his hand on the syringe of Pentothal, but paused to ask, "Who is to offer the prayer for this patient?"

The smallest and youngest of the nurses in the room stepped forward to stand at the patient's side. She bowed her head and in a soft soothing voice spoke Chichewa words of comfort and intercession. After she finished, the old man kept his eyes closed, the lines of worry erased from his face. I doubt he even sensed the anesthetic as he drifted off to sleep.

After I had cleansed his wounds and stabilized his fracture, I couldn't help wondering which was the more primitive way of doing things: my sterile operating room at home with its cold efficiency or the warm, shared prayer of this young nurse and old man?

You are the Comforter. May we accept the peace that You offer, Lord. —SCOTT HARRISON

DAY FIVE—A GLIMPSE OF ADAM'S GARDEN

| 25 | THURSDAY |

...To him that overcometh will I give to eat of the tree of life, which is in the midst of the paradise of God.

—*REVELATION 2:7*

Operating under such primitive conditions was wearing me down. Sally sensed that I needed a break.

"Let's go to Makakola," she said. "It's so beautiful; David Livingstone, the explorer, thought it might have been the Garden of Eden."

So late Friday afternoon we set off in our battered old station wagon. But in the rush to leave I had forgotten our map and directions.

"There are only two paved roads in this entire country," I assured Sally. "How can we get lost?"

"But what if it's on a dirt road?" she replied. "I'm not ready to spend the night wandering among lions."

As we drove past a clump of thatched roof huts, a young child dangled the family chicken, offering it for sale. Stopping to ask him directions brought a polite reply...in Chichewa, not English. I swerved to miss a baboon that ran across the road as I strained to read the road signs. Liwonde, Chiponde, Nchau...unfamiliar names that did little to reassure me. I slowed to weave through a herd of humpback cattle meandering down the center of the road.

Just then I caught sight of a faded arrow pointing us down a dirt road. We bounced along, past elephantine baobab trees, until the shrill cry of a fish eagle, the *ngwaza*, announced our arrival at Makakola.

Beyond our whitewashed cottage, sparkling sand flowed into a gold-sequined bay as the sun receded behind distant mountain peaks. Mango trees bent low, offering their ripe fruit. A cool evening breeze, carrying the sweet fragrance of the protea's flower, began washing away the day's heat.

"I wasn't so sure we'd make it," Sally let out a deep sigh. "I have to admit I was getting scared." After a pause she continued. "But we would have missed a glimpse of Adam's garden if we had stayed home."

Often needless apprehension causes us to miss good things! If there's something you have been hesitating to do...go for it. God may have a marvelous surprise in store for you.

O Lord God, lead us to those special oases that You have scattered about, so we may walk with You. —SCOTT HARRISON

DAY SIX—SHARING PRAISE TO GOD

26 FRIDAY
And after these things I heard a great voice of much people in heaven, saying Alleluia... —REVELATION 19:1

Our last Sunday in Malawi we attended the oldest church in the country, built about 1890 by Scottish missionaries. Many of their predecessors had died in the course of bringing the gospel to Africa, and this crudely eloquent brick structure stands as their monument. An even more eloquent testimonial to their memory were the crowds that spilled down the front steps and around the open church windows to hear that Sunday morning message. Three services couldn't accommodate all who wished to attend.

This middle service was in English, spoken in the clear crisp tones of someone who has learned it as a second language. But the choir sang its anthem in native Chichewa. Although the words were foreign, it was an old familiar melody. Then I heard the word *Alleluia*, and a few seconds later again, *Alleluia*. And my heart too shouted, "Praise God." That same exultation that has echoed through the centuries.

A week later and a thousand miles further north, but still in central Africa, we attended a different church service with a different language, Swahili. A choir of eager teenagers chanted a strange melody. And again, interspersed within the Swahili was the familiar word, *Alleluia*.

One word bound us together. But really it was something greater than that—it was our shared praise to God. Let all hearts, theirs, mine and yours, speak that same language.

Praise to You, Lord! May we shout it from deep within, where we all are one. —SCOTT HARRISON

DAY SEVEN—THE LESSON OF DEPENDENCE

27 SATURDAY
I waited patiently for the Lord; and he inclined unto me, and heard my cry. —PSALM 40:1

At last I have a clear understanding of why I made the trip to Africa. It slowly dawned on me as I talked to people about the experience.

"How was your trip?" was the usual question from friends. My answer kept changing. Remembering our car breaking down on a remote country road, I would reply, "Exciting." Thinking of the threatened invasion by neighboring Mozambique, I'd respond, "Sort of scary." Reminders of the people evoked, "Great." Fear and fascination, beauty and awe, it defied one-sentence answers.

But it was disease, far worse than anything I had ever seen, that remains my overwhelming memory. There were tuberculosis of the spine that paralyzed young legs, limbs torn by crocodile and hippopotamus bites, and even auto accidents, all made worse by long delays before treatment. The medical personnel were earnest and well-meaning, but tragically under-trained. X-ray and laboratory facilities were almost nonexistent.

One common thread tied it all together for me: the knowledge that I couldn't cope with these challenges by myself. A complete dependence on God was necessary if I were to make it through each day. Prayer became an ongoing conversation with Him. My surgical abilities were not sufficient for what was needed.

I was wrong when I talked that Sunday morning in church. It wasn't just that Africans were sick and I was a physician who could treat them. I knew now that I hadn't gone on this mission just for the sake of those Africans after all. God had used that time of danger and fear, the sense of physical and emotional exhaustion and my realization of my own inadequacies to bind me closer to Him. It was for *me* that I went. I just didn't know it until it was all over.

Dear Lord and Savior, thank You! —SCOTT HARRISON

| 28 | SUNDAY |

Honor thy father and thy mother. —EXODUS 20:12

I'd really been looking forward to my seventy-third birthday last year, so when it dawned damp and gloomy, I moped around for most of the morning, feeling sorry for myself. I thought about my father, who never even reached sixty-three, and remembered with regret that our relationship hadn't been very close. The rain prevented my son John and me from playing golf, so I sat in the den recalling my childhood and trying to think if I'd ever told my father, "I love you." Sadly, I couldn't remember one instance.

When the sun broke through the clouds later in the afternoon, my mood lightened. Our daughter Jacqui arrived, and we had a wonderful dinner with roast lamb and mint jelly and my favorite dessert, apple crumb cake with ice cream. The dinner was periodically interrupted by birthday calls from our out-of-town progeny. All three calls ended with, "I love you, Dad."

AUGUST 1988

As I was getting ready for bed, it hit me that even though I could no longer do anything about my relationship with my father, I still had the opportunity to strengthen the good feelings I have with our children! Leaving our bedroom, I went down the hall to John's room and knocked on the door. "Just wanted to say good night and tell you that I'm glad you're here today, John. I love you, Son." My birthday was not a time for regrets, I now saw, but a time for precious opportunities not to be missed.

Today is an opportunity to bring healing to someone. A day to create or restore love and harmony. Why don't you try it?

Lord, help me to find words and actions that will communicate my love to _____ today.
                                    (Name)

—SAM JUSTICE

29 MONDAY
"O God my Rock," I cry, "why have you forsaken me? Why must I suffer these attacks from my enemies?"
—PSALM 42:9 (LB)

One day while looking through a folder of old newspaper clippings, I pulled out an article about the deadly tornado that ripped through the small town of Barneveld, Wisconsin, a few years ago, killing nine people and destroying nearly every home and business in the village.

The reporter wrote, "The wind took almost all of St. Mary's Catholic Church but it left part of page 168. The wind tore it from a hymnal and pinned it to the ground with a chunk of pew. Page 168 is a song: 'O Come and Mourn With Me Awhile.'"

I wondered if that small piece of paper from the hymnal was God's gentle, loving touch, reminding the people of Barneveld that it was all right to lose themselves in grief and sorrow—momentarily. It was as if God was saying, "Cry for *a while,* then get on with the business of rebuilding your lives."

I, too, had been mourning, lonely and depressed, for two years over the fact that my marriage had ended. After I read that article about the tornado, I decided that I'd mourned long enough. It was time to approach life with a positive new outlook. I made some new friends, joined a group of single parents, started teaching a college copywriting class, made an effort to have special moments or hours

240

alone with each of my four children every week, created a daily morning quiet time with God and tried to approach each day with hope and determination.

How about you? Have you taken the time to mourn—*a while*? Now it's time to get on with the business of rebuilding. With God's help you can do it, too.

Lord, when the tornadoes in my life send everything topsy-turvy, let me "mourn a while" and then give me the strength to face the world with renewed courage.   —PATRICIA LORENZ

| 30 | TUESDAY |

FIRESIDE FRIEND

Search me, O God, and know my heart: try me, and know my thoughts: And see if there be any wicked way in me, and lead me in the way everlasting.

—*PSALM 139:23–24*

Whoever heard of fruit flies upstairs?

I certainly hadn't. But that didn't make them any less annoying as hundreds flitted over the bathroom sink. I attacked them with bug killer and glass cleaner, but for every one I annihilated, two more seemed to pop up. What could they be attracted to?

A friend agreed that the only place she'd ever seen fruit flies was—around rotting fruit! Her comment prompted me to check one more spot. Cautiously I opened the cabinet door under the sink and peered into the wastebasket. I was greeted by a cloud of the teeny insects and what appeared to be a dirty, fuzzy tennis ball but was, in fact, a moldy orange. I threw it out and the fruit flies disappeared.

Weeks later I blew up at my husband over a trivial matter. The next day I spent an hour in a department store, allowing myself the uncommon luxury of trying on clothes. In the dressing room, it occurred to me that the real "rotting fruit" in my life had nothing to do with Michael. I was wallowing in self-pity, feeling bogged down with responsibilities but not taking time out for myself. With that out of my system, the irritation left.

Is something "bugging" you? If you will honestly seek the source, even if that means facing up to a fault in yourself, God will help you deal with it.

Lord, show me how to "clean house" of sin that keeps me from You and others.   —B. J. CONNOR

AUGUST 1988

31 WEDNESDAY

And there we saw the giants...and we were in our own sight as grasshoppers... —*NUMBERS 13:33*

My son Chris and I recently loaded up his faithful old car, Junior, and headed eighteen hundred miles across America to the college where he would begin his freshman year. As we talked, his voice was a half tone higher and had a measured cadence as he struggled to control his anxiety. He did not know a single person at the school and had visited it only once. Getting lost in the shuffle wasn't a possibility, it was a certainty. I tried to help with a father-son talk. I remembered how nervous I had been on my first day. But times have changed and nothing seemed relevant.

On our last day on the road, I sat reading my new Bible. The story was of the twelve spies sent by Moses to explore the Promised Land. They all reported back that it was a land of milk and honey. But ten of the spies also described the giants who lived there, who made them feel like grasshoppers.

Perhaps things weren't so different today after all. Thirty-four centuries ago other travelers were as nervous and frightened by the unknown as we were. Chris had a choice: to hop into school like a grasshopper, or stride in feeling like a giant. Later that day, rather than give further advice, I offered a prayer that we all need at certain times of our life. Here it is:

Lord, Who transforms the lowly caterpillar into the delicate butterfly, we ask a second miracle: change us from grasshoppers into giants. —SCOTT HARRISON

Thank-You Notes to God

1.

2.

3.

4.

5.

6.

7.

8.

9.

10.

11.

12.

13.

14.

15.

16

17

18

19

20

21

22

23

24

25

26

27

28

29

30

31

S	M	T	W	T	F	S
				1	2	3
4	5	6	7	8	9	10
11	12	13	14	15	16	17
18	19	20	21	22	23	24
25	26	27	28	29	30	

SEPTEMBER

> BE A GIVER
> *Your Spiritual Pilgrimage*

Freely ye have received, freely give.   —MATTHEW 10:8

When the harvest moon hangs round and placid above the autumn hills, do you ever stop to ponder how generous our good earth is? In September orchards are loaded with fruit, pumpkins glow in the purple dusk, granaries are bursting with grain. Abundance everywhere.

If Nature can be such a lavish provider, why can't we be generous too? If you're not a tither already, try tithing this month. The spiritual rewards may astonish you. And don't limit yourself to giving money. Give time, give attention, give sympathy, give yourself.

Be a cheerful giver in the days that lie ahead. The Bible says that God will love you for it.

Tandem Power for September

1 PRIORITIES

For in him we live, and move, and have our being...

—*ACTS 17:28*

September is a breath-of-fresh-air month when all of life seems to turn a refreshing corner. The days dawn cooler, the leaves glow brighter, the pace of life quickens with new vigor. School starts, routines change, the mail brims with schedules of activities. Before I know it, my desk is piled high with a stack of decisions to make about how I will spend my time and order my priorities this fall.

I used to measure my priorities against an imaginary inverted pyramid entitled, "Put God First." God was at the top with the biggest chunk. Next, in decreasing order came (2) Spouse, (3) Children, (4) Others, (5) Self. Another similar pyramid read (1) Jesus, (2) Others, (3) You—with the first letters spelling out the word *Joy.*

These pyramids frustrated and confused me though, because I found myself worrying more about what I wasn't doing than what I was doing. When I listened to my daughter read aloud, I worried that I should be taking a walk with my husband. When I went to an exercise class, I felt guilty because I wasn't home with my family, two obvious notches above "self" on the pyramid-scale. I often skittered from one activity to another with a vague uneasiness I should be doing something else.

Recently I saw a new chart that changed my outlook—a circle with God in the middle and the words, "Put God in the center of everything you do." Suddenly that visual picture ordered my priorities. Instead of putting God first and then moving on to other agenda items without Him, I now picture Him in the midst of my every moment. Activities don't compete with each other. His presence enriches whatever I am doing: working or fixing dinner or jogging on a country road or talking on the telephone. We are inseparable and together; we have Tandem Power.

As your pace quickens this month, why don't you do what I've done? Draw a circle on a piece of paper; put a smaller circle or heart in the center with the single word *God,* and tape it to your refrigerator door or bathroom mirror or dashboard as a daily reminder that God is in the middle of everything we do.

Heavenly Father, Your presence in the midst of our every mo-

ment helps us glorify You in everything we do.
—CAROL KUYKENDALL

<hr>

2 FRIDAY
*...God hath sent forth the Spirit of his Son into your
hearts, crying, Abba, Father.* —GALATIANS 4:6

Our youngest son John has gone away to college. I miss him so. The
house seems so quiet now that it's no longer a gathering place for teen
activities. John has never liked to write letters, and he doesn't have a
phone yet, so I can't call him. For the past few days, I've had such a
longing to hear from my son. Oh! Can you imagine how thrilled I was
when he called me tonight? He has a big test coming up tomorrow
and lots of school activities going on, so we didn't talk very long. But
that's all right. I just needed to hear his voice. I just needed to hear
those precious words, "I love you, Mom." John's call fed my heart.

I've had a long, busy day today. It's late and I'm tempted to skip my
prayer time tonight. But I wonder...could it be that my heavenly
Father longs to hear from me, just as I longed to hear from my son?
Maybe He doesn't measure the value of my prayers by their length.
Perhaps He just wants to hear my voice. Maybe, on this night when I'm
so tired, He only needs to hear me say...

Abba, Father. I love You so much.
—MARILYN MORGAN HELLEBERG

<hr>

3 SATURDAY
He will not fail or be discouraged...
—ISAIAH 42:4 (RSV)

The year my twin sons were eighteen Jeremy decided to sell his old
car and save for a spiffy new one. His brother retorted, "You'll never be
able to get enough money this summer." Others tried to discourage
Jeremy. I was one of them. But he worked faithfully managing a fruit
stand, and didn't seem to be put off by our constant discouraging
words. He sold his old car and talked the owner of the fruit stand into
buying an old truck that he could drive to and from work daily.

It was a rumbling giant of a truck, bright red with an ancient
black wooden bed. Large signs on either side of the truck said, "Fresh

Corn" and "Georgia Peaches." It made a frightening noise and broke down regularly. Jon ridiculed the monster truck. But Jeremy had little time for his brother's jokes. Sometimes he worked twelve hours a day. Never once during that long, hot summer did I hear Jeremy complain. I saw him very tired, but very determined.

In the fall, a few days before college started, Jeremy spotted the car he'd been dreaming about. And he roared off to school in it, smiling from ear to ear. His dream had come true! Watching him I thought: *The road that led to Jeremy's dream included a bumpy path on which he had to drive a broken down peaches-and-corn truck.* Maybe the way to *any* dream requires the dreamer to travel through unusual, even humiliating situations.

Watching Jeremy drive off that September morning, I decided to fight off discouragement a bit longer. Squinting in the morning sun, I could imagine that one day my sons and I wouldn't quarrel anymore...and even that instead of being a widow I might be a wife again someday.

Oh, Father, let me fight discouragement and disbelief; keep me diligently on the road to making my dreams come true.
—MARION BOND WEST

 SUNDAY
The heavens declare the glory of God; and the firmament showeth his handiwork. —PSALM 19:1

One night when a companion and I were driving through the country on our way home from a meeting, my car suddenly stopped. We had plenty of fuel, but the motor refused to turn over. Neither of us had the slightest knowledge of the internal mysteries of an automobile, so after trying ineffectually to start the engine, we gave up. My companion offered to walk back to a farmhouse we had passed to see if he could phone for help.

I was alone. Total blackness surrounded me. It was a strange sensation, for seldom was I out at night on a lonely road, far away from the city's glow.

Then, for some reason, I looked up. And there stretching above me was an astonishing spectacle. For the first time I understood what the word *galaxy* really means. Thousands, millions, billions of stars were spread across the black sky, making any display of fireworks I'd ever seen weak by comparison. It was awesome.

How many of us have really seen the splendor of God's firmament? This magnificent pageant of His power is on view every night, but you have to move away from man's artificial light to see it properly.

Help me, Lord, to turn my gaze from man-made things to the brightness of Your love. —WALTER HARTER

> 5 MONDAY
> *...The work of a man's hand comes back to him.*
> —PROVERBS 12:14 (RSV)

"That's what Labor Day is for," my husband Lynn cheerfully announced as he sat at the kitchen counter, compiling a long list of tasks to tackle during the day that stretched before us. "It's to labor!"

"Is not," I corrected, reading the morning paper. "It says right here that 'Labor Day was designated as a federal holiday by President Grover Cleveland in 1894 to honor the working man. The first Monday in September was chosen because it comes during the most pleasant season of the year and fills a wide gap in the chronology of legal holidays. Traditionally, it is celebrated with picnics and parades.'" I emphasized "picnics and parades."

"Traditionally," Lynn teased, "we celebrate it by working." His joking was supposed to be the spoonful of sugar to make the medicine go down. Like it or not, he was right. For the last several years, we have used Labor Day as a gift of time to catch up and bring order back into a home that had been neglected during the summer of outdoor activities. And though I resisted, the results were rewarding. Completing tasks that have nagged me for months usually rejuvenates me as much as a picnic or a parade. And the laboring *did* seem appropriate, because I've learned that the attitude and energy I have toward my Monday-through-Friday job has lots to do with the order of the home where I start and end my day.

So that's why the holiday has become a "labor" day at our house, with tasks like the ones on this year's list: update phone number list; sort through recipe and coupon drawer; repot house plants; clean kids' closets. How about you this Labor Day? Do you have a project around the house that is nagging you? The results of tackling it may be as rewarding as a picnic or parade.

Thank You, Lord, for our jobs and our homes, and the gift of time to bring order back into our lives.
—CAROL KUYKENDALL

 TUESDAY   **FIRESIDE FRIEND**
With long life will I satisfy him, and show him my salvation.   *—PSALM 91:16*

My daughter Amy Jo started high school this year. As I drove her to school that first day, I glanced across the seat. A childish flush was on her cheeks, a touch of mascara on her lashes. "Somehow I never thought I'd have a daughter in high school," I said. "I guess I never planned on getting this old."

She turned and smiled at me, a smile remarkably like my own. "Well," she laughed, "you'd better plan on getting a lot older!"

As I drove back home, I thought about those words. *Plan on getting older.* I'd never thought much about aging; I'd been too busy living through diapers and strained peas and scraped knees. How does one *plan* for aging? What things can I do *now* that will make my older years better?

Later that day I made a list:

1. *Invest in people*, not things. Keep in touch with friends, even if the effort costs me valuable time.
2. *Learn more*—about caterpillars and outer space and internal combustion engines. Make learning a way of life!
3. *Listen* to the songs of birds, the dreams of children and the memories of those older and wiser than I.

It's just a beginning, I know. But these simple resolutions remind me that each day is a preparation for the next. And the next. You see, I'm planning now—not only to live a long life, but to live a full life as well.

Show us, Lord, the blessings of old age.
—MARY LOU CARNEY

7 | WEDNESDAY
Blessed is he whose transgression is forgiven...

—PSALM 32:1

I don't know what possessed me—some demonic force perhaps—but immediately after I said what I said to my long-time friend Marguerite I was sorry, *very* sorry.

It happened after my parents had enrolled me in a new school where I'd made a new set of friends. These new friends seemed more sophisticated, more "with it" than the playmates of my childhood. Yet I still saw my old friends regularly, and one day when Marguerite and I were discussing the proper way to act at a party I criticized her manners, her dress, everything. "The trouble is," I blurted out, "you have no class!"

Instantly I regretted my words. But some terrible pride kept me from voicing that regret. Instead I stood there waiting to see what Marguerite would do.

What she did was put an arm around my shoulder. Then she said, "I love you. I forgive you, Eleanor."

Today, more than forty years later, Marguerite says she does not remember the episode. But I have never forgotten it. Nor have I forgotten the marvelous balm that came with those seven wonderful words.

They are words that remind me of Jesus, Who wants us to love and forgive each other because He loved and forgave us.

Dear Lord, may those words I love you *and* I forgive you *be often on my lips and in my heart.* —ELEANOR SASS

8 | THURSDAY
Some trust in chariots, and some in horses: but we will remember the name of the Lord our God. —PSALM 20:7

When we brought Quick Knock home, she was a slick gray filly, full of herself and elated by her strength. Racing through our pasture with her tail erect and her mane flowing, she embodied the spirit of a thoroughbred. As the years went by, Quick Knock became more docile, and her running at full speed lessened. We were relieved because she was much easier to handle. Rather than prancing and chasing about, she came quietly when whistled in from the pasture.

SEPTEMBER 1988

It was our daughter Ann who finally explained the change in Quick Knock's behavior. One evening she burst into the house with a funny expression on her face. "Quick Knock is blind!"

"I don't believe it," was my response. "How can she be blind when she never bumps into anything?"

"But she is. Come out and I'll show you."

As we stood in front of the placid horse, Ann swung her hand alongside Quick Knock's face. The mare didn't blink, but just stood with her head tilted slightly to the side. Ann tried again from the other side...but not a flinch was seen.

Quick Knock had gone blind slowly. During that time she transferred reliance on her own strength and speed to a dependence on those around her, and a calm assurance had replaced her frantic running.

As I start to rush through my day today, I am going to slow down and rely on God's leading. I can find that same calm assurance that Quick Knock demonstrates—when I trust my Master to lead me.

Lord, I step out in faith today and put my hand into Yours.
—SCOTT HARRISON

 FRIDAY

For a thousand years in thy sight are but as yesterday when it is past, and as a watch in the night.
—PSALM 90:4

Sitting behind the wheel in rush-hour traffic, I count the minutes passing. I'm going to be late for dinner, I'm missing an important phone call, I'm definitely off schedule. I start drumming impatiently at the wheel and glare furiously at the driver who appears ready to cut me off—should the traffic start moving. Without knowing it, I'm locked in the gridlock of more than a traffic snarl.

Glancing in the rearview mirror, I glimpse the man behind me singing. Gesticulating with one hand, conducting an imaginary orchestra, he opens his mouth so wide I can see his tonsils. Amidst the honking horns (perhaps he is incorporating them into his accompaniment), he is miles away, on stage or maybe in a Hollywood musical. I wonder, who is using this "lost" time better, he or I?

When you wait for an elevator, do you stare intently at the numbers above, counting the seconds it will take to get from the lobby to the eighth floor? When you're in line at the supermarket, do you glance nervously at the line next to yours, knowing it will move faster? In our world we're often asked to stop quite against our will. But when we do, do we growl with discontent...or read a book, sing a song or say a prayer?

Lord, teach us to number our days. —RICK HAMLIN

---

10 SATURDAY
...I am planning to take a trip to Spain, and when I do, I will stop off there in Rome... —ROMANS 15:24 (LB)

Recently, I saw a statement by a successful animal trainer who threw cold water on the maxim, "You can't teach an old dog new tricks."

"All that a teacher needs to do is repeat a simple lesson several times in succession and the dog will get the idea, regardless of his or her age," the trainer said. "Repetition is the key."

What is true of animals is true of humans. The principal reason most of us quit learning is not that we have become too old, but rather that we take ourselves out of the path of learning. And I think I know why: There is the risk of failure and embarrassment when we try new things, and the older we get the more we choose the security and comfort of unthreatening things we already know.

This is back-to-school time, and several million of this fall's students are forty and over. My wife Shirley just finished work for her master's degree in library science. A retired businesswoman down the street now has the time to take the piano lessons she bypassed as a child. A friend in his fifties has decided he wants to change careers, and he is going to night school studying computer programming.

Fall is a wonderful season for new adventures. Are you out of shape? Maybe it's time for an exercise class at the Y. Are you dreaming of a trip to another country? Maybe you should enroll in a language class. Wish you knew more about the Old Testament? Consider enrolling in a correspondence course or auditing a class at a seminary.

Each of us has some unfulfilled desires of the heart that I believe are prompted by our Creator. The way to bring them to fruition is to begin now. For it is still true that every journey begins with a single step and the best time to lace up your hiking boots is today.

Like a tree, Lord, help us to grow a little new wood each year.
—FRED BAUER

Spirit Lifter
Success comes in cans, failure in can'ts.
—AUTHOR UNKNOWN

---

11 SUNDAY
...Then listen to me. Keep silence and I will teach you wisdom! —JOB 33:33 (LB)

Grandma lived with us all of my growing-up years. No one ever said it was easy for three generations to share one roof. We had our ups and downs; we kids found her old-fashioned notions ridiculous and she considered our newfangled ideas equally absurd.

But it was not the generation gap between us that I remember most about Grandma. It was her total, unshakable faith and confidence in us. I can still picture her, tilted back a bit to see better through her glasses, shaking her head with its small knot of white hair as she read the daily newspaper.

"Tch! Tch! Tch!" was the sound her tongue made against her teeth any time she read of juveniles in trouble. "I am so glad this is not your name here." And then those blue eyes would pierce straight into me. "Oh, but of course it couldn't be. You would never do anything so bad, like that."

And you know, she was right. I had my share of temptations, of course, but any time I felt my resistance weakening where something really *bad* was concerned, Grandma's words would stop me. Somehow, there was no way I could bear to break her trust in me.

Today, I proudly bear the name of "Grandma," and I feel that same confidence in my two grandchildren. I keep reminding myself that I must make them aware of my trust in them. I must give it to them as a buoy to cling to when the going gets rough.

I think this might even be the biggest job God has for us grand-parents to do.

Lord, no joy, such as being a grandparent, comes without re-sponsibility. Help me to fulfill mine in a way pleasing to You. Amen. —DRUE DUKE

12 MONDAY
And he took them up in his arms, put his hands upon them, and blessed them. —MARK 10:16

The big yellow school bus swallowed up Andrew as I dashed for the front stoop to wave vigorously, blew him a kiss, then ended the routine with more wild waving as the bus ground forward.

"Why do you do that silly waving routine every morning, Mom?" asked fifteen-year-old Julie.

"Every single day since Andrew started kindergarten last year, he has left the house with the words, 'Wave to me when the bus comes...and don't forget the kiss part.'"

"You didn't wave to me every day when I was in first grade," reminded fourteen-year-old Michael.

"That's because you had your two older sisters with you. Andrew needs to know he's not alone when he leaves. One of these days he'll get on the bus and forget even to look for me. But for now, I *like* feeling needed."

You know what? After that conversation Julie started giving me a quick kiss on the cheek as she bounded out the door for the bus and Michael made sure to holler, "Bye, Mom!" even if I was in the bathroom getting ready for work. I like the "leaving routines" our family has every morning that tie us together with a string of love and caring.

I've read that it takes seven days to make a habit. This week, why not form a new good-morning/good-bye habit with the people you love?

Lord, let me both give and receive blessings that come from forming daily habits of love and caring with others.

—PATRICIA LORENZ

13	TUESDAY

TUESDAY   **FIRESIDE FRIEND**

...For the Lord thy God, he it is that doth go with thee; he will not fail thee, nor forsake thee.

        —DEUTERONOMY 31:6

As I entered my sophomore year in college, I was discouraged to see old friendships from high school fade. None of us were letter writers and the longer we stayed out of touch, the more I began to question the depth of our friendships.

One night as my friend Rhonda (who is from my hometown) and I were studying for midterms, the phone rang. One of our old friends had been in a minor car accident nearby and needed a ride back to her campus some miles away. She called in desperation knowing we were now living here. Without a thought, we rushed across town to where she was.

When we caught sight of Paula, her face lit up and she ran over to hug us. In the car, we caught up on old times—no hesitation, no apologies, just three good friends laughing together. After we got Paula safely back to her dorm, we stayed another hour talking, really talking—about the past and hopes for the future. I left feeling both happy and renewed. The friendship had not ended; we merely picked up where we had left off. We all vowed to stay in touch, knowing that despite our separate lives, we would always be there for one another.

Perhaps my experience will remind you of a friend with whom you've been out of touch, a friend who can be reached by a phone call or brief letter. As the scouting song reminds us:

> Make new friends, but keep the old;
> One is silver and the other gold.

Lord, _____ is someone with whom I need
               (name of friend)
to rekindle the flame of friendship. Let me take the first step today.   —DAVID CORNELIUS

14	WEDNESDAY

It is a good thing to give thanks unto the Lord...to show forth thy loving-kindness in the morning, and thy faithfulness every night.   *—PSALM 92:1,12*

It was dawn, September 14, 1814, toward the end of the War of 1812, and

Baltimore was under bombardment by the British. On board the British warship *Minden*, the Washington lawyer Francis Scott Key paced the deck. He had boarded the ship to negotiate the release of his physician friend, Dr. William Beanes. The British agreed to release Dr. Beanes, but kept both men captive so that they couldn't warn Fort McHenry of the surprise pre-dawn attack.

As a worried Francis Scott Key tried to peer through the early darkness, all he could see were smoke and haze from the gunfire. Fort McHenry was not a very strong fortification, so Key feared the worst. But when the morning light broke through, the men saw that the American flag still flew over the fort. With joy and gratitude, Key pulled an unfinished letter from his pocket and in minutes scribbled down the words to the now-famous "Star Spangled Banner."

Last Christmas, I too spent some anxious hours pacing up and down in the Boston bus terminal, watching the passengers coming off the buses. My eighty-seven-year-old Aunt Ruth was due to visit us, but she wasn't on the bus when it arrived. Had something happened to her? The bus driver hadn't seen her. There was no answer at her home. As I waited, my feelings of apprehension growing with every passing moment, I thought of Francis Scott Key's long vigil.

"Oscar!" I turned to see Aunt Ruth waving. "I'm so sorry. I missed the first bus and didn't know how to reach you!" Joy filled me. If I had had the talent, I would have written words to a hymn of thanksgiving. All I could do was give my aunt a big, welcoming hug.

Lord, when the outlook is dark and foreboding, I will stay faithful to Thee in my vigil from morning till night.

—OSCAR GREENE

Family Time

15 WELCOMING CHANGE
As we grow toward maturity...as we continue to share honestly with each other, we help one another grow to our full potential as Christpersons.

—*EPHESIANS 4:14a, 15*

"As long as you don't change anything...I'm flexible."

A plaque on our wall with this tongue-in-cheek saying always gets a laugh. Let's face it—change is something we seem to fight against. Yet, if we are to grow and mature as persons, as family members and as Christians, change is inevitable. To remain the same is to stagnate; to change and grow as Christians is to participate in God's new beginnings and to move into the new dimensions of what God is anxious for us to experience.

This thought probably leaves you a bit uncomfortable as it does us. We'd like instant maturity without the pain of growth-change. We're a little like the six-year-old who came home after his first day in school. When his father asked if he had learned everything today, he answered with obvious frustration and disappointment, "No, I've got to go back tomorrow." There's always more to learn and be; we're never "arrivers" but always "becomers" in our pilgrimage of faith. We're on the move, and to move is to invite change.

While God's eternal truth and purposes are changeless, His creation is in a constant state of change. All of nature is a symphony of change—the weather, the seasons, the trees and flowers. Even the shorelines and the earth's surface are always changing. For several years we enjoyed our cottage on the restless Brazos River of Texas. As we watched its flow day after day, we never saw the same river twice.

"Our" river was like the kaleidoscope we had as children. As we stared into that little tube, the arrangement of colors and shapes was breathtaking—nothing could be more beautiful. Yet, as we moved it, new and even more beautiful shapes and colors formed. And as much as we tried, we could never recapture an earlier image—to move was to change.

Dr. Sam Shoemaker, one of God's great spokesmen of a generation or two ago, was heard to ask, "Is your Christianity ancient history or current events?" Good question! Earlier we talked about dreams and goals. One of ours has long been to welcome change, to be open to God's new experiences. Why? Our own lives will be enriched, and as Scripture puts it, we can then "help one another to grow."

We've made a little headway in our "welcome change" pilgrimage, but we've still got a long way to go. It is a matter of attitude. If we *every day* expect new and exciting things to change our lives and ask God to help us anticipate and accept them, something happens.

Plutarch, the ancient Greek writer, astutely observed, "For the wise man, every day is a festival." To grow and change and mature as Christians make every day a celebration!

Help us, Lord, to be deeply rooted in Your eternal truth, but

then to welcome the growth and change that will keep us re-
newed and will help our family and friends to experience the
fullness of Your love.   —HARRIETT AND FLOYD THATCHER

| 16 | FRIDAY |

For thus saith the Lord God; Behold, I, even I, will both
search my sheep, and seek them out.   —EZEKIEL 34:11

A few days ago, my neighbor, a farmer, asked me to help him find some
of his sheep that had wandered from the pasture into a stand of
nearby trees.

"They're so stupid," he complained as we trudged off. "They keep
their heads down, nibbling at the grass, and never look up to see
where they're going. Then suddenly they're among the trees and can't
find their way out. Stupid!"

As we rounded up the vagrants and led them back into the sunlight of the field, I found myself thinking about sheep. They're men-
tionèd as early in the Bible as the fourth chapter of Genesis, when
God looked upon Abel's sacrifice of a sheep "with favor," while ignoring Cain's gift of fruit. Later, Abraham substitutes a sheep for Isaac.
Again and again sheep appear throughout the Bible and on into the
New Testament when Jesus calls Himself "the Lamb of God."

I found myself wondering: If sheep are just stupid creatures, then
why are they used again and again in the Bible? What's good about
sheep that makes them a positive symbol? And then I thought, well,
first, they're innocent. Second, they're useful in every way, from their
wool to their milk to their meat. Third, they are used as sacrifices, like
Jesus Who "taketh away the sin of the world" (John 1:29). And fourth,
as Jesus says in John 10, they "know their master's voice." Yes, humble
sheep have certain qualities worth emulating. They're sacrificial.
They're useful. They're innocent. And they "know their Master's
voice."

Father, help me—always—to know Your voice and to follow it.
                                         —WALTER HARTER

SATURDAY
Though I scatter them among the peoples, yet in distant lands they will remember me.   *—ZECHARIAH 10:9 (NIV)*

When my mother moved into a retirement home she sent me a box of things she wanted me to have. Tucked into a corner of a carton of china was a small silver box I'd never seen before. It contained four small seashells.

Mother later explained that her father, while waiting on the seacoast of Wales for the next boat that would take him to America, had scooped up the shells and put them in his pocket so that he could always "touch a piece of where he'd come from." He homesteaded in Wisconsin and died when Mother was just a young girl. She had kept his shells hidden away in a bureau drawer all these years. Now she wanted me to have them.

On this day as I finger the tiny shells that are the only legacy of the grandfather I never knew, I think of what must have been that young boy's feelings as he left home to seek citizenship in a strange land. And I think of his daughter, my mother, cherishing these shells as she struggled through the Great Depression, raising four children who could one day reap the benefits of life in America.

Our citizenship cost others dearly. Today, let's each of us touch "a piece of where we've come from." And remember.

Father, we have scattered. Help us to remember those who came before us and be grateful for their sacrifice and Your guidance.   —MARILYN MOORE JENSEN

18 **SUNDAY**
…I will sing, yea, I will sing praises unto the Lord.
—PSALM 27:6

On Sunday, September 19, 1937, I was to have a new experience. It was my first evening chapel at Hampton Institute in Virginia. Suddenly, the quiet was broken by a solitary voice singing, "Roll, Jordan, roll!" Instantly, the overflow congregation responded, "I want-er go to heav'n when I die—to hear ol' Jordan roll!"

I sat mute, wide-eyed as the melody swelled. It was a dazzling mixture of love, humor, joy and sadness—the rolling of an emotional sea. I had never heard a spiritual before. Later, during my undergraduate days, I grew to love "Walking Together Children," "We Are Clim'in' Jacob's Ladder," "Joshua Fit De Battle Ob Jericho" and others.

Even though they were enslaved, my people, often without churches and schools, believed with a desperate courage. They knew God saved Daniel, that He preserved the Hebrew children in the fiery furnace, that He delivered Israel from bondage in Egypt and that He would lead them, too, out of two and a half centuries of slavery. The spirituals were a cry of faith from those in bondage, their way of praising God.

Gradually, I saw my slave ancestors in a new light and all feelings of shame vanished. A new respect surged as I saw their courage, their faith, their legacy to me. Joy replaced my sadness over their years in slavery.

Now, fifty-one years later, I still can't carry a tune. But, "Ev'ry time I feel de spirit movin' in my heart, I will pray!"

Gracious Father, when I'm beset with troubles, let my life do the singing! —OSCAR GREENE

| 19 | MONDAY | FIRESIDE FRIEND |

...*Let us run with perseverance the race that is set before us, looking to Jesus the pioneer and perfecter of our faith...* —HEBREWS 12:1–2 (RSV)

I always look forward to the Olympic Games. Every four years, the world honors a sports tradition that first began in Elis, Greece, more than two thousand five hundred years ago. This year is yet another Olympic year.

To me, the most fascinating detail of the Games is the Olympic Flame. This Flame, the symbol of peace and friendship, is lit at the site of the ancient Greek games. A runner carries the Flame for a distance and then passes it to another. This runner accepts the Flame, carries it and also passes it on. Through means of cross-country races, ships and planes, the Flame is kept alive until it arrives at the host nation.

The Olympic Flame reminds me of another Flame, the Bethlehem Flame. It also has an historic beginning. It is also the symbol of peace and friendship—the peace we have in God, and the friendship we share in Him with another. As with the Olympic Flame, we, too, strive to keep the Bethlehem Flame alive by carrying it runner to runner, and always passing it on.

I now pass this flame of faith, this Bethlehem Flame, to you, runner. Will you accept it, carry it for a distance and pass it to another?

Godspeed to you as you run your own race.

O Lord, give us perseverance as we run. Help us to look to You always as we strive to keep the Bethlehem Flame alive.
—DENISE GEORGE

| 20 | TUESDAY | FIRESIDE FRIEND |

…How often would I have gathered thy children together, even as a hen gathereth her chickens under her wings… —MATTHEW 23:37

The dog was small and of undetermined pedigree, and he had taken refuge on our front porch. I chased him away but he returned repeatedly. His matted hair was in desperate need of soap and water. Finally realizing he was hungry, I gave him some table scraps that he devoured ravenously.

In the next few days, he decided our house was "home." I was sure he'd been mistreated in the past: He refused to let me touch him, and although he obviously craved affection, he seemed afraid to accept it. With tail wagging excitedly, he would scamper behind me and through my legs, but when I stooped to pat him, he'd jump several feet from my reach. When I offered him bits of meat, he'd cautiously crawl toward me, grab the morsel and dash away.

Why is he so skittish when I am only trying to help him? I wondered. As I tried other ways to get this small dog to trust me, I thought of how I sometimes react the same way as a child of God. Time and again He displays His love for me and yet I "keep Him at arm's length," refusing to come closer. All He desires is to give me an abundance of His blessings.

I looked down at the stray dog and decided to be patient and give him more time…as God has so often done with me. And perhaps I can learn to trust God more quickly in the days ahead.

Father, remove our fear and fill us with complete trust in You.
—VIRGINIA POEHLEIN

21 WEDNESDAY
Confess your faults one to another, and pray one for another, that ye may be healed. —JAMES 5:16

Yom Kippur is the day of atonement in the Jewish calendar, an annual day of confession and repentance. Its origins can be found in the Bible, "On the tenth day of this seventh month there shall be a day of atonement..." (Leviticus 23:27). And in Jewish households it is the most solemn holiday of the year.

In my heavily Jewish neighborhood, it's easy to remember the day because of the many families I see walking to synagogue, the men wearing *yarmulkes* (black skullcaps), the women dressed in their best. The event of the holiday, though, that touched me most was in a friend's apartment building. Near the front door was a note from the landlord: "At this time of year, it is appropriate to ask you, our tenants, to forgive us for any faults you've found in our management—the mistakes you've told us about (which we've tried to correct) and those you haven't yet mentioned. Thank you. The Management."

I like the honest sincerity of that statement. It's a traditional Jewish teaching that atonement for sin is not complete until things have been put right with both God *and* man. I'm also reminded of something a friend once said, "If I don't confess my sins aloud to someone else, then I have problems confessing them to God." Maybe that's why the Bible says, "Confess your faults one to another...." We can do that on any day.

Forgive me, Lord, for my sins in thought, word and deed.
—RICK HAMLIN

22 THURSDAY   FIRESIDE FRIEND
Long ago, even before he made the world, God chose us to be his very own... —EPHESIANS 1:4 (LB)

I sit outside in a rocker, listening to the melody of the tinkling wind chimes. The sun warms my face and the fresh-scrubbed smell of morning fills me. I need this quiet time. Lately a feeling of doubt has wound its way in, around and through me like a climbing vine. I find myself asking, *What is so special about me? Am I really able to offer God something that no one else has?*

I squint my eyes and search the blue expanse above me. A gust of wind blows through my hair and sets the chimes to tinkling again. That's when I notice the different shapes and sizes of the metal cylinders. Each one, when moved by the wind, creates a different tone from the others.

In the tinkling of the wind chimes I seem to hear God saying, *I need the shape of your life to move in My Spirit. No one else can create your expression of Me. You are needed to complete My song.* Those thoughts pull me free of the vine that has been choking me. No one else can create *my* expression of God!

No one else can create *your* expression of God either. How we each live our lives is our "expression" of Him. Today let's rejoice in that knowledge. Come. Climb onto the wind chime with me and let's sing—in our own special way.

Lord, help us to express Your love and presence in our own special way. Amen. —TERRY HELWIG

---

23 FRIDAY

Then wrought...every wise hearted man, in whom the Lord put wisdom and understanding to know how to work... —EXODUS 36:1

Everybody should have a friend like Ralph.

He can fix a lamp or a lawn mower, refinish furniture, build bookshelves. All by himself he has transformed his garage into a workshop and completely remodeled his mother's house.

One day, marveling at these results over coffee, I asked, "Ralph, where did you learn to do all this? Who taught you—your father?"

Thoughtfully he sipped his coffee, his blue eyes twinkling. "I never knew my father," he said. "But I did meet a good carpenter a long time ago. And He still helps me. In fact, every time I have a problem, all I have to do is stop and ask Him, 'Teach me what I need to know.' And He does. This morning, for instance, those boards just wouldn't work. But after I'd stopped and asked Him, 'What am I doing wrong?' the answer came: I was cutting them too short."

Then Ralph gave me the words of his own special prayer:

Jesus stand beside me.
Guide and direct my life.

> Teach me what I need to know.
> Help me with my work.
> Let me serve You and others,
> That I may be worthy of God's grace.

Ralph's special prayer has become a part of my own life now. I say it every morning. And all day, whenever I am anxious or confused about a situation, one phrase of the prayer comes to my rescue: "Teach me what I need to know." Of all the things Ralph has done to help me, Ralph's prayer has helped most of all.

Dear Father, thank You for this friend and this little prayer. May its words serve You and others. —MARJORIE HOLMES

---

24 SATURDAY
He leads me beside still waters. —PSALM 23:2 (RSV)

FIRESIDE FRIEND

There were unfinished tasks I needed to do, but the gorgeous autumn day beckoned and I sneaked away to enjoy it for a few minutes.

Those golden days when Mother Nature dons her most brilliant gown to bid farewell to the season are so few. I didn't want to miss them. Tucking a sandwich and an apple into my backpack, I pedaled my bicycle up the creek to my favorite spot a couple of miles out of town. Selecting a quiet place along the stream, I settled down for a few moments of tranquility away from the constant pressure of today's world. Gradually, I felt myself unwinding.

The ground around me was carpeted with yellow leaves, the trees lifting almost naked branches to the bright blue sky. Sunlight sparkled on the swiftly moving stream. Near the opposite bank, a huge boulder formed an obstacle, the water churning impatiently to get around it. As I ate, I conversed with a giant dragonfly. He was an excellent listener and seemed to share my love of nature. Together we soaked up the autumn sunshine.

All too soon, I had to return to the busy world I had left behind me. But I took with me the peace that I had found there in God's beautiful world. It would see me through the busy days ahead.

Creator of this magnificent world, help me to pause now and then to appreciate it. Amen. —ROBERTA DONOVAN

SUNDAY

...I will put my trust in him...and the children God has given me. —HEBREWS 2:13 (NIV)

I've had enormous difficulty in the area of trusting my children. Like all youngsters, they made mistakes growing up. But even when their decision-making ability improved, trusting them came slowly, painfully and sometimes not at all. I turned into a detective-mother. Checking, rechecking, questioning, doubting, imagining, remembering....Sometimes my imagination would explode into vivid accusations. Often I was wrong. But I continued to struggle to trust my children (and God). I desperately desired release from my obsessive thoughts that only total trust would bring. I knew the principle. I just couldn't seem to apply it.

While sweeping my front porch one day I noticed the little boy across the street. His father was helping him learn to ride his new bike. The child somehow rode too fast and plowed into a tree. He was bruised, frightened and disappointed as his father picked him up. When the father held the bike for him to try again, the youngster shook his head, "You might let me get hurt again." I knew just how he felt. I turned to go inside.

Suddenly I heard the excited father shout, "Atta boy!" I looked back hopefully. Sure enough the little fellow had decided to trust his father despite his previous disappointment and pain. A few days later the child rode confidently alone. He called out to me, "Hey, Mrs. West, look at me now!"

Thank You, Father, for bruised little boys who climb back on bikes and wave to apprehensive mothers who need to learn about trust. —MARION BOND WEST

 MONDAY

Thou wilt keep him in perfect peace, whose mind is stayed on thee... —ISAIAH 26:3

Peace is something most of us want, whether peace of mind in the world around us or peace of spirit within us. Many people, I'm sure, encounter as much difficulty as I in attaining such peace. If you have, as I do, a nineteen-year-old grandson living with you, peace is bound to be elusive.

Rocco has the world's loudest stereo in his room, where he concentrates on heavy metal music. He leaves his door open so he can hear the phone when his buddies call. His whole scene, including several car accidents, keeps me close to the ragged edge.

Then I ran across the above verse from Isaiah and I grabbed it like a drowning man. I wasn't quite sure how to "stay" my mind on the Almighty. Finally, I decided that when things got borderline, I'd repeat the verse. In fact, I kept repeating it, embroidering it with assurances to the Lord of how much I love and trust Him. The more I repeated it, the better I felt. Others who experience similar stressful situations might find this approach helpful. I recommend repeating the verse until peace rolls over you like a gentle wave.

And when that peace comes, I find it easier to once again count my blessings as far as Rocco is concerned...*after* I've asked him to turn down his stereo a tiny bit!

Lord, help me love and trust You so completely that the peace
You personify will always be with me. —SAM JUSTICE

| 27 | TUESDAY |

Evening, and morning, and at noon, will I pray...
—*PSALM 55:17*

A Christian friend and I were headed to a favorite but crowded restaurant for lunch one recent Indian-summer day. She was in town from Oklahoma and I hadn't seen her for over a year, so we both looked forward to our time together. I hate to admit it, but a silly thought nagged me as we sat on a bench outside, waiting for a table.

Would we pray together before we ate?

Sometimes I prayed in restaurants and sometimes I didn't, depending on the other people at the table. I had no set rule, but usually I felt self-conscious, and now I began to dread the potentially uncomfortable moment of decision.

Soon our table was ready. We were seated, our orders taken, and soon our meals were served. The moment had arrived. Without hesitation, my friend looked across the table at me, eye to eye, and said, "I thank God for you and our time together today and for this food. Amen."

In an instant, I was touched with her simple and direct way of saying "thank You" to God and embarrassed that I had worried about how to pray in public. Her open-eye prayer was a warm and honest reminder that I can thank God in prayer by looking down or looking up...or looking someone else squarely in the eye.

Lord, may I never be self-conscious about thanking You for the blessings of food or friends at any time or any place.

—CAROL KUYKENDALL

|28| WEDNESDAY
...For a man's life consisteth not in the abundance of the things which he possesseth. —LUKE 12:15

I love books, and for twenty years I collected biographies. Not just any biographies, but those out-of-print, hardcover, first-edition ones. I would even visit local libraries to compare their collections with mine, and come away swelling with pride. Mine was larger.

Then one Sunday our pastor told the story from Luke about the man whose storehouse was filled. What did the man do—thank God for giving him so much? No. He built larger barns! I felt ashamed. I had so much—in fact, I'd run out of space, and books were piled up in my study, attic and cellar—far too many books for one person to enjoy. I resolved to start clearing out my collection immediately.

Gingerly, I picked through my collection to see what I could part with. Although it was hard to let go, I gave my prized first-edition Handel biography to a music lover. His delighted face as he leafed through the book told me that this dusty old volume came alive for him. After that it became easier to weed out my collection. I gave books to other friends who had similar reading interests, and still others I gave to hospitals and charitable bookstalls. Soon my shelves were orderly and manageable, and I glowed with the satisfaction of having given joy to others.

Are you sagging under clutter? Do you feel like Midas, collecting useless "gold"? Try letting some of your possessions go—to people who can give them new life.

Father, help me let go—not just of things I don't need, but also of things I know others will enjoy. —OSCAR GREENE

Spirit Lifter

*If a man's Bible is coming apart, it
is an indication that he himself is
fairly well put together.*
—JAMES JENNINGS

 THURSDAY   **FIRESIDE FRIEND**
*...Add to your faith virtue; and to virtue knowledge;
And to knowledge temperance...*   —II PETER 1:5, 6

At the college I attend, there is constant pressure on young women students to be thin. They starve themselves and become anorexic, or fall victim to the "binge-purge" syndrome, bulimia. People who wear anything above a size nine are seen as overweight, and most girls will do anything to keep the pounds off. Result: some become victims of malnutrition. Some even wind up in the hospital.

That pressure got to me, too. I started dieting, and what began as a discipline became an obsession. I found myself fasting several days a week and only eating meager suppers other days. When I finally came to my senses, I found I was a victim of anorexia and needed counseling to avoid ending up in the hospital like my friends.

Anorexia is a serious problem all over America today. Ninety percent of its victims are female. How do you know if you or someone you love has anorexia? Psychotherapist Susan Rudnick lists the following symptoms:

1. Inability to stop dieting even after normal weight has been attained.
2. Ritual eating. One meal a day or fractional meals when the victim is at normal weight or less.
3. Rigid dieting in public but hoarding food to eat in private.
4. Excessive or compulsive exercise.
5. Use of laxatives, diuretics or induced vomiting to lose weight.
6. Overconcern about personal appearance, especially body image.

A person with some or all of these symptoms needs therapy. It's only through learning about themselves and why they feel the need to starve themselves that victims of anorexia can be helped.

It was hard for me to admit that I had an eating problem. But now, with help, I'm learning about myself—and food. Just in time.

Father, help us to use Your gift of food as You intended we should use it—wisely and well. —TAMMY RIDER

30 FRIDAY
...And Adam and his wife hid themselves from the presence of the Lord God... —GENESIS 3:8

Some years ago there was a plea on TV by some parents who were trying to find their son. He had run away with his girlfriend because her family didn't approve of the relationship. The boy's parents were trying desperately to find the young man because a dog that had bitten him had died of rabies. Police had been called in and had almost caught up with the young people several times, but the couple kept running and hiding.

Sometimes I try to hide from God because of my sinfulness. Oh, I don't do it consciously, but I've found that when I start skipping my daily prayer time or missing church, it's time to examine my conscience. Often it's because there's something I'm feeling guilty about. I need to remind myself that God pursues me in order to heal me, not condemn me.

When you find yourself neglecting your spiritual life, consider that you might be hiding from God. Then tell Him your sins and ask His forgiveness. He wants to save your life!

Lord, You know everything about me. Help me to stop hiding from You. —MARILYN MORGAN HELLEBERG

Thank-You Notes to God

1

2

3

4

5

6

7

8

9

10

11

12

13

14

15

SEPTEMBER 1988

16

17

18

19

20

21

22

23

24

25

26

27

28

29

30

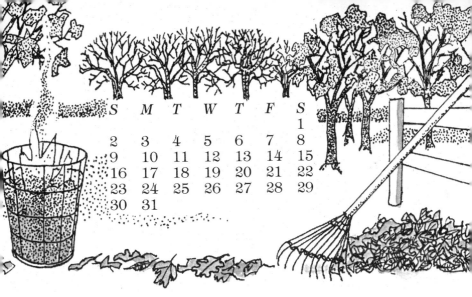

S	M	T	W	T	F	S
						1
2	3	4	5	6	7	8
9	10	11	12	13	14	15
16	17	18	19	20	21	22
23	24	25	26	27	28	29
30	31					

OCTOBER

BE A LIFE-LOVER
Your Spiritual Pilgrimage

Consider the lilies of the field, how they grow...
—MATTHEW 6:28

Welcome blue October, hazy in the sun.

A glorious month just about everywhere. Think how it appeals to all five senses. The smell of burning leaves. The blaze of scarlet and gold on the hillsides. The roar of a football crowd, or the lonely cry of wild geese winging south. The taste of pumpkin pie. The cold nudging nose of a pointer or setter urging you to take him into the field.

This month why not try to heighten your awareness of the marvelous messages your five senses bring you? The more aware you are, the more wonderful life will seem. And the more your gratitude to the Giver of life will grow.

Tandem Power for October

1 | RISKING

The Lord recompense you for what you have done.
—RUTH 2:12 (RSV)

One weekend each fall our church sponsors a women's retreat at an inspirational mountain setting. As a new member, I resisted going. What if I don't have anyone to talk to during the coffee breaks? What if six people share one bathroom? What if I wish I hadn't come? I know the worries sound shallow, but going far away from the comforts of my home and family for two nights seemed too much of a risk. So I manufactured excuses: The children were too young, I had conflicts or deadlines. But the nudges inside me kept getting louder and stronger.

"Okay, okay, Lord," I responded reluctantly one year, "I'll try it just this once." So I gave in and signed up. I felt a little uneasy as I checked in that Friday evening, but soon all two hundred of us gathered in the main meeting room to get acquainted, sing songs and hear a speaker. Her lesson that night was about the risks Ruth took leaving everything familiar and comfortable in Moab in order to accompany her mother-in-law Naomi back to Judah, Naomi's homeland. Ruth was an ordinary woman who demonstrated extraordinary faith when she chose to step out of her comfort zone and take a risk. Little did she know that eventually her risk would be rewarded with her marriage to Boaz.

I carried Ruth's story back down the mountain with me on Sunday afternoon as I drove home. Certainly my risk was less life-altering, but I too was experiencing unexpected rewards: some new friendships, fresh spiritual insights, and no more fears about attending retreats. As I rounded the curves of the canyon road, I had a silly childhood flashback. I remembered how my mother used to urge me to taste breakfast sausage. Always, I refused even the teensiest bite, until finally I tried a nibble. To my amazement, I loved the taste! And then I was sad, thinking about all those years of sausages I'd missed.

When we refuse to risk, we get stuck in ruts and miss out on the blessings God has in store for us in the unknown. But if we cooperate and use Tandem Power when the Spirit nudges us toward a risk, we often find we like the taste. Is the Spirit nudging you in the direction of a risk, to apply for a new job, make a difficult phone call, enter a contest, tell a friend about Jesus? Why not respond this October, and take some teensy tastes?

Lord, we know that when You nudge us toward a risk, we do not step into the unknown alone. Please help us cooperate with Your calling this month. —CAROL KUYKENDALL

---

2 SUNDAY
Be devoted to one another in brotherly love. Honor one another above yourselves. —ROMANS 12:10 (NIV)

We were talking about family relationships, this business acquaintance and I, when he volunteered, "I haven't spoken to my brother in fifteen years." When I asked why, he said they had disagreed over the settlement of his parents' estate. How different their relationship from the one in this old legend....

There were once two brothers named Stephen and Aaron, who labored diligently in their father's fields. They were fiercely loyal to each other, to their parents and to God. When their father became old and his days numbered, he called the two together and divided the land between them, and Stephen and Aaron set up homes of their own. But they and their families remained close, helping and caring for each other. And they prospered...until a drought came and their wheat fields yielded only a fraction of previous harvests.

One night, concerned that his brother and his family might not have enough grain for their table, Stephen took a sack of wheat to his brother's barn and secretly added it to Aaron's storage. The next morning Aaron was amazed—his supply seemed even greater than the day before. With more than enough for their needs, Aaron told his wife that that night he was going secretly to take some grain to Stephen's barn—just in case he was in need. Then it was Stephen's turn to be amazed, and he repeated the favor. Back and forth they went, until one dark night the two brothers met on their way to each other's barn with grain sacks in hand. At first they laughed, then they cried and then they hugged. They didn't say a word because no words were needed.

> *More than people with loving creeds,*
> *Lord, make us people of loving deeds.*
>
> —FRED BAUER

3	MONDAY

A soft answer turneth away wrath... —PROVERBS 15:1

As I read the letter, anger boiled within me. "I am very disappointed by your discourtesy...it seems to me that just a few short lines....the least you could do...."

The writer was complaining about the length of time I'd taken to answer her request for information. I had been slow, no doubt about it. But there had been so many deadlines to meet, so many more important things to do. *She should know how busy I am right now*, I thought resentfully. *There's no reason for her to write such a nasty letter!*

I whipped out a piece of stationery and rolled it into my typewriter. "Dear Mrs. ..." I typed. "You obviously are unaware..." I accused her of being inconsiderate, ill-informed, thoughtless. I really let her have it.

Just as I got to a frosty "Sincerely," a friend stuck his head through the door of my office. "How are you doing?" he asked. Ignoring his question, I held out both letters. "Read these!" I commanded. He sat down and read.

When he had finished, he handed the letters back to me with a smile. "You won't send yours," he said cheerfully.

I hesitated, then answered, "No, I guess I won't."

And I didn't. Instead, I bowed my head over my machine and said a quick prayer, thanking God for sending my friend at just the right moment. Then I threaded another piece of stationery into the typewriter. "Dear Mrs. ..." I typed. "I'm sorry it took so long...Please forgive the delay...You see..." It was a soft answer. And when I finished typing it, my hot anger was gone.

Dear Father, help me to cool down and speak with understanding instead of acting on impetuous anger too quickly.

—ELEANOR SASS

4	TUESDAY

My heart is fixed, O God, my heart is fixed...

—PSALM 57:7

On this day, many churches remember St. Francis, who wrote the beautiful prayer that begins, "Lord, make me an instrument of Thy peace." Recently, I heard about an incident in the life of this man who lived outdoors, communing with God in nature. One bitter cold night, a man who tended the fire periodically during the night woke up and found that Francis wasn't there. He found him kneeling on a hill, completely unprotected from the blizzard that raged about him. Arms uplifted, his ragged friar's cloak whipped by icy winds, Francis stayed that way all night, completely unaware of the cold. When he was later asked how he could do that, he replied, "God gives *His* warmth, when the heart is fixed on Him."

I could never do what St. Francis did. Yet I've found that, during the stormy times in my life, if I can just withdraw my attention from whatever my trouble is and "fix my heart on God instead," He gets me through the storm. If you're going through a stormy time right now, try to focus on God instead of on your problem. It's a way to peace.

With Your warmth in my heart, Lord, I'll get through this storm! —MARILYN MORGAN HELLEBERG

| 5 | WEDNESDAY |

By this shall all men know that ye are my disciples, if ye have love one to another. —JOHN 13:35

I recently read that some years ago a group of people visited Dr. Albert Schweitzer in Africa and tried to persuade him to leave his jungle hospital and return with them to Europe. They told him of great praise and honor awaiting him there.

As they talked, an African mother with a small child in her arms came to thank the doctor for saving her child's life. She grasped his hand, kissed it and left two tears shimmering there. Looking down at his hand, Dr. Schweitzer said, "Those two diamonds of love are the only reward I want."

My Lord Jesus left the glory of heaven and came to earth to save my eternal soul. But He doesn't want empty plaudits. The only reward He asks of me is a contrite and loving heart in which He can live.

It's the same as He asks of you. Are you giving it to Him?

Thank You, Lord, that You do live in my heart. Life would be meaningless without Your presence. Amen. —DRUE DUKE

6 | THURSDAY

The Lord gave the word: great was the company of those that published it. —PSALM 68:11

It's October 6, the day on which I say a prayer for the soul of William Tyndale, an Englishman whose short life has made *my* life a joyful and happy one. For it was he who, in 1526, made the first English translation of the New Testament. He had decided that the Bible should be read by *everyone*. Until then the marvelous words of that great book were in Latin, a mystery to the average person, and priests jealously guarded them and their meanings.

Forbidden by the bishops to print this translation in Henry VIII's Catholic England, Tyndale fled to Europe. But he persisted with his dream that all his countrymen should be permitted to read God's words, and eventually hundreds of copies of his translation were smuggled into England. Even after King Henry broke with Rome, he still proclaimed Tyndale a heretic, and demanded that he return to England for punishment.

And the priests didn't forgive the man who had torn the veil of mystery from God's words. They hounded and hunted him until he was captured in Belgium. There he was tried for heresy and condemned to death.

On October 6, 1536, he was strangled, then burned at the stake.

That's why, whenever I open my Bible, I think of the man who gave his life so that people like you and me could find solace and God's love in its pages. And why, on the anniversary of his death, I say a small prayer of thanks for his strength and conviction to perform a spiritual service that has changed infinite lives now and in the ages to come.

Father, thank You for the example of William Tyndale. May my actions always reflect the courage of my convictions for goodness and truth. —WALTER HARTER

7 | FRIDAY   FIRESIDE FRIEND

…First be reconciled to thy brother, and then come and offer thy gift. —MATTHEW 5:24

I discovered a note of hope in a consumer study. Researchers found that by settling a complaint promptly and well, a company can often generate greater customer loyalty than if the problem never occurred.

I think of the time our pizza order was lost, and we were given a larger one for the same price, or when some take-out fried chicken was late, and we got a discount. Yes, I'd go back. Both restaurants owned up to their shortcomings and compensated us.

Sometimes I'm afraid to take action for fear of making a mistake. But that's not what the study says, and it's not what I see in God's word. We are imperfect creatures in an imperfect world; so the question is not whether I will make mistakes—everybody does—but how I will handle them.

After repenting of his adultery and deadly plan for Uriah, David seemed closer to God than ever. Peter, who denied Jesus three times, got a second chance to declare his love for his Savior, and went on to become the spokesman for the disciples. My bond with my husband, when I am wrong and finally swallow my pride enough to ask for his forgiveness, grows steadily stronger.

Is there anyone you avoid because you think you "blew it" and it's too late to make amends? If your heart is beating, it's not too late.

Father, give me the humility, wisdom and courage to press on despite my errors.   —B. J. CONNOR

| 8 | SATURDAY |

Let us walk honestly, as in the day...not in strife and envying.   —ROMANS 13:13

For several months a dear friend and I walked in a local mall early each morning. After four rounds we stopped for coffee and conversation. I cherished this time with Ruth, and so, I thought, did she—until another friend of Ruth's began to join us. They enjoyed each other so much that I felt miserable and left out. Soon I stopped joining them. When Ruth called, expressing concern, I was deliberately cool.

Then one afternoon my husband brought home a tiny kitten. Our gentle collie accepted her immediately. Soon they were playing together. But our little beagle resented this intruder. She even stole a small teddy bear I'd placed in the kitten's basket and hid it in her own. Then she sat and glowered.

"Jealous?" I chided, cuddling the beagle. "Look at the fun you're missing!" *Oops. I saw myself in that sulky little beagle!* I whispered a little prayer of thanks for a timely lesson. Then I called Ruth, asked her forgiveness and agreed to meet my walking companions the next morning. In the next weeks, I found that instead of losing a dear friend, I had gained a new one.

Dear God, keep me from the sin of jealousy, because it keeps me from the joy of love. —ALETHA JANE LINDSTROM

Spirit Lifter

Things turn out best for the people who make the best of the way things turn out.

—AUTHOR UNKNOWN

9	SUNDAY

...I will fear no evil... —PSALM 23:4

In one of my Bibles is a picture of Daniel in the lion's den. It's a beautiful painting, a work of art. What I like most is the position Daniel has taken. He has turned his back on the lion. His hands are bound behind his back. Nevertheless, Daniel is looking up toward a small window, praying. He is looking at his source of strength instead of the menacing problem.

I like to study the crouching lion too. One day it occurred to me that the mighty beast had a baffled expression on his giant face. He wasn't accustomed to coming up against fearless men. Confused, maybe even fearful himself, he sat there and did nothing. Daniel walked out of the den the next morning without a scratch.

Sooner or later all of us find ourselves in a lion's den of some sort. Maybe you're shut up in one today. Like Daniel, walk to a window and look up to God, Who is bigger and stronger than any enemy in the world. Turn your back to your fearful problem and face a God Who is waiting to hear from you.

Thank You, Father, for truly Your strength does show up best in weak people. —MARION BOND WEST

| 10 | MONDAY
Practice hospitality ungrudgingly to one another.
—I PETER 4:9 (RSV)

Not long ago our old springer spaniel, Captain Marvel, had to have surgery. When I left him at the vet's, he looked at me with big, sad eyes. Back home I glanced at his quilt nestled on the carpet. He'd curled up on that old lap quilt day and night for years. It was where we knelt to scratch his ears and where he retreated after his baths. Remembering his sad look, I had a thought. *Carry Captain the quilt.* But it seemed like such a silly idea. Drive all the way back just to take a dog a quilt...the vet would think I'd lost my grip. Besides, I was very busy.

But Captain had washed the children's faces with sloppy kisses, pulled their wagon and chased their sticks for eleven years. I picked up the quilt and drove back to the vet.

I felt awkward handing it to the receptionist. But she smiled. (I think she'd seen my type before.) She left, then reappeared a moment later. "Poor dog's been crying all morning," she said. "But when I slipped the quilt in his pen, he curled right up on it and closed his eyes."

That little quilt had made all the difference. And driving home, I had a new sense of just how important even the smallest gesture of love can be. I felt a prayer rising in my heart....

Oh, Father, help me take more time to love all *Your creatures, great and small.* —SUE MONK KIDD

| 11 | TUESDAY   **FIRESIDE FRIEND**
Children are an heritage of the Lord. *—PSALM 127:3*

"Yo!"

"Yo? This is your *mother* calling you. You always answer the phone that way?"

"Yeah. Everyone here does."

"Everyone in the college answers the phone with a 'Yo'?"

"Yup."

"Huh! So how are you? You coming home soon?"

"Fine. In three weeks. I have to pick up my skis."

"How're you doing?"

"Okay. No problems."

OCTOBER 1988

"Marks okay?"

"I'm not failing anything."

"Well...okay. We'll see you in three weeks, then. Take care of yourself."

"Okay. Bye."

So it's not great communication. I know he's okay (he's healthy enough to go skiing). I know he's not getting any F's (or A's). I know he's making friends (he knows how they answer the phone). I know I'll see him in three weeks (and he'll sit and really talk to me, then). *Yo!* It's enough.

Lord, sometimes loving is letting go. Teach me, too, to trust to Your care all who are dear to me. Amen. —TONI SORTOR

12 WEDNESDAY
...Then thou shalt have good success. —JOSHUA 1:8

He was really quite a colossal failure. Everybody said he'd never reach his outrageous goal. They were right. He didn't. His name was Christopher Columbus. Whoever heard of such a thing as traveling west to get to the east? Of course, he was a very determined young man (only thirty-three at the time), and he had a dream. But dreams sometimes fail. His did. He never reached India nor the Asian mainland. And yet, because of him the gateway to a new continent opened up, and the West Indies and the Bahamas were discovered.

I know how failure feels. I've often had work projects rejected. Yet, when I look back on those failures, I very often see that they led to something much better than the original would have been! Or else I find that something I've learned in the process has helped me to grow—mentally, emotionally or spiritually.

Next time you fail to reach a goal, take a close look at the land you've traveled through along the way. I think you'll find that there was something of value there. It may, in fact, be more precious than the goal you sought!

I know that there is purpose, Lord, even in my seeming failures. With Your help, I'll find it!
—MARILYN MORGAN HELLEBERG

13	THURSDAY

Moses was 120 years old when he died, yet his eyesight was perfect and he was as strong as a young man.
—*DEUTERONOMY 34:7 (LB)*

Someone once said that life is made up of:

> The tender teens
> The teachable twenties
> The tireless thirties
> The fiery forties
> The fretful fifties
> The serious sixties
> The sacred seventies
> The aching eighties
> Shortening breath
> Death, Sod, God.

It all sounds so neat and orderly, doesn't it? But when I first heard this little version of the stages of life, I was in my late thirties, which hadn't been "tireless" at all. In fact, with four young children and various part-time jobs, I'd been "exhausted" most of the time.

Now that I'm in my "fiery" forties, believe me, there are days I don't feel fiery at all. Most days, in fact.

What's "fretful" about the fifties? None of my friends in their fifties are fretful… "tireless," perhaps, and other times "aching" with exhaustion from working and playing so hard. And a dear aunt in her sixties is "seriously" enjoying life and friends and discovering new things from her numerous grand nieces and nephews, who also enjoy her "fiery" enthusiasm for life. A dear friend, in her seventies, is quite "teachable" as she takes one college course after another in her spare time. The white-haired octogenarian down the block who just retired is as "fiery" as they come, actively involved in politics, especially issues concerning the elderly.

It's a fact to be accepted and treasured: We can all be exactly what we want to be at *any* stage in life.

Lord, help me not to stereotype myself or others according to age. Let me be myself to the fullest, using my talent, my gifts, my life to serve You always with joy and gladness.

—PATRICIA LORENZ

OCTOBER 1988

14 FRIDAY
Return unto thy rest, O my soul... —PSALM 116:7

I'm a compulsive reader of plaques. I pull off highways to read historical markers, stop before signposts on nature trails. It makes travel
slow and walking non-aerobic, but over the years I've made some
lovely discoveries.

Beside a mountain stream in North Carolina a sign calls attention to the slope of the banks. Their V-shape, the plaque points out,
can be wide or narrow depending on the material the bank is made of.
Solid rock erodes to steep-sided banks while softer soil melts to a
gentle slope. In either case, when the bank no longer tumbles into the
river with every passing storm it is said to have reached its "angle of
repose."

Do people too have an angle of repose? Can we reach a place
where the storms of life no longer threaten our stability? I suspect
that this is true. Our resting places will be as different as our personalities. But for each of us it will be the place where we find God's
undergirding strength. When we rest in Him through downpour and
drought, freeze and thaw, we have found the position nothing can
shake.

Lord, teach me to rest in You. —ELIZABETH SHERRILL

Family Time

15 THE VALUE OF FRIENDS
...I have called you friends... —JOHN 15:15

Certainly among the most beautiful words Jesus ever spoke to His
disciples was the electric statement, "I have called you friends." Again
and again we see that having friends and being a friend are very much
a part of our Bible story.

Perhaps the most celebrated friendship story is the one about
David and Jonathan. But equally rich, if not more so, was the friendship of Barnabas and Saul of Tarsus, later known as Paul the Apostle.

Luke describes the scene vividly. Following Saul's conversion
and his escape from the irate Jews in Damascus, Saul traveled south
to Jerusalem for some fellowship with and encouragement from the
disciples. But he was rebuffed; they were all afraid of him because of

284

his past. In fact, they refused to have anything to do with him until Barnabas befriended Saul and vouched for the sincerity of his Christian conversion.

Upon leaving Jerusalem Saul then returned to Tarsus and dropped out of sight for a while. But some time after that Barnabas went to Tarsus and brought Saul back to Antioch where they worked together in the church for a year. In his support and concern for Saul, Barnabas was a caring and nurturing friend following the model Jesus gave His disciples.

Christianity begins in friendship and continues that way. First, we accept the friendship Jesus offers us. Then, it is friendship that converts a house into a home as our loved ones move from being relatives to friends. In addition to being lovers, a wife and husband become friends, and the parent-child relationship combines friendship with love.

But to have friends we must work at being friendly, and to be a friend exacts the cost of caring more for another person than for ourselves. A friend can never be taken for granted.

Samuel Johnson, the eighteenth-century English author, understood the importance of friendship when he wrote, "If a man does not make new acquaintances as he advances through life, he will soon find himself left alone. A man, sir, should keep his friendships in constant repair."

It has been a practice of ours for many years to work at establishing one new friendship a year. Try it this year...work at it...enjoy it, for friendship is one of God's special gifts; it is our gift to the world.

Lord, thank You for being our friend. Help us to be the kind of a friend that lifts others up.

—HARRIETT AND FLOYD THATCHER

| 16 | SUNDAY |

...Let patience have her perfect work...   —JAMES 1:4

Often I have wondered why God seems so slow to answer my prayers. Recently something happened to help me understand His timetable.

For twenty years, as an ambitious young man, I often grew impatient because my prayers for rapid advancement in my work never seemed to be answered. For those same twenty years I often drove the main route east to Hannibal, Missouri. During that time I was dimly aware of a construction project going on out in the rolling prairies to my right. I would see a bulldozer gobbling up a hill or a train of trucks disgorging dirt into a ravine.

"Wonder what they're doing?" my wife Sharon would always ask, and I would just shrug my shoulders. "Don't know, but they're sure taking their time."

Each time we passed the area we could see something new—a road to nowhere, an isolated bridge, a ribbon of rocks snaking through the fields.

Then one bright Sunday morning as we passed by the construction area, I almost swerved off the road from shock.

"Look at all the water," Sharon blurted out. I stopped the car. As far as we could see were the golden waters of the new Mark Twain Lake. At once it made sense—the roads to nowhere, the strange bridges, the rock piles. *The water had been held back until the earth was fully ready to receive it.* Too early and it would have been a disastrous flood, not a welcome lake!

If I had been given too much responsibility too quickly in my work, the same thing might have happened. I've decided that God holds back His best gifts until we are ready to receive them. A blessing given too soon could be a curse.

O Lord, when I get impatient, help me to trust Your calendar of love.   —DANIEL SCHANTZ

PRAYING AND PRAISING HIM
Three Days in the Psalms

Many Christians are rediscovering the prayer book that Jesus used—the Psalms. Praying the Psalms can be an exciting form of personal prayer, as relevant to everyday life in the 1980s as in the time of Jesus. We invite you to join Marilyn Morgan Helleberg during the next three days, as she shares some of her experiences in praying the Psalms. Maybe you'll decide to make it a daily habit!

—THE EDITORS

Psalm for My Choices

MONDAY
Guide me in your truth... —*PSALM 25:5 (NIV)*

Since I've been starting each morning by reading a Psalm or two, I've been amazed how often the psalmist's words are just exactly what I needed to hear that day! Recently, I had a tough decision to make, in which all the choices had serious drawbacks. I woke up with anxiety and uncertainty stabbing me in the chest. My marker was at Psalm 25, and as I began reading it aloud, certain phrases seemed meant just for me. "Show me your ways, O Lord, teach me your paths; guide me in your truth and teach me...." Then came blessed assurances: "...He instructs sinners in his ways. He guides the humble in what is right and teaches them his way. All the ways of the Lord are loving and faithful...He will instruct him in the way chosen for him."

What a healing balm for the fearful ache in my chest! I carried verse 15 in my heart all day: "My eyes are ever on the Lord, for only he will release my feet from the snare." Near the end of the day, an alternative I hadn't thought of occurred to me, and I was able to make a truly freeing decision.

You probably have some choices to make today. Maybe reading Psalm 25 aloud will help you, too.

"Show me Your ways, O Lord, teach me Your paths."
—MARILYN MORGAN HELLEBERG

Psalm When I Am Weak

TUESDAY
God is our refuge and strength... —*PSALM 46:1 (NIV)*

Every day, the horrors of the world leap out at me from the headlines and blare into our family room via TV. Nuclear buildup...failed arms-limitation talks...terrorist attacks...hostages taken...Chernobyl. Sometimes my hope for our world gets so weak it almost dies. That's when I turn to Psalm 46 and read it over and over and over, until gradually, like a strong ship that will not sink, I sense my heavenly Father's unfailing strength. "We will not fear, though the earth give way and the mountains fall into the heart of the sea...The Lord Almighty is with us; the God of Jacob is our fortress...He makes wars cease to the ends of the earth; he breaks the bow and shatters the spear...."

As I pray those shining words of the Psalm, I begin to know, deep within, that God's love is more powerful than all the hatred and darkness and evil in the universe. Then I'm finally able to let go and just soak for a while in the wisdom of verse 10: "Be still, and know that I am God." And my ailing hope is healed.

If your hope sometimes weakens, praying Psalm 46 can make it strong again!

You, Lord, are my refuge and my strength.
—MARILYN MORGAN HELLEBERG

PSALM FOR THE BLUES

19 WEDNESDAY
Why are you downcast, O my soul?
—PSALM 42:5 (NIV)

I used to be bothered by the negative things in the Psalms, such as complaining and vengefulness, but now I realize that the psalmist was just being utterly honest with God. Every human emotion is in the Psalms, and praying them aloud has a wonderfully healing effect! Identifying with the deep emotions—even the negative ones—helps me to get rid of my own mental garbage. Once that's out, there's room for love and praise and affirmation to enter in.

When I'm feeling depressed, for instance, I read Psalm 42. The first time through, I pour out my pain with the psalmist: "My tears have been my food day and night...my soul is downcast within me... I say to God my Rock, 'Why have you forgotten me? Why must I go about mourning?'"

Then I read the Psalm again. Now that I've had my mental "scream," I'm ready to be lifted up by such healing words as, "By day the Lord directs his love, at night his song is with me—a prayer to the God of my life...Put your hope in God, for I will yet praise him, my Savior and my God."

If you sometimes feel a little blue, try praying Psalm 42. Twice.

I will praise You, my Savior and my God.
—MARILYN MORGAN HELLEBERG

Psalms to pray when:

you can't sleep—Psalm 4
you're feeling guilty—Psalm 51:1–17
life seems to have lost its lustre–Psalm 8
you are afraid—Psalm 18:28–36
doubts overtake you—Psalm 19:7–14
you are ill—Psalm 41:4–13
you've suffered a loss—Psalm 73:21–28
a storm is raging–Psalm 29
you feel spiritually dry—Psalm 63:1–8
you need protection—Psalm 91
*a friend has wronged you—Psalm 55:12–14 and
     20–22*
you are overburdened, tense—Psalm 23
you are thankful—Psalm 136.

20	THURSDAY	FIRESIDE FRIEND

Fear ye not, neither be afraid...   —ISAIAH 44:8

There is a full house in the theater tonight. I step out on stage, take a deep breath and begin a ten-minute monologue from *Saint Joan.* Yes, there are a few butterflies in my stomach...but I am not afraid. It was not always like this, however.

When I was in junior high school, I was painfully shy. Ordering a meal at McDonald's was an ordeal for me, and if for some reason they mixed up my order—forget it! I was not one to complain. My first week of high school was dreadful. If I lost my way to a class, I couldn't ask for directions. If I didn't understand the algebra in my assignment, I couldn't ask for help. So imagine my surprise when my English teacher asked me to join the debate team! Automatically, I started to decline, but then I remembered Moses, who pleaded with God to send someone else. But what did God do? Provided Moses with a mouth-piece: his brother Aaron.

Perhaps God was pushing me into using my own mouthpiece at that moment. I joined the debate team, and then in the spring, the speech team. During my freshman year of college, I tried out for a major play on campus. And this spring, I'll graduate in theater arts!

God doesn't want us to be dominated by fear. He has given us a spirit of strength. Do you have a fear that's holding you back from enjoying a full life? If we trust in God, saying, "Lord, send me," He will provide the necessary strength to do His will.

Father, I put my fear into Your hands: Place in me a spirit of strength and courage. —TAMMY RIDER

---

21 FRIDAY
Judge not, that ye be not judged. —MATTHEW 7:1

For several years my mother lived in a New Jersey nursing home and I commuted by bus each weekend to visit her. It was a boring trip, but it gave me time to catch up on my paperwork.

One day on the return trip to Manhattan, in an effort to discourage anyone from sitting next to me, I took the outside seat in the row that is right over the wheel. Then I placed my briefcase and belongings on the adjoining seat. All went well until the last stop before the bus headed into the Lincoln Tunnel. At that point, two people boarded, a young girl and an elderly cane-carrying woman. I looked around and saw that the seat beside me was the only unoccupied one left, so I lifted my papers and moved over. As I did, the young girl quickly slid into the seat I'd vacated.

She should have let the elderly woman sit there! I fumed. For several minutes I mentally threw daggers her way. Finally, I got up and offered the woman my seat. Graciously, she accepted it.

Standing in the aisle I looked down at the young girl. *I hope you feel guilty*, I thought. Then, in the midst of my anger, like a still, small voice, the biblical verse came to me: "Judge not." I knew what I must do.

At first it was hard, but I began to pray silently for the girl. *Father, bless her...help her...let her see Your light....* As I prayed, a feeling of peace enveloped me. It was as if, in doing something positive rather than condemning, I had taken another step forward in my spiritual growth.

Isn't that what God wants us to do?

Dear Father, renew a right spirit within me. —ELEANOR SASS

22 SATURDAY

...The patient in spirit is better than the proud in spirit.
—*ECCLESIASTES 7:8*

In the early 1930s, many young men came expectantly to George Washington Carver's cluttered laboratory at Tuskegee Institute to serve as lab assistants. Each was greeted warmly, then mostly ignored by the famous, but preoccupied, Dr. Carver. Eventually many departed, bewildered and discouraged.

In 1935, Austin W. Curtis, Jr., arrived fresh from Cornell University, and with him this pattern began to change. Each morning, Dr. Carver nodded, then moved off to work alone as usual. For six weeks Curtis stood around—disappointed like the others. Except, unlike the others, Curtis didn't leave. Instead he began working independently, experimenting with the *magnolia grandiflora*, a flower whose oil might improve soap or produce a suitable paint.

One day, unexpectedly, Dr. Carver paused and asked, "What are you doing?" Curtis answered and more questions followed. Carver began to walk away, but stopped and said, "Let me know if you need some help." Curtis's patience and persistence had opened the door to Dr. Carver's treasury of knowledge. And later the two became supportive colleagues in their work.

When I was newly married, almost forty-five years ago, I would ask my wife Ruby if she needed help. "No, thanks," she would answer, and I'd take her at her word. As the years passed, however, I found ways to take the initiative: setting the table when six o'clock rolled around, straightening up the house just before company arrived, getting out the paper towels when a child spilled a glass of milk. As I persisted, our relationship grew stronger, and Ruby began to depend on me for help and support—just as I found I needed them from her.

Are there people in your life who need your help but won't ask? You can change the situation—try a little initiative and see if appreciation doesn't follow.

Lord, with Your help, I will not wait to be asked for assistance, but will find ways to demonstrate my love.

—OSCAR GREENE

SUNDAY

The Lord also will be a refuge for the oppressed, a refuge in times of trouble. —PSALM 9:9

Most of the time I manage to convince myself I've got a certain amount of inner strength. Then along comes something like this energy-sapping virus that's been with me for several days now, and I have to admit there's still a quivering little girl in me, wanting to be comforted. As I reach for Mother's afghan and pull it up around my shoulders, I can still see her fingers knitting as she and I sat quietly talking and John (only a baby then) unraveled her skeins of yarn. Has it really been eighteen years?

Ah. That's better. The love Mother knit into this afghan still comforts me, even though she's been gone many years now. Some things just never leave you. It's like those comforting words from Isaiah [40:11] that drift in and out of my mind as I lie in bed alternating between groaning and dozing... "He shall gather the lambs with his arm, and carry them in his bosom." I probably learned them in Sunday school, but like the love in Mother's afghan, some things just never leave you.

Is there a lamb in you who needs to be gathered into loving arms today? Find refuge in God's loving words.

Lord, wrap me in Your love when I am weak.
—MARILYN MORGAN HELLEBERG

24 **MONDAY**

I will not leave you comfortless... —JOHN 14:18

I have a friend, Pat, whose father died, leaving her mother in a deep, enduring depression. Pat did all she could, but adjustment for her mother was slow and trying.

Pat prayed for a way to help. Finally she decided to make up a booklet titled "One Day at a Time." Each page contained one activity selected to help her mother overcome inertia and self-pity by renewing her awareness of God's goodness and encouraging her to reach out to others. For example:

Monday: Get up early and take a dawn walk. Watch the world wake up.

Tuesday: Take the time to bake bread from scratch. Enjoy

the cool feeling of dough in your hands. Notice how the more you punch it down the more it rises.

Wednesday: Go to the town library and browse. Just follow your inclinations—you may find yourself gravitating toward a book that can help you.

Thursday: Write a thank-you letter—to an old teacher, to a friend, to your child. Make a list of people you feel grateful to, and why. Pray to God and thank Him for them.

Friday: Do something today for someone else who was close to Dad—find a picture they'd like to have, or think of something Dad said about them they'd like to hear. They're grieving too, and would really love attention from you.

Saturday: Go for a drive. Pick a different direction and explore a little bit. Feel the wind on your face, the peaceful solace of movement on an open road. Then thank God for your life and living things.

Sunday: Spend quiet time thinking of dreams for the future. Touch your toes ten times. Thank God for something each time. Get up and go to church, even if you don't feel like it. Above all, don't isolate yourself from people or God at this crucial time.

In due time Pat's mother was able to overcome her deep grief, and renew her joy in living. How about you? Do you have a loved one who might benefit from a similar booklet you could prepare? Why not copy these helps down (or make up your own) on sheets of paper and tie with a colored yarn or ribbon? It's a sure way to be cheered on those dark days we all experience.

Father, remind me that there are so many ways I can help others be aware of You. Let me start today.

—ALETHA JANE LINDSTROM

25 TUESDAY
A generous man will prosper; he who refreshes others will himself be refreshed. —PROVERBS 11:25 (NIV)

My dachshund Phoebe is seven years old. She's my constant companion, a lovable creature. I hadn't realized how fat and lazy she had become until one day she couldn't get out of her basket. The vet gave me a stern lecture. "This dog is obese. No doubt," he surmised correctly, "you feed her what you eat. She needs exercise. Get her a companion, a puppy to play with."

So Phoebe became a substitute mother to our newest addition, Hans, a small red dachshund. (His complete name is Hans Ludwig van Beethoven!) As she plays and runs with the puppy, I can almost see the pounds falling from her body.

One day I stopped to look at myself. "I'm as out of shape as Phoebe. Little exercise, little interest in anything. I certainly need help." When I confided in my wife Edna, she suggested that God might want me to help someone else in the process: "How about being a Big Brother?" This organization, which matches up adults with boys who need substitute fathers, is active in my area.

I'm now a Big Brother. I see my young friend for a couple of hours every weekend, and we make quite a foursome—Phoebe, Hans, Tom and I. I eat healthy food (so does Phoebe), and if the exercise we get playing games with Tom hasn't made my excess pounds melt away, I do feel better. Best of all, I love the feeling of affection that Tom and I have for each other.

Father, as You take care of me, let me reach out today to help someone. —WALTER HARTER

| 26 | WEDNESDAY | FIRESIDE FRIEND |

Now the God of peace...make you perfect in every good work to do his will, working in you that which is well-pleasing in his sight. —HEBREWS 13:21

When my children were in the sixth grade, they were fortunate enough to have a teacher who insisted that her students do every lesson to the best of their ability. "Pretend this assignment is your ticket to heaven," she used to tell them.

I had not thought about this for years until I was reminded of her words a few days ago. My daughter, an artist, was beginning a new painting. She smiled as she repeated, "Pretend this assignment is your ticket to heaven," took up her brush and began to work with the determination to achieve excellence that has become her ingrained habit.

The perfection of God's handiwork is convincing evidence that He is not pleased with careless workmanship. Happy is the person who early in life develops the habit of doing work well.

Heavenly Father, help us to do our work to the best of our abilities—in such a way as to please You, Who created us for good works. —GAIL BROOK BURKET

---

27 THURSDAY
Lord, thou hast been our dwelling place in all generations. —PSALM 90:1

My husband Terry breezed into the house, uttered a breathless, "Jim stacked up his plane. Phil was in it, but they're both all right," and rushed out the door again, leaving me staring after him wide-eyed and speechless.

Terry, his cousin Jim and our son Phil (nine at the time) were supposed to be doing a routine spring changeover from skis to wheels on Jim's four-passenger Cessna at nearby Big Lake—still frozen in late March. I found out later that the plane's throttle stuck as Jim taxied toward the shoreline. Suddenly he and Phil were racing full bore for a row of steel posts encased in a snowbank. At the last minute he slowed the plane, but a wing nicked the bank, flipping the Cessna onto its nose.

Jim had the plane inspected immediately to discover why the throttle jammed. He learned three of four motor mounts had broken, causing the engine to rattle about loosely. It could have *dropped out* of the airplane at *any time*!

Terry had recently flown over two thousand miles in that plane across some of Alaska's remotest mountain terrain. This was one of those times when what we didn't know could have hurt us—in the worst way.

Jesus, in His infinite mercy, often allows us "warning signals" that point to a potentially serious—perhaps hidden—condition. Are there signals in *any* part of your life alerting you to trouble up ahead? Health? Job? Marriage? If so, don't ignore them. Talk with a doctor, a pastor, a counselor, a friend. Jesus promises to take care of us...but that's not to say we can't help make it easier for Him.

Lord Jesus, teach us to heed warning signs—those urgent messages from You, our Protector. —CAROL KNAPP

| 28 | FRIDAY

Trust in the Lord with all thine heart; and lean not unto thine own understanding. In all thy ways acknowledge him, and he shall direct thy paths. —PROVERBS 3:5, 6

John Spilsbury was a mapmaker by trade and a drawing master at Harrow school in England during the eighteenth century. He spent his leisure hours searching for ways to make learning enjoyable. "How can I make my students learn faster and remember longer?" he asked himself. Then he discovered a way by using his maps as teaching aids.

Spilsbury glued a map of England and Wales onto a smooth board. Using a thin blade he cut the maps into pieces sawing along the border lines of the various counties. His pupils were delighted and they remembered their lessons! Soon such maps and pictures appeared all over England. These were called jigsaw puzzles after the saw used for cutting.

Often my life resembles a jigsaw puzzle. Pieces are scattered everywhere, refusing to fit. One day I stumbled upon the reasons. I make promises, lacking the time to fulfill them. I accept responsibilities, knowing I haven't the skills to perform. I create battles of will to get my own way. Finally, in exhaustion, I turn to prayer.

In the quietness, God showed me He holds the perfect plan for each of us in *His* mind. Through faith, then, I can fit some pieces here and discard others there, trusting myself to His perfect will. Then, as I reassemble my life within His boundary lines, knowledge and joy become mine.

Lord Jesus, when parts of my life do not fit, help me replace them with the parts that complete Your perfect plan.
—OSCAR GREENE

| 29 | SATURDAY

He restoreth my soul... —PSALM 23:3

It's been a very busy week, with fall cleaning, houseguests, meetings, appointments and desk work. Each has siphoned away little drops of me, leaving me feeling...well, spilled out. But late this afternoon, I drove out into the country, parked the car along a quiet road and went for a walk. With the crunch of dry leaves and roadside gravel under my sneakers and my dog Oscar dancing around in the weeds by the edge of the road, I began to fill again.

There was just enough breeze to twirl gently the blades of an old weatherworn windmill in a nearby pasture. The trees were bare, the cornfields stripped and only the winter wheat was green. Yet it was with that greenness that I identified this afternoon. There is a certain greening of the soul that comes only during those incredibly precious moments of being alone in the natural beauty God created. It's a greenness that enables me to go back to my busy life feeling filled and once more ready to give.

If you're feeling spilled out, find some time to be alone outdoors, even if it's in a city park. It will fill you.

Thank You, Lord, for Your beautiful world of nature, and the greening of my soul. —MARILYN MORGAN HELLEBERG

30 SUNDAY
And the Lord God planted a garden eastward in Eden.
—GENESIS 2:8

A friend of mine journeyed from California to New Hampshire a while ago to help his parents celebrate their fifty-fifth wedding anniversary. His father had been the town barber in Ashland all the years he could remember; his mother had kept their home on nearby Squam Lake, a little bit of heaven that became Golden Pond for the Academy Award-winning film with Henry Fonda and Katharine Hepburn.

"My mother gave me her secret for their long years of amity," Art smiled. "She got it from her father on her wedding day. 'Whenever your man wants to go fishin' let 'im,' he told her. 'A body needs to get off by himself to pray.' So, even though they knelt side by side in church every Sunday, when Dad wanted to go fishing, she 'let 'im.'"

I thought about that a lot, remembering that our Lord, too, needed to "get off by himself to pray." When he heard that John the Baptist had been beheaded "he departed thence by ship into a desert place apart" (Matthew 14:13). After he fed the five thousand he "went up into a mountain place apart to pray" (Matthew 14:23). On the eve of His crucifixion He led His disciples to the Garden of Gethsemane and told them to sit "while I go yonder and pray" (Matthew 26:36).

If this could increase my intimacy with God, I surely wanted some. But I couldn't just "go fishin'" or descend into a garden of olive trees. What I did was start a "Retreat Book," retreat as in "a quiet, secluded place." Into a scrapbook I paste color photos of solitary beauty spots from round the world. My friends and relatives contribute. So now I can "get off by myself to pray" using only my scrapbook, my imagination and my deep desire.

A "Retreat Book." Why don't you start one? Make it a place where you can go and "get off by yourself and pray."

Lord, let me walk with you in the garden in the cool of the day.
—ELAINE ST. JOHNS

| 31 | MONDAY
I press on toward the goal for the prize of the upward call of God in Christ Jesus. —PHILIPPIANS 3:14 (RSV)

One October when I was a girl, we had an old-fashioned apple bob at the school Halloween carnival. We knelt in a circle around the pail of water, hands behind our backs. The first one to nab a floating apple with his mouth would be the winner.

The prize, as I recall, was a genuine, plastic, canary-yellow kazoo. "I'm gonna win that kazoo," said a small, music-loving boy named Neil. We smiled knowingly at each other. Neil never won anything. He was too shy and invariably the last boy picked to play kick ball.

"On your mark. Get set. Go!" called the teacher. Most of us were chasing the impossible, spinning apples around on top of the water, when splash! Neil plunged his head and shoulders beneath the surface, grasping his apple against the bottom. Up he came, looking like one of those roast pigs with an apple in its mouth.

He stood there, making a puddle in the third grade room. "Why Neil, you're...you're sopping wet!" the teacher exclaimed.

"Yes ma'am," he replied. "But I got myself a kazoo."

Somehow I've never forgotten that Halloween event. It says to me that when it comes to a worthwhile goal, it never pays to sputter around on the surface, afraid of getting wet. If you want to achieve your goal, you must believe in yourself and go after it headfirst, despite the cost. After all, a little water never hurt anybody!

May we set our eyes on You, Father, and pursue Your will with a determined spirit. —SUE MONK KIDD

Thank-You Notes to God

1

2

3

4

5

6

7

8

9

10

11

12

13

14

15

OCTOBER 1988

16

17

18

19

20

21

22

23

24

25

26

27

28

29

30

31

S	M	T	W	T	F	S
		1	2	3	4	5
6	7	8	9	10	11	12
13	14	15	16	17	18	19
20	21	22	23	24	25	26
27	28	29	30			

NOVEMBER

BE A COMFORTER
Your Spiritual Pilgrimage

I will lead him also, and restore comforts unto him…
—ISAIAH 57:18

Now comes November with its gray, rainy days. But what is more comforting on a chilly afternoon than an open fire that mutters contentedly on the hearth as dusk sweeps over the world?

You can be a source of comfort too, you know. An unexpected word of praise or encouragement. A sudden reassuring hug. Even a loving glance can work wonders on a rainy afternoon.

Or any afternoon—all month long!

Tandem Power for November

1 GIVING THANKS

And whatsoever ye do in word or deed, do all in the name of the Lord Jesus, giving thanks to God and the Father by him. —*COLOSSIANS 3:17*

The phone rang just as I dumped hamburger into the smoking-hot skillet. I reached for the phone with one hand and a lid to cover the sizzling meat with the other. Immediately I knew my friend Carole was suffering. She had just received word her parents had been in an accident. They were pried from their demolished car and air-lifted to a hospital where they were now in satisfactory—but painful and frightened—condition. She was leaving the next morning to join them, so would I pray for them and her?

"Of course," I assured her. "How should I pray?" Together, we decided to pick the "praise" pieces out of this jumbled heap of turmoil and fear. Obviously, we were thankful they were alive and thankful for their opportunity to experience God's protective presence and thankful Carole was able to respond to their needs. Soon our thankful-thinking helped us respond positively to this negative situation, and Carole sounded calmer when we said good-bye.

For the next several days as I prayed thankfulness into their lives, I found myself getting into the habit of picking the thankful parts out of my own daily frustrations and fears. I dropped a contact lens on the bathroom carpet. On my knees looking for it, I thanked God for the wonder of contact lenses. I faced an irritation in a personal relationship. I thanked God for that person's good qualities and my thankfulness soon outweighed the irritation. I got lost looking for a house but I spent the drive-time giving thanks for my friend who lived there. We can't be thankful *for* all circumstances, but we can be thankful *in* them.

There's an old saying, "Life is ten percent what happens and ninety percent how you respond." I've also heard that if you practice something daily for fifteen consecutive days, it becomes a habit. How about putting these two ideas together in the month of November? If we practice giving ninety percent of our responses to thankfulness *in* all our circumstances for the next fifteen days, just imagine how brimming our hearts will be by Thanksgiving!

Lord, You tell us "in everything give thanks." Please help us make a habit of that response and use Tandem Power this month. —CAROL KUYKENDALL

| 2 | WEDNESDAY |

...If ye continue in my word, then are ye my disciples indeed. —JOHN 8:31

There is an expression that I heard often as a child but seldom hear now: "He (or she) is a saint!" I wonder why? Are saints more scarce these days or has our manner of speaking changed? With that question came another: What *is* a saint?

I asked the last question of a dozen people, theologians and laypeople, and got a dozen different definitions. All were sincere, all applicable, according to the dictionary. But the one I liked best was this:

> Someone—
> Anyone—
> Immovably
> Nestled
> To
> JESUS
> (This could mean YOU)

I read this one again and again and it gave me shivers. I wished it *could* mean me, but I knew I could not qualify at this point. Who could? I got a paper and pencil and began to write down names that tumbled into my mind. A dear ninety-year-old man, always first at church service. A mother who straps her baby into the car seat while she delivers meals to the poor. The little boy who told his parents to forget his new bike at Christmas and put the money in the mission offering.

My list also answered my other question: Saints are not more scarce these days, it's our manner of speaking that has changed, and that's a shame. Why not revive the old way, if only on paper? Make a list of the saintly people you know and what sets them apart. Perhaps you can add your own name. If not, why not join me? For I am striving toward someday qualifying on somebody's list.

It's Your list that I am most anxious to be on, Lord, the list of those who cannot be separated from You. Amen.

—DRUE DUKE

---

3 | THURSDAY
Blessed be the God and Father of our Lord Jesus Christ, who according to His great mercy has caused us to be born again... —1 PETER 1:3 (NAS)

After fifteen years as a college teacher, I'd run out of gas. I felt dried up, empty, burnt out. So I decided to take a year off.

I slept the summer away. But I was forced to wake up by fall. My six-year-old was starting first grade, and his teacher suggested at the first open house how parents can help their kids read. And then the Sunday school superintendent roped me into leading the high school discussion group. And then my thirteen-year-old began a big project on the Revolutionary War and needed advice....

All of a sudden, my mind was afire! I was making up rhyming games and hunting up interesting street signs to sound out with my first grader. I dreamed up an Old Testament board game for the teenagers at church. I was haunting the local hobby shops for miniature replicas of cannons for the scale model of the Surrender of Yorktown that my thirteen-year-old was building.

It occurred to me finally that I wasn't burned out at all. My year off was a fallow time, a healing time, when new seeds of wisdom were being sown in the old, rich soil of the past. I couldn't wait for the next fall, for the eager faces of students, for the new harvest of understanding in store for them and me.

How about you? Do you find yourself pushing too hard and getting nowhere? Not everyone needs a year off. Renewal can come in small ways: Change your routine, claim solid resting time, get up a half hour early to look at the sun, shut the door on the world and listen to your own whispering voice. Sometimes it's in these small ways, faithfully practiced, that you will feel the energy flow back in.

Jesus, Who rose from the dead, assure us that from the ashes

*of self-doubt spring forth a new life of wisdom and faith when
we trust in You.* —LINDA CHING SLEDGE

 FRIDAY
...He hath opened mine eyes. —*JOHN 9:30*

Last fall I was a guest in a lovely home located in a wooded area on a
mountainside overlooking a majestic river. Imagine my disappointment when I discovered I'd forgotten my camera! Not wanting to let so
much beauty slip away, I decided to try to take some mental photos,
and I discovered a fascinating thing. The scenes in my mind are even
better than snapshots! That's because I deliberately memorized the
sounds and smells and even the *feel* of my lovely surroundings.

Now, when I'm feeling tense, I can close my eyes and call back the
scene I memorized while sitting on the end of the pier, watching the
sailboats drift by and listening to the gentle lapping of the waves. On a
recent snowy day, I called up my mental snapshot taken on the deck of
my hostess's house, complete with the feel of the warm sun on my
bare arms and the sound of the birds singing in the tall trees.

Next time you're in a beautiful place, use all of your God-given
senses to record it in your mind. Then call it up when you're tired or
bored or tense. You'll be inspired and refreshed!

*Thank You, Lord, for the beauty of Your world and for my
senses to record it.* —MARILYN MORGAN HELLEBERG

5 **SATURDAY**
*Let each of you look not only to his own interests, but
also to the interests of others.* —*PHILIPPIANS 2:4 (RSV)*

When my oldest daughter Tamara was eleven, she really wanted a
black jacket that she saw in a store. It looked part hoodlum to me. I
told her she would have to pay for it herself. Since I knew she didn't
have thirty dollars I thought she would drop the idea.

I underestimated her. She earned the money and soon she was
wearing that awful jacket. I might have continued to resent the jacket,
and her for buying it, if I hadn't remembered the fish skeleton....

One day our family had picnicked near a river. Tamara plucked a salmon skeleton from the water. I found a much better treasure, an agate, which my husband stashed in his pocket. At the end of the day, when we were leaving, I remembered Tamara's fish skeleton lying on the picnic table. I thought, *She doesn't need that old thing. She'll never miss it.* I didn't go back for it.

On our way home I asked to see my agate, and guess what my husband replied: "Oh, didn't you get it? I laid it on the table beside the fish skeleton."

I'm still learning that just because something isn't important to me doesn't mean it isn't important to someone else. Jesus made it clear to me that I had better stop dismissing Tamara's choices...or I was going to lose a whole lot more than a pretty rock.

Dear Lord, no two of us are alike. Help us to understand we need each other's differences, and to respect them.

—CAROL KNAPP

6	SUNDAY

...This do in remembrance of me. —LUKE 22:19

During communion at our church, parishioners walk to the front of the sanctuary where they are given a piece of bread, which is then dipped into a communal cup.

In order to facilitate the procedure, laypeople frequently help the pastors in serving communion. I often feel a twinge of jealousy when longtime friends or new members are asked to participate. Why not my husband and me, I ask myself?

On World Communion Sunday, I again battled resentment, trying to ignore the words in the invitation: "Ye that do truly and earnestly repent of your sins, and are in love and charity with your neighbors...."

Were my jealous thoughts a sin? Of course! Was I in love and charity with those taking part in the service? No!

"Oh, God!" I prayed. "I've created a barrier between You and me. But I can't control my feelings."

The usher signaled our row to go forward. When our neighbor Charlie broke a piece from the loaf, he spoke softly, "Shirley, the body of Christ, broken for you." I dipped the morsel into the cup and his wife whispered, "Shirley, the blood of Christ, shed for you."

Human hands, to be sure, administering the elements. But it wasn't Charlie or Jo serving me—it was the Lord Himself! I walked back up the aisle to my seat, flooded with thanksgiving for what Jesus Christ did for me on that cross long ago. The resentment and jealousy were gone.

Thank You, Jesus, for shedding Your precious blood for me!
—SHIRLEY POPE WAITE

7	MONDAY

But encourage one another daily…
—*HEBREWS 3:13 (NIV)*

After twenty-eight years of being a homemaker I took a temporary job. That meant driving into downtown Atlanta daily. With butterflies in my stomach I started out on my first day. The early morning traffic was so heavy that I almost turned around. I groaned as I approached a line of cars waiting to get onto the expressway. There was no traffic light. How would I ever get on? I began to get cold feet, and going out into the world to work suddenly seemed ridiculous.

I thought I heard the Lord suggest: *Watch, Marion.* After a few panicky moments, I was moving along toward the stop sign. As I got closer I saw something that still amazes me as I remember it. Each person with the right of way deliberately slowed up and motioned the next car in the long line to come on into the line of fast-moving traffic. As I waited my turn it was almost like watching a giant pigtail with two strands of hair being braided. The rhythm was beautiful. So was the gesture. Day after day the same thing happened. The smiling man who had signaled me in front of him that first day will never know how much he encouraged me. I zipped onto the expressway feeling ready to face the world…and a new job.

I've been thinking what a marvelous thing it would be if I could apply that principle to discouraging situations in life. When I have the "right of way" in some incident, if I could simply forego it, smile and motion to some helpless, discouraged person, to…move forth. I think it's called encouragement. And like costly perfume, the smallest amount of it lasts a very long time.

Show me, Father, what a simple thing real encouragement can be. Let me practice it with gladness today.
—MARION BOND WEST

| 8 | TUESDAY

For as the body is one, and hath many members, and all the members of that one body, being many, are one body... —I CORINTHIANS 12:12

"Have you voted?" I asked a drugstore salesclerk one election past. "Nope," she said, "I gave up on politicians a long time ago. Anyway my vote wouldn't change a thing."

Unfortunately her attitude is shared by too many others. One of the myths of our age is that the individual is powerless to bring about change in society, that one voice will not be heard, that one vote doesn't matter. That flies in the face of the evidence. Presidential elections have been won because as few as one vote in a precinct swung key states. And one famous presidential election went undecided because Samuel J. Tilden fell one electoral vote short in 1876. Congress appointed a committee to resolve the stalemate and it selected Rutherford B. Hayes, 8-7.

Today, this country will choose its president for the next four years. But many other key offices need to be filled, too, and there are issues of national, state and local importance that need to be decided. Millions of voters will exercise their democratic right, unrestricted by sex, race, religion or creed. But if past records hold true, almost as many millions will relinquish it, which is a pity and a tragedy considering the sacrifices our forefathers made to secure the privilege.

Your prayerful consideration of the ballot is needed today. Your prayers—and your participation.

When we feel we have no influence, Lord, remind us that one with You makes a majority. —FRED BAUER

9 WEDNESDAY
...A word spoken in due season, how good is it!
—PROVERBS 15:23

It had been one of those weeks. Rain every day. Too much to do, not enough time. The older children snapped at me, I snapped at them.

At church that Sunday our minister challenged, "Each time someone hurts you, snubs you, is unkind to you or puts you down, give that person a compliment that same day."

Give that person a compliment! I thought. *Impossible!*

By mid-week life was so grumpy I decided to give it a try.

I left my older son, the talkative one, a note, "Thanks for making your bed. Your room looks great!"

The next time Andrew threw a temper tantrum I scooped him off the floor, told him I loved him and read him a story.

When the girls were complaining about chores, I changed the subject. "You girls sure are good baby-sitters. Two people have told me this week how good you are with children."

You've probably figured out what happened next. My son actually gave me a spontaneous hug on his way to catch the school bus the next day. Julie offered to watch Andrew so I could go shopping by myself. Andrew asked me if he could help set the table for supper. And Jeanne invited me to go to a high school musical with her.

Lord, when I'm hurt by those around me, help me to fight fire with water and to find creative ways to show my love.
—PATRICIA LORENZ

10 THURSDAY
For my thoughts are not your thoughts, neither are your ways my ways, says the Lord. *—ISAIAH 55:8 (RSV)*

Sometimes I find I can learn about life—and death—from unexpected sources, but the last place I expected to find wisdom was from a scatterbrained, five-month-old colt named Duobs. Selfish, always wanting his mother, interested only in sleeping, eating and playing, he didn't seem to qualify as a profound thinker.

As a physician I have seen many reactions to death. Patients and family can be angry, frightened, ranting, resigned, sometimes all at once. Frustration at being unable to understand the "whys" is the only common emotion.

One recent morning, Duobs' mother, an apparently healthy mare, suddenly dropped dead in the pasture. I was surprised to find her a few hours later because Duobs had not uttered a sound of protest. A few weeks before, when temporarily separated from her, he had run along the fence bleating like a lost sheep, banging against the rails to get back to his mother. But now he lay quietly beside her in the pasture. When I approached, he stood up, looked down at his mother's still body and then trotted to me for the walk back to the barn.

Perhaps I am reading too much into it, but I saw respect, dignity, resignation without despair and a practical acceptance of God's order of things in that little foal as he trotted away. He understood, perhaps better than I, God's plan.

Heavenly Father, allow me to accept Your orderly plan. Not only for life but for death as well...and thank You, Lord, for giving me the additional assurance of life eternal.

—SCOTT HARRISON

| 11 | FRIDAY |

They shall beat their swords into plowshares, and their spears into pruninghooks: nation shall not lift up sword against nation, neither shall they learn war any more.
—ISAIAH 2:4

In the summer of 1969, at the request of President Nixon, I went to Vietnam to talk to our fighting men there. I visited hospitals where the wounded lay, cheerful and uncomplaining. I flew in a Navy jet to the great aircraft carrier *Kitty Hawk* and spoke to many of her crew, which totals almost five thousand.

But my most vivid memory is of a place called Hill 55, far up in the combat zone, where I was asked to conduct a memorial service for the men of the Seventh Marine Regiment who had died in battle. There had been hard fighting around that hill. A little altar had been set up, and in front of it were seven hundred marines, faces etched with fatigue. A military band played. All of us together joined in singing the old majestic hymns: "Nearer My God to Thee" and "My Faith Looks Up to Thee." Then I tried to tell them how proud their country was of them, how much we owed them. I found it hard to speak, my throat was so tight.

The service had to be short; our position was too exposed to be safe. A helicopter came and whisked me away. Looking down, I saw the whole regiment standing at attention, saluting me. Not knowing what to do, I simply waved at them. They all broke ranks and waved back. I watched until they were out of sight. Then I went back to my seat and put my face in my hands and wept like a child.

We should never forget these brave men and women. Not on Veterans Day. Not on any day. Not ever.

Father, we thank You for these brave souls who gave their lives. Keep them in Your eternal care, always.
—NORMAN VINCENT PEALE

| 12 | SATURDAY   FIRESIDE FRIEND
And it shall be for a sign and for a witness unto the Lord of hosts...   —ISAIAH 19:20

The branch scrapes against the window and bids me to look out upon the cold, gray day. I am depressed. Even the steaming cup of tea in front of me, and the warm slice of banana bread, with butter oozing over the edges, do little to lift my spirits.

My daughter Mandy passes through the kitchen sipping juice through a straw. She is on her way to watch *Sesame Street*. She lifts her hand and gives me "the sign"—her thumb, forefinger and little finger raised in the air. I smile and do the same. Without words we have just said "I love you" in sign language.

I feel as if a ray of sunlight has just streamed through the kitchen window. Mandy has brightened my morning and given me an idea. Why don't I use some sign language of my own to say "I love you."

I called my sick aunt, sent a card to Ruth to let her know how much we missed her since she moved away and pulled out a recipe for play dough that Mandy had been wanting to make.

How about you? What type of sign language can you use today that says "I love you"?

Father, as I go about my day, help me to "sign" love to those around me.
—TERRY HELWIG

13 SUNDAY

Then Samuel took the horn of oil, and anointed him...
—*I SAMUEL 16:13*

When I was younger I could never wait for results; I wanted everything *now*. I am happy to say that I have improved in this area. I have learned that some things take time. When God wants to grow a weed, that can be done overnight; an oak tree takes longer.

The Bible verse above tells us that Samuel anointed the boy David. This was God's promise that he would be king. But where was David the next day? On the throne? No! He was back keeping the sheep. *It would be years before the promise became a reality.*

Do you have God's promise for something in your life? Have you been like me, telling God that you must have it *now*? Instead, as we sit under our tree watching our flock, let's remember the anointing oil, God's promise for our futures. Then with newfound patience, let's wait, keeping foremost in our hearts the thought that *our time* is not necessarily *God's time.*

Dear Lord, give me the patience to trust Your grace today as I await Your promise for tomorrow. —LEE WEBBER

14 MONDAY — FIRESIDE FRIEND

...I have called you friends... —*JOHN 15:15*

One day as I was setting the table for guests, my mother said to me, "I wish you had a service of sterling silver, Faye. All of your sisters have sterling to use. It makes their tables so pretty."

I thought a moment and then replied, "Mama, plate silver is all right for our table. Anyway, I do have some sterling."

My mother looked at me quizzically.

I continued, "You see, I have *sterling friends.*"

This statement was true, for my dearest friends have all the qualities of sterling silver:

Sterling silver is beautiful; my friends are lovely.
Sterling silver is useful; my friends are of service.
Sterling silver is lustrous, shining; my friends are radiant.
Sterling silver is precious metal; my friends are
    beyond price.

Sterling silver is treasured; my friends are cherished.
Sterling silver is of great value; my friends are of great worth.
Sterling silver is of high quality; my friends are of lofty
character.

*Dear God, thank You for Your example of friendship and love.
And thank You for friends who are of sterling, inestimable
value.* —FAYE FIELD

Family Time

| 15 | GIVING THANKS
*...Giving thanks to our God the Father for everything
...with gratitude in your hearts...*
—*EPHESIANS 5:20 & COLOSSIANS 3:16*

I was alone and desperately lonely in a drab hotel room. It was
Thanksgiving Day, 1942. Harriett and our two-year-old daughter were
at home many miles away. As far as I was concerned, there wasn't
much to be thankful for, and they were feeling much the same.

The company for which I worked had given me a six-week assignment in San Diego. I didn't have either time or money to take the
train home for the holiday, so along with thousands of sailors
stranded in that Navy town I was away from my loved ones, adrift in a
strange and impersonal city.

In our childhood homes both Harriett and I had been accustomed to celebrate Thanksgiving with family. And so after we were
married we, too, planned festive occasions in celebration of Thanksgiving. We were young and in a hurry. Things were going our way most
of the time, and I don't remember giving much thought to the idea of
being thankful except for making it from one payday to the next.

Out of the loneliness of this day, though, I began to be more aware
of something that up until then I had taken for granted: the joy of
being with loved ones on the special day set apart to express gratitude to God for His blessings. Sometime after that we heard Dr. E.
Stanley Jones, missionary statesman to India, say that Christians
should live each day in an "attitude of gratitude." And with that we
began to understand as a family that Thanksgiving wasn't just a date
on our November calendar; it was an attitude, *a way of life.* Then we

began to feel just a little bit of what the Apostle Paul meant when he wrote that we were to "give thanks everyday for everything" and "be filled with gratitude."

Don't misunderstand—we had our moments then, and now, when this whole idea seemed not only unreasonable but impossible. And it is impossible without God's help. But we've come to see that when we are faithful each day in asking the Lord to give us an attitude of gratitude, that day is Thanksgiving even if it is July.

Here's a suggestion. Try it with us this year. Every morning when you get up between now and Thanksgiving Day, pray this prayer: "Thank You, Lord, for *everything* and fill me with gratitude for the hard things as well as the good things." Then, read the words of Paul from our Scripture lesson along with one of the thanksgiving psalms. Stop for a moment at noon and pray the prayer again. And, finally, just before you drift off to sleep at night, pray the "Thank You, Lord" prayer once more. You will find this to be a life-changing experience. Exciting things will happen! We know!

These words from President Lyndon Johnson's 1964 Thanksgiving Proclamation might well become a habit with us every day: "Let us…give thanks to God for His graciousness and generosity to us—pledge to Him our everlasting devotion—beseech His divine guidance and the wisdom and strength to recognize and follow that guidance."

Lord, give us thankful hearts today and every day.
—HARRIETT AND FLOYD THATCHER

| 16 | WEDNESDAY |

Strength and honor are her clothing…

—*PROVERBS 31:25*

Last night I was rereading my copy of David Grayson's *The Countryman's Year*, a book filled with wisdom that I've treasured for years.

The entry for November 16:

> I got up this morning,
> I put myself on
> Like a comfortable old coat.
> Holes in the elbows?

I do not mind,
I made them myself.

So like me, I thought. I have worn myself for over sixty years. I, too, don't mind the holes in the elbows. I'm accustomed to them by now.

Dear God, I only hope that these "holes in the elbows" of the coat I wear daily became worn in service for You.
—ALETHA JANE LINDSTROM

| 17 | THURSDAY |
I will therefore that men pray everywhere…
—*II TIMOTHY 2:8*

Bob had been sick and coughing for several days when I took him to the doctor. But instead of a quick prescription, he sent us to get an X-ray. *What can possibly be wrong*, I worried, waiting for Bob in the radiologist's office. Around me nurses scurried about calling out names, patients wandered in and out, phones rang. I could feel my anxiety building. *If only I could steal away to a quiet place and pour out my heart to God,* I thought, turning toward the receptionist's counter. There my eyes fell upon a white sign. It said: *Pray Here.*

Amazed, I blinked, focusing my eyes on it again. This time I read it more clearly. It read: *Pay Here.* I'd misread the first word. But perhaps in some mysterious way, I'd seen what God wanted me to see—a reminder that prayer doesn't have to wait for some quiet, holy place. We can pour out our hearts to Him wherever we are, whatever we are doing.

Right there in the waiting room, I began to pray silently. And in the midst of that swirling activity, I found peace.

Father, help me seize every opportunity to pray.
—SUE MONK KIDD

| 18 | FRIDAY   FIRESIDE FRIEND
If God be for us, who can be against us?
—*ROMANS 8:31*

I admit it—I'm a contest freak. I'm a sucker for any dangled trip to

Disney World or the prospect of a new car. In the past few years I've probably wasted about ten dollars on postage.

But you know what? For describing "Why My Cat Is Special" in one hundred words or less, I won ten pounds of cat food. For taking some neighborhood photographs, I won a family membership to the zoo. And for being the fourth caller to a local radio station, I won two tickets to a symphony concert.

I even entered a nationwide story writing contest. I worked hard and entered in 1980, and was one of about four thousand "losers." In 1984, I was one of about seven thousand rejected. But in 1986 I received a Mailgram with those glorious, terse words: "Happy to inform you that you have been selected...."

I believe there's a saying, "You can't win if you don't play." Now, playing doesn't guarantee that you'll win. But it's certain you won't win if you don't try.

Is there some dream you're afraid to pursue because the odds of attaining it seem so slim? Pray for the courage to try—and go for it!

Lord, remind me when I'm reluctant or afraid that I can't be a loser as long as I'm a try-er.   —B. J. CONNOR

 SATURDAY

For everything there is a season, and a time for every matter under heaven.   —ECCLESIASTES 3:1 (RSV)

It's almost Thanksgiving. Here in Alaska another long winter has begun. The lakes are a frozen playground that will soften and disappear in May.

Open water in spring signals the return of the loons. Their stay is brief—barely three months. When they leave I hear their haunting call as they pass over in the night, and I wonder if I dreamed them.

Tall stalks of fireweed begin to open bright pink blossoms in early July. They will top out in August—a sign that summer, too, is on its way out.

Autumn is a yellow sea of birch trees cresting on a September tide. For a handful of days I have a longing to dive into the leaves and swim for miles—until they drop, or I do.

Once again the branches are bare and the lakes are frozen...

stark reminders of how quickly Alaska shuffles the seasons.

The months are passing swiftly in my life, too. There is no time to waste on quarrels or complaints or anything that robs me of my precious opportunity to enjoy this corner of the world God has given me...for a season.

Teach me, God, to value my days. They are irreplaceable.
—CAROL KNAPP

20 SUNDAY
But be doers of the word, and not hearers only...
—*JAMES 1:22 (RSV)*

One year in Sunday school my daughter Ann was asked to memorize a Bible verse, II Corinthians 9:7 to be exact. It had a lot of words for an eight year old. It goes, "Every man according as he purposeth in his heart, so let him give; not grudgingly, or of necessity: for God loveth a cheerful giver."

She stumbled over the words all week, repeating them over and over in her head. Finally the day came for her to recite them. After Sunday school she rushed up to me. "Mama, I did it! I knew the whole verse *by heart!"*

Later during the worship service the ushers passed the collection plate. From the corner of my eye I saw Ann pull six shiny quarters from her purse and drop them in with a grin, suddenly putting the verse she had learned into action.

That's when I understood what it really meant to know God's word *by heart*, as she'd declared. It was more than knowing it with one's head. It meant *living* the Bible's majestic, lifegiving words and making them flesh in our lives.

I looked down at the "cheerful little giver" beside me in the pew. *How much of* my *Bible knowledge is heart-knowledge*, I wondered. Today on National Bible Sunday, maybe that is a question we all should ponder.

Lord and Author of all, may we respond to Your words, not only in thought, but in deed. —SUE MONK KIDD

Spirit Lifter

HOW TO GET THE MOST OUT OF THE BIBLE

1. *Come to the Word unexpectantly.*
2. *Come surrendering to the truths here revealed.*
3. *Come expecting to use the truths here revealed.*
4. *Come unhurriedly.*
5. *Come with a proper emphasis.*
6. *Come to it even if nothing apparently comes from your coming.*

—E. STANLEY JONES

---

21 MONDAY

...And God said...replenish the earth, and subdue it: and have dominion over...every living thing...

—GENESIS 1:28

"This is a scrumptious dinner," I said to my wife Sharon the other night. "It's the best beef we've had in years."

She grinned. "It's not beef; it's buffalo."

"Buffalo?" I asked incredulously. She then went on to explain that it *was* beef, but not from a cow. She'd bought some bison meat at the grocery store.

I shouldn't have been surprised. Even though Missouri is known as cattle country—Charolais, Brangus, Texas Longhorn and other "designer cows" forage the pastures of our spacious farms—we have also seen another kind of cattle grazing within our city limits: bison or "American buffalo." A large herd of buffalo dot the fields west of town, near the pecan groves. They are fun to watch, and twice a year our little airport turns into a major terminal as ranchers from all over the west jet into Moberly to bid on cattle and breeding rights.

These fine animals are a reminder to Sharon and me that mankind, using God-given talents, has taken God's basic creation and improved it to meet the needs of an expanding population. In fact, I know that there is hardly any limit to what I can do when I cooperate with my Creator. He has given me the raw materials, and it's up to me to make the world a brighter place. This week, I've offered to prune an overgrown apple tree in the yard of a disabled friend. Next week, if I till the soil in that unused garden plot, some retired neighbors can plant some vegetable seeds and enjoy a summer harvest.

Perhaps there is something in *your* neighborhood that could use some re-creating. Will you join me?

Inspire me today, Father, to use my talents for the needs of others. —DANIEL SCHANTZ

22 TUESDAY
Come unto me, all ye that labor and are heavy laden, and I will give you rest. —MATTHEW 11:28

Thornton Wilder's classic, *Our Town*, was first staged in Princeton's McCarter Theater in 1938, and last year the play was revived in my hometown. There are many quotable lines from the cemetery conversations that Wilder wrote, but none more memorable than the lament of young Emily, who asks, "Do any human beings ever realize life while they live it?"

Those haunting lines came back to me yesterday while I was running hither and yon, taking care of myriad daily tasks...delivering some materials to church, telephoning a friend who is ill, sending off a child's tuition payment, getting the car serviced, on and on. Mornings magically become afternoons, Mondays turn into Fridays, Januarys change into Decembers. How can we keep life from becoming one big blur?

The answer, for me at least, is drawing back occasionally from the "what must be dones" and taking time for the "ought to be dones." Reading time, meditation time, daydreaming time, good-neighbor time, walk-in-the-woods time, music time, museum time—those breaks from regular routine are not wasted time as some would have us think, but restorative time, renewing time, revival time.

Socrates told his students once that the unexamined life is not worth living. Today, I'm going to find some time to appreciate the abundant life God gave me. If you're feeling hassled and weary from the wars of daily duties and responsibilities, maybe you'd like to join me.

Lord, help me to experience the main attractions in life and not get distracted by the sideshows. —FRED BAUER

23 WEDNESDAY   FIRESIDE FRIEND

Whatsoever thy hand findeth to do, do it with thy might...   —ECCLESIASTES 9:10

I came home for college break this evening to an empty house. I hadn't called Mom this week, so my visit was unexpected. Or so I thought.

As I lugged my dirty laundry back to my room and tossed it on the floor, I noticed a small pile of papers waiting for me on the bed. Each item had a little note from Mom explaining it. "I was in the drugstore and Mr. Hoyt said to tell you 'Hello'" or "This card is from Auntie Mae; thought you'd like to see her second paragraph." As I was reading the messages, I realized that Mom may not have known *when* I was coming, but she did expect me at some point.

The same realization hit me when I went into the kitchen to check out the food supply. In the cabinet were all our favorites—pizza mix, peanut butter, even some Halloween candy. I knew my mother had no need for those items, but she'd stocked up because she never knew when one of her boys was coming home.

There are things I can also do for people today, before they ask. And I see that the grass is about three inches long, so I'll get the trusty mower out, before Mom asks. I know Mom loves popcorn but really hates to make it, so tonight I'll surprise her with a batch. And my girlfriend is working late tonight, so I'll drive downtown to pick her up so she won't have to take the long bus ride home.

What are the little "unexpected" gifts you can give today?

Dear Lord, help me to do things unexpectedly for others—and to enjoy their surprise when I do.   —DAVID CORNELIUS

24 THURSDAY

I thank my God upon every remembrance of you.

                           —PHILIPPIANS 1:3

Every year, when Thanksgiving Day comes around, I remember Johnny Ray.

Johnny Ray was a popular singer in the early fifties, whose recording of the song "Cry" sold millions of copies and sent thousands of teenage girls into a state of rapture. I was one of those teenage girls.

But in order for me to listen to my Johnny Ray records, it was necessary to sit very close to the record player. I'm hard-of-hearing, and at that point, though I'd been told—*and knew*—that a hearing aid would help me hear better, I refused to wear one. I was afraid of what my friends and classmates would think. I worried that they'd laugh behind my back. Somehow, I hoped they wouldn't find out about my handicap.

Then one evening my hero appeared on Ed Sullivan's TV show. After he sang his songs and the audience stopped applauding, Ed Sullivan came onstage and spoke to him.

"Just a minute," Johnny said. He put his hand into his coat pocket and lifted out a hearing aid. Casually he fitted it into his ear. Then he smiled and reminded Sullivan that it helped him hear better.

I stared at the TV screen. My mind whirled. *Here's someone,* I thought, *someone I admire, who isn't afraid to go on national TV and let millions of people know he has a handicap!*

Shortly thereafter I, too, began wearing a hearing aid.

Today I will attend a Thanksgiving service. I'll listen to the glorious hymns of praise. I'll thank God for all my blessings, including Johnny Ray and the positive influence he had on my life.

Thank You, Father, for the many people You put into our lives to inspire us. —ELEANOR SASS

 FRIDAY
...He will give his angels charge of you...
—MATTHEW 4:6 (RSV)

"I'm going out tonight," my seventeen-year-old son Jon insists. The weather is bad out; road conditions are unsafe—I've already told him why he should stay home on this night.

"Oh, no, you're not," I say angrily. Raising twin sons after the death of their father has been harder than anything I've ever known. We shout at each other and Jon storms out the door and I follow, prepared to continue arguing.

But suddenly a Scripture pops into my mind, something about: "Are there not ministering angels..." (Hebrews 1:14). Jon glares at me, but I feel a sudden rush of peace, and only smile. "I'm sending angels with you, Jon. They're in the back of your truck!"

I turn back to the house, calm even as I hear the motor revving up. I know I can't stop him, but the image of Jon with a truckful of angels makes me smile. It does more, too. I feel a reassurance in the image that reminds me of that simple truth: that maybe I can't always be around to protect my children. But fortunately, God—and His ministering angels—are always around to look after His.

By the way, fifteen minutes later Jon showed up, looking a little sheepish. *Something* had made him change his mind. Angels? Who can say?

Dear Father, help me let go when I cling too tightly and worry too much about my children. Let me hand them over to Your angels. —MARION BOND WEST

THE MEANING OF CHRISTMAS
Advent: Season of Paradoxes

Prepare for Christmas with writer Elizabeth Sherrill as she explores Advent as a season of paradoxes. And as the meaning of Christmas becomes more alive for us in these next four weeks, may our hearts be ready, also, to receive the Christ Child as we declare:

Come, Lord Jesus, come!
Blessings and joy to you and yours this Holy Season.
—THE EDITORS

A CONTRADICTORY SEASON

|26| DAY BEFORE THE FIRST SUNDAY IN ADVENT
Surely I am coming soon. Amen. Come, Lord Jesus!
—REVELATION 22:20 (RSV)

The four weeks of preparation for Christmas: what a strange, contradictory season!

We're turning the last pages on the calendar
...and the church says the year is just beginning.

The event we celebrate happened two thousand years ago
...and the church calls our attention to the future.

It's a time of eager expectation: angel choirs and "tidings of great joy"
...and the church drapes itself in mourning.

322

They're the most hectic weeks of the year: more activity, more expenses, more pressures

...and the church announces Peace on Earth.

The shortest days come now: the longest, darkest nights

...and the church proclaims it the Season of Light.

The dictionary defines *paradox* as "a statement that is seemingly contradictory, yet true." Christians through the ages have affirmed that the paradoxes of Advent are in fact true—the greatest truths we know.

It is only when we try to eliminate one extreme or the other, to pick and choose the elements of truth that appeal to us, that we miss the totality of what God is doing among us.

"Truth," wrote the Danish theologian Søren Kierkegaard, "is the tension between paradoxes." This Advent let us seek the meaning of Christmas in the very tensions of the season themselves. In the noise as well as in the Silent Night. In the darkness as well as in the light of the star.

Come is the root meaning of the word *Advent*. Let us keep the word *come* in our minds throughout this Advent season.

Come, Lord Jesus, over these next four weeks, into every part of our Christmas preparation. —ELIZABETH SHERRILL

THE PARADOX OF SOLEMN JOY

27 FIRST SUNDAY IN ADVENT
And Mary said, Behold the handmaid of the Lord; be it unto me according to thy word. —LUKE 1:38

Happy New Year!

The secular New Year, January 1, can fall on any day of the week. But for Christians each year begins, as each week begins, on a Sunday.

But what a strange subdued Sunday this Christian New Year is! In our local Episcopal church the folding panels behind the altar are closed, hiding the painting of Jesus Transfigured. There are no flowers on the altar. The pulpit cloth is purple, the color of mourning. Is this any way to welcome in the new year?

Yes, believers over the centuries have answered. Beginnings, real beginnings, are like that. Painful...hidden. No dance bands. No noise-makers and confetti. True beginnings happen in silence and in secret.

The seed sprouting in the earth. The idea germinating in the mind.

Nor at the moment of beginning can we ever know the outcome. That's the reason for that blank and shuttered wall behind the altar. As the Baby stirred in Mary's womb she could not foresee the events of the Life she was bringing into the world. As John the Baptist called the crowds to repentance, he did not know which one among them would prove to be the promised Messiah.

And beginnings, real beginnings, involve death. The death of the grain of wheat so that a new crop can grow. The death of false idols to make room for the true.

Advent summons us to die to the old as we await the birth of the new. To examine our hearts and put to death anything there that cannot welcome the Child in the manger.

As we prepare for Christmas during these next four weeks, let's watch for signs of death to the old self-centered life. A smile for the others in the long line at the post office. An extra bit of patience with a slow salesperson. A gift for someone others may forget. It's not a spectacular way to celebrate. No crowds will gather in Times Square to cheer. But in heaven angels will sing.

Happy New Year!

O Christ, help us to remember that Your coming depended on the courageous and joyful submission of a young girl to the word of God. May we this season live with that same attitude.
—ELIZABETH SHERRILL

 28 MONDAY
The Spirit itself beareth witness with our spirit, that we are the children of God. —ROMANS 8:16

The November day was gray. Sleet was beginning to pepper against automobiles and make little white ribbons in gutters. The temperature had fallen all day and the wind was now a cold, stabbing knife.

The display window of the bakery shop frosted as the warm inside air swept against it. A small girl in a thin jacket peered through the frost at the freshly baked cookies and pastries. How wonderful they looked with their sugar frostings and oozing fruit fillings! And, oh, how she longed to taste them!

A voice behind her said, "Don't they look delicious?" She turned to see a fur-coated woman smiling down at her. "Would you go in and share some with me?"

At the round table in the fragrant shop, seated on a padded white chair, the child watched as the woman ordered cocoa and cookies. The steaming cups were set on the table and the woman put a cookie on a small plate in front of the little girl. "Eat," she said softly. "They're good!" And the child began to eat hungrily.

After the second cookie, she looked up into the woman's face and asked, "Are you God?"

"No," the woman replied, "but I *am* His child."

The little girl gave a contented sigh and, for the first time, she smiled. "I knew you had to be *some* kin to Him," she said.

I'm watching for opportunities today to let others know that I am "some kin to Him." Won't you join me?

To be recognized as Yours, Lord, is the greatest identification I
could want. Amen.   —DRUE DUKE

 TUESDAY
I have set before you life and death, blessing and curs-
ing: therefore choose life, that both thou and thy seed
may live.   —DEUTERONOMY 30:19

John Wesley, the founder of Methodism, is supposed to have said, upon seeing a man being taken to the gallows, "There, but for the grace of God, goes John Wesley." I think he meant that we all have many choices in our lives. And we don't know beforehand which path might lead to happiness and fulfillment, and which one to misery and disappointment. We *do* have a little voice inside us, however, that can guide us. Perhaps that voice comes from our parents' training, perhaps it comes from God. In any case, it can help when we are at a crossroads.

Many years ago, when Prohibition was in full swing, I was a young man of twenty-one living in New York City. There had been no jobs in my hometown of Bethlehem, Pennsylvania, so I wrote to 390 drugstore managers and finally got a job in New York. The hours were very long—seven A.M. to six P.M. plus from seven A.M. to eleven A.M. every other Sunday—and the pay was low. I met some "friends" who urged me to join them in running in liquor from the ships at sea. "Walter, you can earn more in one night with us than you can working a month at the drugstore!" What a temptation.

In my head I heard the questions, "What would Mom or Pop say? What would God say?" and I followed the choice that my little voice suggested. I said no to the rum runners. I went on to a successful career in the drugstore business, but several of those acquaintances were later found floating in New York Harbor.

You may have some difficult choices to make today. I can assure you that the answer is right there—in your heart, in your head.

God, with Your help, I will make the right choice today.
—WALTER HARTER

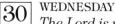 **30** WEDNESDAY **FIRESIDE FRIEND**
The Lord is near to all who call upon him...
—PSALM 145:18 (RSV)

Our cat Lu-Lu recently had surgery. She is recuperating nicely but is still unable to jump around with her usual ease. This morning as I was having a cup of coffee and reading my devotional, she put her paws on my chair and attempted to leap onto my lap. She jumped part way and fell backward. To me, she seemed to be saying, "I want to be near you. Please help me up."

I tried to hoist her up, but she stiffened in pain. For some reason, I thought of how God works in my life. Sometimes I'm in pain, not so much physically but mentally as I agonize over some decision I have to make. I want God to be near, but my troubles make Him seem far away.

Thinking of Lu-Lu again, I moved from my chair down onto the floor next to her. She moved easily into my lap. Lu-Lu curled up happily, contentedly, and went to sleep. Her reaction made me realize that I need not struggle to be near God; I can merely reach out to Him, and He lovingly comes to embrace me with His presence.

Perhaps *your* cat can teach you a heavenly lesson today!

Lord, help me to remember that when I reach out, You're always there.
—CORA PETERS

Thank-You Notes to God

1

2

3

4

5

6

7

8

9

10

11

12

13

14

15

NOVEMBER 1988

| 16 |
| 17 |
| 18 |
| 19 |
| 20 |
| 21 |
| 22 |
| 23 |
| 24 |
| 25 |
| 26 |
| 27 |
| 28 |
| 29 |
| 30 |

S	M	T	W	T	F	S
				1	2	3
4	5	6	7	8	9	10
11	12	13	14	15	16	17
18	19	20	21	22	23	24
25	26	27	28	29	30	31

DECEMBER

BE A STAR-GAZER
Your Spiritual Pilgrimage

When they saw the star, they rejoiced with exceeding great joy. —*MATTHEW 2:10*

"The stars are brightest on the darkest night."

So goes the old saying, and certainly it is true of this frosty month when the jeweled heavens blaze with a special brilliance—and the most brilliant of all is the Star of Bethlehem.

Star of wonder, Star of light, emblem of God's supreme Gift to mankind. Keep your eyes on it steadfastly this month. And let it lead you triumphantly from this old year into the new.

Long ago it guided the Wise Men. Wise men and women follow it still.

Tandem Power for December

1 | NURTURING HIS MIRACLE

I appeal to you therefore, brethren, by the mercies of God, to present your bodies as a living sacrifice, holy and acceptable to God... —ROMANS 12:1 (RSV)

Imagine this. You are sitting alone at the kitchen table early one morning, sipping coffee, and suddenly an angel of the Lord appears and announces that you have been chosen to carry out a precious, important part of God's plan today. In fact, you will be participating in a miracle.

Would you gulp and resist? After all, this is the Christmas season and you know what that means. Cards. Gifts. Decorations. Entertaining....

Stop and think back to Mary, the mother of Jesus. She too had a full agenda—she was planning her wedding. Yet the angel Gabriel appeared with the shocking news that the Lord intended to use her in His most incredible of all miracles—the birth of His son. What was the reaction of this innocent teenage girl? Much like ours might be, according to the Bible: "She was greatly troubled." But soon she made the choice to cooperate with God's plan. "Let it be to me according to Your word," she surrendered.

We have an opportunity to participate in a measure of the same miracle during this Christmas season. God asks us to present our bodies as a "living sacrifice"—even as Mary did—in order to nurture His miracle of Christmas: the internal presence of Jesus in our lives. There's just one hitch. Nurturing His presence means reading the Bible, praying, adoring Him, writing Him letters of confession and commitment. It means giving Him *more* time, not *less* time, which may seem inconvenient or impossible in the midst of this hectic season!

So we have a choice: To cooperate or resist. Respond or be distracted with busyness. If we cooperate, we are bound to feel the stirrings of new life growing within us, as Mary did, which is the miracle of Christmas working in us and through us from inside out. And surely we will reach the brink of another new year, ready to cooperate with God by accepting His plan for our lives. That's Tandem Power!

Will you nurture the Christmas miracle of His presence in your life during this Christmas season by giving Him more time, not less time? An extra fifteen minutes each morning, a portion of your lunchtime or a quiet moment before bed?

Heavenly Father, I commit myself as a living sacrifice to nurture Your presence within me during this Advent season. Please fill me with new life. —CAROL KUYKENDALL

---

2 | FRIDAY
For unto you is born this day in the city of David a Savior, which is Christ the Lord. —LUKE 2:11

Years ago when my husband and I were traveling through the western part of North Carolina, I bought a small wooden manger scene that had been made by someone living in the area. It has become my favorite Christmas ornament because it is so simple and so lovingly carved. Over the years, some of its more delicate parts have been broken and mended, but there it stands today, under my tree. It means even more to me now.

In many ways each one of us is very much like that little carving. We are made of simple materials, but lovingly crafted by our Creator. There are no two of us exactly alike. We are not perfect; we haven't always held up well under life's pressures, but we have always been tenderly mended by a caring God. Even today, *especially* today, God looks upon us with deep love.

What can we give to God in return? Nothing. Christmas means that we can't give anything to God. It is He Who gives to us—His love, His care, His concern for our well-being, our struggles, our failures and our victories.

But Christmas also means that we can give to one another—not things, exhaustion, short tempers or heroic achievements, but simply the kind of undemanding, tenderly caring love God gives to us. That is the way each one of us can truly bring joy to the world!

Beloved Father, as You blessed us with the gift of Your Son, let us love one another—not only on Christmas Day, but every day. —PHYLLIS HOBE

3 SATURDAY

If ye...know how to give good gifts unto your children, how much more shall your Father which is in heaven give good things... —MATTHEW 7:11

One December when my daughter Ann was only six, she tucked two gifts beneath the Christmas tree, one for her daddy, the other for me. "What do you suppose they are?" I asked my husband. He shrugged, as puzzled as I.

On Christmas morning I opened my gift to find a pair of slightly familiar-looking silver earrings. In her daddy's package was a navy tie with little tan ducks on it.

"Why, Ann," I exclaimed, genuinely amazed. "Where did you get these lovely gifts?"

"The old chest," she answered.

That's when I recognized the earrings as some I'd retired to the chest at least ten years before. The tie had been discarded long ago, too. Ann had given us gifts we already possessed!

And she had reminded me of something important. Christmas should not be simply the experience of getting more, but waking up to what we already possess. For God has already given us everything we need: a Savior, love, hope, eternal life, beauty, peace of mind, joy, faith, community...so much. Only we don't always experience them. With time and familiarity we tend to lose touch with God's abundance.

So this Christmas let's not just open what is new beneath the tree, but *re*open what is already ours!

You have given me everything, Lord. Help me to embrace it again. —SUE MONK KIDD

THE PARADOX OF THE CROSS AT THE CRIB

4 SECOND SUNDAY IN ADVENT

And she shall bring forth a son, and thou shalt call his name JESUS: for he shall save his people from their sins. —MATTHEW 1:21

Like many families, we've picked up Advent traditions over the years. Such as setting up our creche-set three weeks before Christmas. Only the stable goes on the mantelpiece this early, with the shepherds and sheep nearby. Mary and Joseph are still a long way from Bethle-hem—on the other side of the room—and the Wise Men remain upstairs (they won't reach the stable until the feast of the Epiphany on January 6).

Something else goes in the stable today, though; a small wooden cross beside the manger where the Baby will go on Christmas Eve.

We added the cross to the set twenty-five years ago. That was the year I wrote a children's book called *Our Christmas Story* with Mrs. Billy Graham. Meant to be read aloud in Advent, the book begins not in Bethlehem but in the Garden of Eden, and follows the whole human story, from the time we drew apart from God to the stable where He drew close to us.

The publisher seemed happy with the concept—until the time came to design the cover. We all agreed on a manger scene. "With a cross, of course," Ruth Graham said, "behind the crib."

The editor was horrified, the artist aghast. A cross? At Christmas? And on a children's book! Children would never understand. Anyhow, Christmas should be a happy time!

"Yes, but what are we happy about?" Ruth asked quietly. "Not just His birth. That alone changed nothing for you and me." It was the cross, she explained, that made the difference. "It was in order to die that He was born."

And of course when the cross appeared on the cover, children understood perfectly. Pain and comfort, laughter and tears, wander-ing from home and being found again... it's we adults who make op-posites of these things. The cross in our cribset reminds us of a mystery: Not only was He born to die. But also He died so that we might be born to everlasting life.

Father, we accept the gift of Your love this Advent season, Your Son whom You lifted up on the Cross to save us from our sins.
—ELIZABETH SHERRILL

| 5 | MONDAY |

And we urge you, brothers, warn those who are idle, encourage the timid, help the weak, be patient with everyone. —*I THESSALONIANS 5:14 (NIV)*

"Our marriage was on the way to the trash heap," the attractive woman of about forty told her fellow panelists on a television program I watched the other day. "The problem, I thought, was my husband and his unwillingness to conform to my wishes. I nagged him about how he dressed and how he ate, about his low-paying job, about how he disciplined the kids, about his poor church attendance. His response was defensive, and we fought like wildcats, but nothing changed."

Then one day, the woman said, she read an article on behavior modification. "It stated that the only way a boss can get an employee to change is through either reward or punishment. I wasn't a boss, but I was certainly bossy and I'd given my husband a lot of verbal punishment. Maybe it was time I tried the carrot instead of the stick. So instead of nagging him I began looking for ways to compliment him. Suddenly the whole atmosphere of our marriage changed. It was miraculous! That was eight years ago and now I have a sweetheart of a hubby."

Her discovery should not have surprised her. We give lip service to the maxim "love conquers all," but our actions often deny it. "If any man be in Christ (that is, filled with Christ's love)," Paul wrote, "he or she is a new creature; old things are passed away; behold, all things become new" (II Corinthians 5:17). Even marriages ready for the trash heap.

We will never be able to see ourselves as others see us, Lord, but help us see ourselves as You do. —FRED BAUER

| 6 | TUESDAY |

... He stedfastly set his face to go to Jerusalem.
—LUKE 9:51

My wife Joy and our three sons have convinced one another that sliding across snowy terrains in sub-freezing temperatures builds family togetherness. They love cross-country skiing, and I've chosen to go along with them, even though I think they're a bit crazy.

Recently, we were out on a lake practicing. We were doing quite well; then Joy mentioned that the reason crossing the lake was so easy was that a fifteen-mile-an-hour breeze had been pushing us. "Now we're a half mile from the warmth and comfort of the car!" she said as we headed back with a sub-zero wind in our faces and no trees to break the gale force.

Six-year-old Jonathan turned to me and said simply, "I don't want to ski that way, Dad. It's too hard."

He was right, of course, but we had to go into the wind since it was the only way home. Once we made it to the car, warmed the engine, rubbed toes and fingers back to life, and poured out some cocoa from the thermos bottle, Jonathan piped up, "Hey, we did it!"

His sense of pride reminded me that sometimes the only way to accomplish something in life is to "head into the wind." Jesus did it when He set His face toward Jerusalem. Today I have a letter of apology to write that has been on my mind for a month. I keep putting it off because it's a hard thing to put into words. This day will be a good time to pick up my pen and make a start.

Lord, help me make the right choices in life, even when the choices are difficult or uncomfortable. —ERIC FELLMAN

---

7 WEDNESDAY
...Whatever you ask in prayer, you will receive, if you have faith. —MATTHEW 21:22(RSV)

My friend's business came to a halt because an important piece of machinery broke down. A frantic call to the factory produced a serviceman who replaced a small screw. My friend was aghast when he received a bill for $100. "That screw cost no more than ten cents," he complained, "and the workman was here only a few minutes!"

He demanded an itemized bill. The factory sent one: "One screw—10¢. Knowing where to place the screw—$99.90."

The cost of that little piece of metal was insignificant. But its *value* to the factory was enormous.

Sometimes a small, hurried prayer can seem insignificant too. But the difference it can make in a life may be beyond all reckoning.

Lord, let me never underestimate the power of even the smallest prayer, and the great mountains it can move.
—WALTER HARTER

DECEMBER 1988

8 | THURSDAY
...He placed it by great waters, and set it as a willow tree. —*EZEKIEL 17:5*

As I walk along the road at the edge of the river I loved as a child, my shoes make tracks in the soft silt. How long has it been since my smaller footprints, planted here so many years ago, have blown away? Yet the God-planted willows that line the river banks are the same.

There is a part of me that longs for that kind of rootedness, but my life keeps turning and shifting. My husband Rex has changed careers, Karen and Paul have both married and moved away, and now John has gone away to school. God keeps calling me to change myself, too—to vary my routines, to shift the direction of my work, to relate to others in new ways. Maybe the secret to staying rooted in an up-rooting world is to keep myself firmly planted near my God, like the willows by the river.

If there's an unsettling condition in your life, consider it an opportunity to discover *God's* changelessness through frequent, deep-rooted prayer. He will hold you firm and steady.

Thank You, Lord, for rooting me in Your love.
—MARILYN MORGAN HELLEBERG

9 | FRIDAY
When I was a child, I spoke like a child, I thought like a child, I reasoned like a child; when I became a man, I gave up childish ways. —*I CORINTHIANS 13:11 (RSV)*

"Auntie," a delightful old woman I knew, lived alone and always did things *her way.* One day, after her friends had told her she no longer needed to bake cakes "from scratch" because instant mixes did just as well, she reluctantly decided to give it a try. This new-fangled idea was a failure.

"What a mess!" she complained. "The cake ran all over the oven. I told you it wouldn't work."

We were truly surprised. "Auntie," we asked, puzzled, "did you follow the instructions?"

"Why, of course I did," she replied with a little edge to her voice. "But, you know, no cake tastes good without butter, so I added a big gob."

We all protested and explained carefully the instructions. We thought we'd convinced her, until Auntie replied, "Well, I *still* like a bit of butter!"

She wouldn't give in! But you know, sometimes I'm like Auntie. I stubbornly cling to old-fangled ideas, refusing to try new ways. I've combed my hair the same way since grade school and I always put my left shoe on first. When I was a kid, I hated all vegetables, especially spinach, and the only fruits I ate were pears and bananas. But finally I learned to put away childish things. Now I enjoy persimmons, apricots, kiwifruit, mangoes...I even grow spinach in my garden! My life feels richer since I started opening myself to new things.

Maybe you're ready to open yourself to something new-fangled today. After all, what have you got to lose?

Dear Father, don't let me get stuck in a rut. Let me try something new today. —LEE WEBBER

10 | SATURDAY
Break forth into joy, sing together...for the Lord hath comforted his people... —ISAIAH 52:9

What do you do when you're alone at Christmas? Hope you'll be invited out to dinner? Sit by yourself, remembering how good it felt to have a family around you? Take a trip to get away from your loneliness? Perhaps you think that hospitality has no place in your life anymore. Well, if you do, then you're mistaken. Over a third of the adult population in the United States lives alone—and Christmas is for them, too.

Jesus was alone. We often forget that because we think of Him in the company of others. But there was hospitality in His heart. He didn't wait to be invited somewhere; He invited friends—and strangers—to be with Him. He didn't have a home as we know it, yet He welcomed people into His life. And they brought Him joy.

My friend Peggy Bates tells me that after she had been widowed for two years, she decided it was time to stop shutting Christmas out of her life. "So I told my children, and my grandchildren, and all the aunts and uncles, that that year I wanted them to come to my house. It was a lot of work, and I cried at times because it brought back memories of my husband. But we all had such a happy Christmas that I've been doing the same thing every year. It brings me back into life!"

Yes, hospitality can do that. So, if you don't want to be alone this Christmas, open your home, your heart and your life to the people you know.

As we celebrate Your coming, Lord, lead us out of our solitude and into each other's hearts. —PHYLLIS HOBE

THE PARADOX OF THE UNEXPECTED SURPRISE

11 THIRD SUNDAY IN ADVENT

Blessed are those servants, whom the lord when he cometh shall find watching...Blessed is that servant, whom his lord when he cometh shall find...doing.

—LUKE 12:37, 43

"If Jesus tarries," Mr. Weber would say, "I'll come again Tuesday."

He was an odd-jobs man who, in fact, came to our house every Tuesday for many years. As a child I always wondered if he wanted Jesus to come before next week, for as he put up screens or repaired my bicycle bell he whistled like a man who was totally content. One thing I was sure of: For Mr. Weber the imminent appearance of Jesus was as daily a fact as the weather. Unpredictable, like tomorrow's sunshine, but certain to occur before long.

When, years later, I took some Scripture courses, I discovered that Mr. Weber's expectant attitude was also the Bible's. The New Testament has little to say about the birth of Jesus—only St. Luke's Gospel gives any space to it—but it has a very great deal to say about the Second Coming. For two thousand years the church has maintained the same emphasis, urging believers to watch with "feet shod and lamps lit."

Advent was the season the early church set aside to contemplate Jesus' coming in glory, as King of Kings. If we find it somehow easier to think about His coming in humility, as a Baby in a manger, that's understandable. The birth of a baby is a human-sized event. We can picture it, relate to it.

How can we relate to an event of cosmic proportions, a day without a date? It will come, Jesus tells us, when we least expect it. Not when a century ends or a comet lights the sky, though at such times people have always rushed to the mountaintops to await Him. That's not the way He tells us to keep Advent.

He says when He comes that He wants to find us doing the work He has given us to do. Putting up screens and repairing bells. Now in December: shopping and wrapping and baking. If He comes tonight, may He find us discharging such small errands of love. Preparing our great Christmas celebration two weeks from now...if Jesus tarries.

O Jesus Christ, help us to do all our work, to live each day, as though You were going to be spending the day with us. We eagerly watch for Your coming, and we joyfully work for Your approval. —ELIZABETH SHERRILL

12 MONDAY
Many are the plans in a man's heart, but it is the Lord's purpose that prevails. —PROVERBS 19:21 (NIV)

Today did not go as planned. When we went to bed last night, the wind was howling and heavy wet snowflakes began swirling around our windows. When we woke up, drifts were piled high in front of our door, and the radio announced there would be no school. The blizzard had given our three children the gift of an unplanned holiday and at first I shared their joy, remembering that kind of a day from my own childhood. But my mood deteriorated steadily.

"Will you make a fire and some hot chocolate?" ten-year-old Kendall asked. I did, followed by pancakes in three shifts and more hot chocolate. At mid-morning, I surveyed the mess: a sink full of half-finished cups of cold hot chocolate, and a floor covered with globs of melting snow and soggy wool mittens. The pot of chili I made for dinner was being devoured for an early lunch. My patience waned, especially as I caught a glimpse of my desk, piled high with work I had intended to tackle alone in a quiet house today. Suddenly the blizzard seemed to be suffocating me.

But just as suddenly, the advice of a friend flashed through my mind: "Make the most of life's irretrievable moments." I hardly heard her words at the time, but here they were, wrapped around a real-life situation. Surely, a no-school blizzard day was an "irretrievable moment," even though it was an interruption of my anticipated agenda. I

339

couldn't change the circumstances, but I could change my attitude. Instead of wishing myself finished with this day, I could appreciate it for what it was—a minute in life that would never happen in the same way again.

"Hey," I said, turning around to face the very same day. "Anyone want to make some chocolate chip cookies?"

Lord, help me recognize and savor life's irretrievable moments. Today and every day. —CAROL KUYKENDALL

| 13 | TUESDAY | FIRESIDE FRIEND |

Give us this day our daily bread. —MATTHEW 6:11

Sometimes being a cowboy is a solitary business.

It was winter in the High Absaroka Mountains of Wyoming. I was all alone in a little cabin. Snow was deep and travel was impossible. I wore snowshoes to feed the livestock. When you're alone like that there are times when the solitude gets to you and you wonder if even God has forgotten you. When that happens you begin to look for a sign from Him.

To feed myself I had a supply of staples planned to last the winter, but I was getting low on flour. Finally I decided to use what was left to make some bread. I mixed enough for five or six small loaves and sat the pan of dough on the back of the stove to rise. But it wouldn't rise. Late in the afternoon I got so disgusted that I threw the whole pan of dough out on the south side of the cabin. I was pretty depressed. I was fifty miles from anywhere, and spring was a long way off.

Later as I looked out the kitchen window I couldn't believe my eyes. The dough I had thrown away had risen up until it looked like a plastic balloon. The sunlight on the cabin wall had warmed it just right. I ran out and picked up the dough. Pine needles had stuck to it, but I made five loaves and baked them anyway. Pine-scented from the pine needles in it. Best bread I ever ate.

Was there a Higher Power at work in the sunshine? Of course there was! Did God know that was the last of my flour? You bet He did! He never forgets us. Anywhere. Ever.

Lord, help us recognize Your signs when You give them.

—DON BELL

14 WEDNESDAY   FIRESIDE FRIEND
But if we walk in the light, as he is in the light, we have fellowship one with another...   —I JOHN 1:7

I must have been six or seven years old when I learned the truth. Before then, at the Christmas midnight service each year, I would stare at the big stained glass window at the front of our church and see Jesus' face light up as He saw us coming down the aisle. As the magnificent glow spread over the gathering congregation, I knew that I was somehow special because I saw a miracle happening.

Then one Christmas Eve my mom happened to comment on how beautiful the stained glass looked "with the light bulb shining behind Jesus' face." "Light bulb?" I croaked. Reality came crashing into my young existence, and for many years, I didn't believe in miracles.

More than a decade later, my faith in miracles returned. As I sat in the pew, wrapped in the holy darkness of Christmas Eve, a lovely glow caught my attention. I looked around in amazement and saw faces aglow, lighted with the joy of His coming! One couple, who had touched so many lives in small ways, squeezed each other's hand. I saw Morrie, a former street person, enter our pew with a youngster from our church's inner-city program. Across the aisle sat Eddie, the eight-year-old terror who had squirmed through every service. I realized that somehow he had wriggled his way into our hearts.

Here, in the faces of this fellowship, was the light of Jesus, illuminating the darkness of Christmas Eve. I'm sure if you look at the people around *you*, you'll see the same "miracles" in their faces.

Father, let the miracle of Your love shine through my face today.   —TAMMY RIDER

Family Time

15 BUILDING FAMILY TRADITIONS
...And they will call him Immanuel—which means, "God with us."   —MATTHEW 1:23

For us, Christmas and the month of December have never been an ending, but a glorious beginning, a time of anticipation. As children, there was the excitement of the Christmas program—little boy shepherds in bathrobes carrying crooks, three kings in gold paper crowns and the rest of us being prompted through Luke's familiar description of the birth of Jesus. And that excitement peaked over the years as Christmas morning produced a red wagon, a baby doll complete with wardrobe—later a bicycle and perfume and a necklace. The traditions of our families were pretty much the same, and in a childish way we were aware of "God with us."

Then as adults with our own family, some sense filtered into the "December confusion" as we have focused on our inherited traditions and established our own. Purchasing and decorating our tree has been a ritual shared and enjoyed with our daughter. The colorful decorations and lights serve to remind us that Jesus is indeed the light of the world. The stockings hanging from our fireplace point to the presence of God in the ordinary as well as in the extraordinary.

Spiritual preparation has always been important in our anticipation of Christmas Day. Each rereading of the nativity story in the Gospels fills our hearts and minds with the wonder of God's greatest Gift. Then as we wrap the gifts for our own loved ones, we are reminded of the gold, frankincense and myrrh the "wise men from the east" brought to Jesus. Have you ever wondered what Mary and Joseph did with those gifts? We have.

And "God with us" seems especially real as we welcome Christmas Day in a midnight service of praise and worship. Then, too, our celebration has been joyful as the family circle has expanded with grandchildren, even as it has been painful because of the "empty chairs" of father and father-in-law. But as we've built our own traditions of celebration, the continuity has held us together both in fact and in spirit.

Patterns of celebration are most likely different between your family and ours as we center on the presence of God with us. But we can share in this marvelous truth expressed by a little boy on the meaning of the season when he said, "Jesus is the nicest picture God ever made." And Robert Louis Stevenson captured the pulse of Christmas as he prayed...

Loving Father, help us remember the birth of Jesus, that we may share in the song of the angels, the gladness of the shepherds and the wisdom of the wise men.

Close the door of hate and open the door of love all over the world.

Let kindness come with every gift and good desires with every greeting.

Deliver us from evil by the blessing which Christ brings, and teach us to be merry with clean hearts.

May the Christmas morning make us happy to be Thy children, and the Christmas evening bring us to our beds with grateful thoughts, forgiving and forgiven, for Jesus' sake. Amen.   —HARRIETT AND FLOYD THATCHER

| 16 | FRIDAY
...Behold, I bring you good tidings of great joy, which shall be to all people.   —LUKE 2:10

A few years ago some neighbors invited me to go caroling with them a few nights before Christmas. I didn't think I should because I had so much to do, but the idea appealed to me. Somehow I found the time, and I'm glad I did. Because on that windy, bitterly cold night, as we trudged from house to house, singing those beautiful carols, greeted by smiles of surprised delight, I felt the joy of Christmas. For a few hours, I was free to think of nothing but the coming of Christ to earth and all that means.

Joy is the ability to give to others the love God gives to us, something I'd forgotten in the midst of holiday distractions and the usual complaint, "so much to do, and so little time."

But on this night the true meaning of Christmas returned to me—I saw that Christ isn't Someone we have to find. He has already found us. We don't have to follow a star or wait on a lonely hillside for a sign of His arrival. He is here, not only on earth, but in our hearts and in our lives.

This year, will you join me in truly celebrating Christ's coming? Let Him be a part of everything we do, from our quiet moments to our hurried attempts to do more than we can. Let Him enable us to put His love into our efforts. Let us not look far...He is here.

Lord, open our hearts to Your presence, here and now.

—PHYLLIS HOBE

| **17** | SATURDAY | FIRESIDE FRIEND |

And Jesus came and touched them… —MATTHEW 17:7

Christmas carols filled the hallways and brought many residents to the doors of their rooms. Some sat in wheelchairs while others swayed on their walkers. The young carolers were Sunday school children from our church and were dressed in their Christmas finest.

We had come to the nursing home "to make some lonely people happy," my daughter told me. She did not question her ability to make someone happy. But as I looked around at the hunched men and women robbed of their faculties, their health and, in some cases, their families, I wondered how much happiness we could really deliver. I sang with the children, hoping my tears would go unnoticed.

As we filed down the last hallway, singing "Away in the Manger," a lady wearing a faded print dress shuffled to the doorway. She waved to the children and reached out her hand. Three-year-old Katie grabbed hold of it. The woman smiled, her eyes lit with some sparked memory, as her fingers stroked Katie's smooth white skin.

I branded that image upon my mind. I want to remember it. Because, sometimes, I think too big. I forget that a song, a smile or even a handshake can indeed make "some lonely people happy."

Lord, when I feel helpless to help others, let me remember that even a handshake can say, "I care." —TERRY HELWIG

THE PARADOX OF LIGHT IN DARKNESS

| **18** | FOURTH SUNDAY IN ADVENT |

…The dayspring from on high hath visited us, to give light to them that sit in darkness and in the shadow of death, to guide our feet into the way of peace.
—LUKE 1:78–79

Today we light the fourth and final candle in our Advent wreath. The first candle, lit on New Year's Day, November 27, is little more than a purple stub. Each Sunday we've added another, until now in this darkest week of the year, our wreath is its brightest.

It's another of the Advent traditions we share with Christians all over the Northern Hemisphere. And like so many Christian customs, its roots are very old, tapping human experiences we might have forgotten, if faith had not claimed them for her own.

Our wreath with its base of evergreens takes me back to the dark forests of Europe, where families wrapped in animal skins against the cold watched in terror as the sun rose less high each day, lingered less long in the sky. I see a wheel to represent the sun built in a clearing, and watch the shivering people build fires around the rim in a desperate effort to call back light and warmth.

Why do we Christians celebrate Jesus' birth in December? The actual month is not recorded in the Bible but it was probably springtime, lambing season in Judea, the only time shepherds remained in the fields at night.

But when the church settled on a date to commemorate His coming—His coming in time, His coming at the end of time—it chose not spring, but this darkest hour of the year. In replacing the ancient midwinter ceremonies with the Advent celebration, it did what Christianity has always done, spoke God's word into the fear-filled pagan world.

It is not what men do, Advent tells us, that brings back the light. Not our fires, our candles, even our prayers. The initiative is always God's. When things are darkest, when times are hardest, when the case is most hopeless: Look up! Someone is coming into our need...and now He is very close indeed.

O God, it is hard to remember the light in the blackness of discouragement and despair. But I thank You that Christ came for our darkest time. I thank You for the light that even now is shining in the darkness. —ELIZABETH SHERRILL

 MONDAY
Without having seen him you love him; though you do not now see him you believe in him and rejoice with unutterable and exalted joy. —I PETER 1:8 (RSV)

No game to test a student's knowledge of the Bible goes on very long without the inevitable question: *What is the shortest verse?* The answer is, of course, "Jesus wept." *Where is it found?* (John 11:35) and *Why was He crying?* (because of Lazarus' death) are sure to follow.

Not long ago on a speaking trip in the Midwest, I was asked, "What is the shortest devotional thought you've ever written?" I told the woman I had no idea, but that the shortest one I could imagine would be "God is love."

"But that would need some amplification, wouldn't it?" she asked.

"If I were writing to believers," I said, "maybe not. Otherwise, if I were allowed just a few more words, I would add that as undeniable evidence of His love God sent His only Son to die for our sins in order to save us from death—both death in the hereafter and the death of aimlessness, peacelessness and selfishness in the here and now."

All that is true and yet, for most of us, I think, "God is love" is message enough.

Let our lives speak our gratitude, Lord, for Your unspeakable gift. —FRED BAUER

 TUESDAY   **FIRESIDE FRIEND**
...In all his thoughts there is no room for God.
—*PSALM 10:4 (NIV)*

My son Brett had been chosen to play the part of the innkeeper in our annual church Christmas pageant, and I was upset. No noble shepherd or diligent wise man. Instead he was to be the one who offered a lowly stable as the birthplace for the Son of God! As we drove home from rehearsal, I asked Brett how he felt about being the innkeeper.

His face broke into a big smile. "I like it! He's the hero, you know. If it hadn't been for him, Baby Jesus wouldn't have had a place to be born."

As we rode on in silence, I thought about the innkeeper in this new light. A hero? No doubt his inn was full. And he was probably tired from dealing with the demands of guests forced by Caesar's census to make the long journey to Bethlehem. Then had come this man named Joseph and his pregnant wife, whose time was very near. The innkeeper could have brushed them aside. Instead he took the time to consider their plight. He offered the best he had available— his stable.

I looked over at my son. I knew he would do well in the Christmas pageant, giving his best effort to play the "hero" of the story. *Giving*

346

your best.... I thought of the lesson in my son's attitude. It was a lesson I could apply that very day—as I finished cleaning my house, as I took my elderly neighbor to the grocery and as I planned the best-ever costume for my little innkeeper.

This Christmas, Lord, I offer You my best effort in all that I do.
—MARY LOU CARNEY

21 WEDNESDAY
...God so loved the world, that he gave his only begotten Son, that whosoever believeth in him should not perish... —JOHN 3:16

Have you ever wondered about the origin of the word *noel*? We sing it in carols and see it on Christmas cards, but what does it mean? Last year I decided to find out.

I discovered there are several explanations. But the one I like the best goes back to medieval England. It was common then to abbreviate a common phrase into one word in order to save time; for example, the phrase *God be with you* gradually became *good-bye*. During Christmas, it seems our ancestors cried out a greeting to one another as they passed in the streets. "Now all is well," they shouted, referring to the event of God sending His Son. The theory goes that with time the phrase was contracted into one word, *noel*.

Today I cannot sing the word or read it upon a card without its full meaning filling me with new peace. Christ is born into our darkness. *Now all is well!*

Father, fill my heart with the peace of noel!
—SUE MONK KIDD

22 THURSDAY
...For your Father knows what you need before you ask him. —MATTHEW 6:8 (RSV)

When I was growing up I loved Christmas Eve because it was the night Mom would sing "Sweet Little Jesus Boy" at our candle lighting church service. Her pure soprano voice cradled each note, making the song a prayer that reached shadowed corners of church and hearts alike. I'd sit entranced, thinking that's how an angel must sound.

After I was married, with children of my own, I still loved hearing Mom's "Sweet Little Jesus Boy" every Christmas. One year, on a whim, I asked if I could tape-record her. She paused on her way out my door, wearing a bright red scarf over her white hair, and began to sing.

The very next year found us thousands of miles apart. My family had moved to the woods of Alaska. It was Christmas Eve. A lonely time when you're in a new place far from "home." I remembered the tape recording I had made and quietly slipped outside and crunched up and down the frozen drive playing "Sweet Little Jesus Boy" over and over. Mom's voice hung in the clear night air like an angel song. Not even the frigid temperature could keep my loneliness from melting away. I looked up at the stars...and God, and whispered, "Merry Christmas!"

Isn't it comforting to know God sees ahead? He understands our every need and prepares an answer *before* the need arises! What just-right answer has He planned for you today? Have you looked for it...maybe the answer hovers in the "air like an angel song" and you just need to listen more closely.

Lord, here is my need today: _____.
Now show me the answer You already had in mind for me.
Amen. —CAROL KNAPP

---

23 FRIDAY

And the Word was made flesh, and dwelt among us...
—JOHN 1:14

It was Christmas Eve and I was in a crowded airport, on my way home. I was fortunate to have a ticket on a flight that would get me back to Philadelphia in time to attend a midnight church service, something I didn't want to miss.

Then I heard the announcement: My flight was delayed—something about heavy air traffic. No one could say when we might take off, and I knew I would miss the midnight service.

It's not fair! I thought as I turned away from the flight information desk. I was too upset to sit down, so I walked to the glass wall overlooking the runways. It was dark and the glass looked like polished onyx until I got close to it. Then I could see the runway lights—and above them, bright and distinct, a skyful of stars.

I felt tears coming to my eyes as I stared up at the sky. I thought of some shepherds, thousands of years ago, looking up into the darkness. Perhaps they, too, longed to be home. I realized how many anxious delays three Eastern kings must have experienced on their long journey. Yet how quickly they must have forgotten life's inconveniences once they saw the Child.

And how little my inconveniences now mattered—because I too had seen the Child. I felt peaceful as I sat down facing the dark, star-sprinkled wall. Whether I was still in the airport or up in the sky at midnight, I knew I would have my own quiet service. Because we don't have to be back home, or even in Bethlehem, to celebrate Christ's coming. Nor do we have to seek Him to adore Him. He is here, with us, wherever we are.

Praise the Lord, O my soul!   —PHYLLIS HOBE

THE PARADOX OF PEACE IN PANDEMONIUM

|24| CHRISTMAS EVE

And all went to be taxed, every one into his own city. And Joseph also went up...unto...Bethlehem...to be taxed with Mary his espoused wife, being great with child.   —LUKE 2:3–5

This is the Silent Night, the Holy Night. The night before Christmas when all through the house not a creature is stirring. When the world in solemn stillness lies to hear the angels sing.

Not in our house. Here everything's astir. We have twelve overnight guests, four of them unexpected, and the phone is ringing, and the skirt I'm wearing to the midnight service has a jammed zipper and the callers at the door with gifts are the ones I forgot to get anything for. And I'm pressured and anxious and angry at myself for once again failing to hear the angelic song. O little town of Bethlehem, how still we see thee lie!

But isn't this part of the problem? That we've come to see Bethlehem this way, over the centuries: that hushed and holy manger scene painted by artists? No doubt there was a hush in heaven that night; this is what artists with their gifted vision are showing us. But in Bethlehem I suspect it was more like pandemonium.

We have twelve extra people to house tonight; Bethlehem had additional hundreds. Could Mary and Joseph have been the only travelers lodged in that overflow space in the stable?

It's the unforeseen that upsets Christmas plans. But because of a sudden order from Rome, their whole journey was unforeseen. How many painstaking preparations for the birth did Mary have to leave behind in Nazareth?

I chafe at crowded stores, but what about the press of people in those narrow streets? I've witnessed jostling, shouting market days in Israel—and those are willing crowds; two thousand years ago it would have been an angry one as well, herded together by order of a foreign dictator.

I'm distressed at what we've spent for Christmas. But I wonder—what was the price of bread in Bethlehem that night? How much did Joseph have to pay for the water Mary needed?

Silent night. Holy night. It was holy, of course, in the only place that matters—in the hearts of those who understood what was happening. But the holiness occurred in a noisy world. A tense and pressured time of history. Come, Lord Jesus, tonight, into this chaotic world of ours.

O Jesus Christ, I will make room for You in my heart as I celebrate Your coming this busy Christmastide.

—ELIZABETH SHERRILL

CHRISTMAS...ALL PARADOX RESOLVED

 CHRISTMAS DAY

We who have been made holy by Jesus, now have the same Father he has. That is why Jesus is not ashamed to call us his brothers. —HEBREWS 2:11 (LB)

It's Christmas, the "Feast of Christ"! Time to open the stockings, unwrap the gifts, eat the holiday meal. After weeks of getting ready, today is the time awaited. Advent was the season of coming; Christmas is the season of arrival. Advent looked to past and future; Christmas celebrates the now.

This year we've watched for signs of His coming in the paradoxes of our lives. We've looked for Him in our light but also in our darkness, in peace but also in pandemonium.

Today we experience Him as the great Resolver of all paradox. He is both Alpha and Omega, the first and the last. He is priest and sacrifice, servant and king, infant and Ancient of Days. He did not come to abolish the poles of our experience, our heights and our depths, but to unite them in Himself, so that nothing that can happen to us, now or ever, will fall outside His all-seeing love.

Paradox is a Greek word meaning "contrary to expectation"— and how contrary to all preconceived ideas that first Christmas was! The Jews expected their Messiah to be a military conqueror; Jesus was born a carpenter's son. The Wise Men looked for Him at the court of the king; they found Him in a stable. Scholars foretold His birth; illiterate shepherds celebrated it.

His arrival is still like that: contrary to expectation. Today we meet Him not as we imagine Him to be, not as artists have painted Him nor saints extolled Him. But as we find Him in our own hearts at this moment, just as we are…with all our ambivalence, all our incompleteness…gathering all our contradictions into Himself.

At Christmas the Son of God becomes human so that you and I can know ourselves this very day as children of God. Merry, merry Christmas!

O Jesus Christ, how blest I am that You call Yourself my Brother. I thank You for the gift of Your love this Christmas. Help me to live in Your love today and always.

—ELIZABETH SHERRILL

| 26 | MONDAY |

Fix your thoughts on what is true and good and right…
—*PHILIPPIANS 4:8 (LB)*

Now comes what professional counselors have come to recognize as "the letdown season." Christmas has come and gone, and something is missing. The prospects of going back to work, returning to the old routine and the dark dreariness of winter put many of us in a blue funk.

Fortunately, with God's help most of us can turn ourselves

around. The fact is He gave us the wherewithal to deal with such problems at creation when he fashioned our brains. The Bible says, "As people think in their hearts, so are they" (Proverbs 23:7). God gave us the power, through our thoughts, through prayer, through studying and applying His Word, to reverse negative patterns. Science now knows that the body contains both healthy and unhealthy chemicals that are released by our thoughts. The choice is ours.

If you are looking for a New Year's resolution, you could do worse than pledge to give yourself away daily, to share your time, your talents and your resources, not as if there were no tomorrow, but as if there were millions. That kind of love not only testifies to our faith in Christ's promises, but is a guaranteed chaser of post-Christmas letdowns and a sure cure for winter's worst blue funks.

> *Live each day, each hour, each minute*
> *With all the love that life has in it.*
>
> —FRED BAUER

27	TUESDAY

FIRESIDE FRIEND

...I have learned, in whatsoever state I am, therewith to be content. —PHILIPPIANS 4:11

Rachel and I have been friends since college. We keep in touch not only by phone, but also by exchanging chatty letters about our work and our problems and our children. I finished typing one such letter to Rachel and paused to proofread it before pulling it out of the typewriter. When I came to a typo in the last paragraph, I laughed aloud. I had meant to say, "Amy Jo gave a shining performance in the school play." Instead, the sentence read, "Amy Jo gave a whining performance in the school play." Only one letter differentiated the two words, but what a difference that one letter made!

I thought about those two words the next day when a salesman was rude to me. *Whining* or *shining.* I remembered them again when I had to miss a church luncheon to stay home with my measle-covered son.

Whenever trouble or disappointment comes our way, we have two choices. *Whining* or *shining.* We can choose to complain and become bitter, or we can choose to trust in God's presence and purpose and become better. What a difference in our lives that choice will make!

I choose to "shine" by trusting You, Lord, in the midst of what could be a "whining" situation. —MARY LOU CARNEY

28 WEDNESDAY
And to stand every morning to thank and praise the Lord, and likewise at even. —I CHRONICLES 23:30

I recently heard of a prescription that a doctor gives his patients whom he diagnoses as "nervous, overanxious, tense and/or unable to sleep." It reads:

> Purchase a calendar that has a page for each day in the year. Every morning look at the current day's page, ask God's guidance through the day and then proceed to live it fully. Upon retiring at night, tear that page from your calendar and thank God for giving you the day and for His blessings during it. Ask His forgiveness for any sins you committed during that span of time. Then crumple the used day's page and throw it in the trash can. Already the next day's date is looking up at you, fresh and clean and promising. Lie down in your bed, put the old day out of your mind and rest peacefully in preparation for the new tomorrow.

I think it is such a good prescription that I have bought my 1989 calendar and have it on my night table, ready for use.

Don't you want to get yours today?

Every day is a gift from You, Lord. Help me to live it for Your glory. Amen. —DRUE DUKE

29 THURSDAY **FIRESIDE FRIEND**
The Lord is my shepherd; I shall not want. He maketh me to lie down in green pastures: he leadeth me beside the still waters. He restoreth my soul...
—PSALM 23:1–3

My job at the moment was to clean the combine to put it away for the winter. It had been a long harvest season, for we started four long months ago in the middle of September. We had worked long hours and late into many nights this year, but we were finally done!

I finished oiling some chains and parked the big machine in its spot in the shed, where it will sit until next fall. The grain bins were full, and despite some bad weather, we had harvested a bumper crop, one that would last us well into the following harvest season. I glanced at my watch and saw it was time to start milking. As I opened the barn door, I saw a vibrant sunset in front of me. The blues, pinks, purples and reds were painted across the sky in a beautiful yet peaceful picture.

As I sanitized the milkers, I started to think about the crop we would have next year. *I hope it will be a lot easier than this year has been.* Then I caught another glimpse of the sunset, took a deep breath and started after the cows as dusk started to set. In those few minutes—because of His lovely sunset—God really had fulfilled His promise to restore my soul. I felt filled with the Spirit of God and now I could hardly wait for spring planting to start.

God, give us the vision to see Your touch every day in the things around us. —JOHN COEN

Spirit Lifter
BENEDICTION
The sun be warm and kind
to you.
The darkest night, some star
shine through.
The dullest morn
A radiance brew.
And when dusk comes—
God's hand
to you.
—ELEANOR POWERS

30 FRIDAY
...As thou hast believed, so be it done unto thee.
—*MATTHEW 8:13*

"My mother, my grandmother and both of my sisters died before they were seventy," a woman told me some years ago. "This year I turn seventy. I've resolved to stay in good health, but I expect this will be my last year, too." Four months later she died.

Today we stand on the threshold of a new year, and if you're like me you'll be making out a list of resolutions. But keep in mind that what you *expect* in 1989 may be far more crucial than what you *resolve.*

Expectation is one of the most powerful, creative forces in the world. My dictionary says that *expect* means to consider a thing probable or certain. When we do that deep within our minds and hearts, it has a transforming effect upon our lives. It is based on a sound principle—an internalized expectation becomes an externalized motivation. This simply means that all the faculties of our mind—our thinking, feeling, believing—will create conditions that tend to make whatever we expect a reality. If I expect the worst I will immobilize my abilities and set up patterns around me that produce the worst. But if I hold positive expectations, I will generate energies and potencies that will help bring them about.

So this New Year's Eve I hope you'll join me in creating not just resolutions, but expectations. Great expectations! Stretched before us are three hundred and sixty-five new days. God is the source and fulfiller of them all. With Him and faith-filled expectations planted in our lives, this year may be our most wondrous adventure yet!

I'll be expecting You, Lord, every day of this glorious new year.
—SUE MONK KIDD

31 SATURDAY
Judge not, and ye shall not be judged: condemn not, and ye shall not be condemned: forgive, and ye shall be forgiven. —*LUKE 6:37*

"New Year's resolutions remind me of wishes made before you blow out the candles on a birthday cake," a cynic once observed, "and the common denominator of both is hot air." I must confess that as a new year "resoluter" I have been something of a bust...the spirit has been willing, but the flesh...well, you know the rest. However, I am tempted to make one more try this year because I see a personal shortfall that needs improvement, and my prayer is that God will help me accomplish it.

That shortfall is this: Too often I find that I am less than generous in my attitude toward two groups of people—the young, particularly those in their teens and early twenties, and the aged, those whose slower speech and movements are patience testers. The other day I overreacted when a white-haired driver slowed to a stop in front of me, signaled left and then turned right into his driveway. My reaction was not dissimilar to the one I had had when a young woman, her mind wrapped in earphones and music, obliviously careened into me in a department store—without apology.

It's so easy to take umbrage when others take over our time or space, to bark at youthful exuberance and thoughtlessness or aging immobility and forgetfulness. But how much more compassionate, how much more gracious to withhold judgment and smile in the realization that someday, God willing, all of us will complete the cycle and come to know the follies and foibles of both ends of life.

Maybe you'd care to join me in this New Year's resolution.

Help us to love one another, Lord, in the knowledge that You created each of us the way we are and when You were finished You said it was good. —FRED BAUER

Thank-You Notes to God

1.

2.

3.

4.

5.

6.

7.

8.

9.

10.

11.

12.

13.

14.

15.

DECEMBER 1988

16

17

18

19

20

21

22

23

24

25

26

27

28

29

30

31

Hospitality House

Friendly faces. Friendly conversation. Friendly atmosphere.

Friendliness abounds here at *Hospitality House* and we're happy you dropped in. The door's always open. Any time of day, afternoon or night. Don't wait for an invitation. Don't even knock. You're family, you know. And you're always welcome.

So, step in, step in. Mingle and chat and visit. Look at all these friendly folks waiting to make your acquaintance—again and again.

FRED BAUER'S trying to take time for the little things this year: laughing with friends at golf shots he's duffed, really seeing sunsets, talking with folks whose lives are short of friends and listening to little people ("Why do birds like worms, Grandpa Fred?"). But that's not all that happened this past year. The last of Fred and Shirley Bauer's children left the nest: Daniel, 18, is now a freshman at Penn State. Shirley finished her master's degree in library science at Rutgers, so now she "only" has a full-time job as an elementary librarian to keep her busy. Daughter Laraine, 32, is expecting her third child after Jessica, 4, and Ashley, 2. And Fred continues to write, edit, publish, consult and speak from his home base in Princeton, New Jersey. Caring teachers shaped Fred's life most, beginning with his mother, a lifetime student of the Bible who still teaches a Sunday school class for young adults. When Fred has questions about the Bible, he still calls her.

Last year DRUE DUKE and her husband Bob packed their camper for a leisurely trip up north from their Sheffield, Alabama, home. Included were visits to New York, to Bob's sister Florence in Connecticut and to the best man at their wedding 43 years earlier. They even stopped at Niagara Falls. "Looks like our marriage is going to last, so I figure it's worthwhile to take you on a real Niagara Falls honeymoon," Bob told Drue. She loved every minute of it. The Dukes returned home to find a notice of Drue's 50th high school reunion, so they headed for Macon, Georgia. "How wonderful to see so many 'old' faces," Drue laughs. Drue had a cornea transplant last year, and now with her new vision, she says, "I'm convinced that spring's exceptional beauty this year was provided by God for my personal enjoyment." Bob nursed Drue through her recovery, "continuing," she says, "to teach me patience by example, and enriching my life beyond measure." (She also adds that he does a mean jitterbug!)

Family life is very important to ERIC FELLMAN, his wife Joy and their three sons, Jason, 10, Nathan, 8 and Jonathan, 6. Not only does Eric go fishing at a nearby lake with his sons just about every week the ice is off, he coaches all three boys in Little League teams. Eric, who is the editor-in-chief of the Foundation for Christian Living, and Joy, who is a board member of the local YMCA, live in Pawling, New York, but they took time last year to travel with their family to the Adirondacks and Poconos, to Virginia, Washington, D.C., to Chicago and even to Acapulco, Mexico. "It's a super way to learn about other people and places and about each other," Eric says of his travels. Eric and Joy also started a group Bible study for a growing number of couples who meet weekly for Scripture study and fellowship. A college English professor, Glenn Arnold, set writing standards for Eric that he's been trying to reach ever since.

ARTHUR GORDON is *Daily Guideposts'* General Editor. He also writes for *Guideposts* magazine and gives occasional talks. Arthur and his wife Pam have been busy this past year as they traveled around the country from their Savannah, Georgia, home: to California and Pepperdine University, where Arthur received an honorary doctor of laws degree and gave the commencement address; and to New York where a famous department store had an elaborate promotion featuring Savannah and where Arthur signed books. Always remembering his businessman-father's kindness when he thinks of the people who have shaped his life, Arthur says, "He never put any pressure on us kids, but somehow he responded so enthusiastically whenever we did anything worthwhile that we all knocked ourselves out trying to please him." Once, when Arthur was at college, he broke his squash racquet before a tournament. Arthur wrote his dad, knowing money was tight, "Guess I won't play." But somehow his dad managed to scrape together the money and said to Arthur: "Why don't you win that tournament?" "I was by no means the best squash player, but I did win—just because he wanted me to."

Last year OSCAR GREENE and his wife Ruby took a leisurely trip through the narrow highways and rolling hills of Vermont and New Hampshire, haunting bookshops and antique stores, and stopping in on Oscar's 50th high school reunion in Williamstown, Massachusetts—where Oscar was in a graduating class of only 34 students. At home, Oscar enjoys life in Medford, Massachusetts, just outside Boston. "There are many outlets for my literary interests here, like conferences and wonderful bookstores," Oscar says. He also speaks once a month at the Medford Public Library on some of his favorite books—he especially likes biographies. "I get in three days the wisdom it took the subjects a lifetime to acquire," he says. He also draws wisdom from the memory of his Aunt Lillian, who bought him his first suit and lent him the train fare to get his first job back in 1941. "You can repay me," she said, "by being good to your family." Oscar still tries to live up to that promise today.

Last year RICK HAMLIN and his writer-wife Carol were busy "nesting" as they bought a two-bedroom apartment in upper Manhattan, overlooking the Hudson River. But the Hamlins had only six months in it to themselves—in March the extra bedroom was filled with their first baby, William Thornton Hamlin. Since William, named for both his grandfathers, was born, "our lives have simply not been the same," Rick says. For Rick, the diapers, the tears, the doctor bills, the lack of sleep are more than made up by "the giggles, the smiles, the shadowboxing at the mobile over his crib...." Rick reports that William has his mother's hair and smile, his grandfather's round face, "my long, skinny fingers, and, alas, my long, flat feet." Now that Rick and his wife have started on a new generation, when asked who most influenced him, Rick can only say diplomatically, "It was either my mother or my father, but how can I pick between them?"

C. SCOTT HARRISON attended Guideposts' 1984 Writers' Workshop, but he has to squeeze his writing time into a busy career as the chief of orthopedic surgery at Harrisburg Hospital not far from Mechanicsburg, Pennsylvania, where he lives, and from his teaching work at the Hershey Medical Center of Penn State University. He also finds time to help at a local shelter for the homeless. He and his wife Sally have an "empty nest" now: Lynn, 25, will soon be the mother of their first grandchild; Ann, 22, recently got married, graduated from Wesleyan University and headed off to Europe to work. Their son Chris, 19, is enjoying his first year at Colorado College. "What we save in food bills we're losing to long-distance calls, but it's fun to relive those years through his eyes," Scott says. In 1988 Scott and Sally are revisiting Malawi, Africa, to celebrate Scott's 50th birthday. (You can read all about his first trip as a "missionary-doctor" in a series of devotionals in August.) "A schedule like mine would be tough if I tried to do it alone. But by sharing our faith together, Sally encourages, reassures and mirrors a Christ-likeness that challenges me. It is humbling to be 'one flesh' with her," Scott says.

WALTER HARTER and his wife Edna celebrated their 47th anniversary last fall, but they haven't slowed down. They've had visitors from as far away as Australia, including many young friends they made through English classes Walter has taught at Flagler College in St. Augustine and Bethune-Cookman College in Daytona. The Harters also took train trips to spend time visiting retired friends. They are excited to be in St. Augustine, the oldest city in this country (founded by the Spanish in 1565), at a time when it's "blooming into a large city with permanent residents from all over the world." In addition to visiting and writing, Walter also tells stories for young children at schools and speaks to writers' groups. He credits his father with shaping his life: "A simple man, he believed in all the basics," Walter says, "reliability, honesty, you name it, and he encouraged me, too. Whenever I've felt temptation, I've wondered, 'What would Pop say,' and that helps me resist it."

MARILYN MORGAN HELLEBERG of Kearney, Nebraska, shared a year of joys and busyness with her husband Rex, which included seeing their son John, 19, graduate from Wyoming Technical Institute; taking several trips to New York; writing; and playing with grandchildren Matt, 11, Joshua, 7, Dawn, 5 and Zackery, 2. Marilyn balanced her busy life by arranging a week of alone-with-God time in the Colorado Rockies, finding quiet time at home and going to a nearby retreat center. Her remarkable first-grade teacher, Miss Hellerich, is someone she's always admired. She set Marilyn's first poem to music, "published it on the ditto machine and had the class sing it. Miss Hellerich taught me to trust the gifts God gave me," says Marilyn.

PHYLLIS HOBE continues to love her country life in the small town of East Greenville, Pennsylvania. She takes time from her seven-days-a-week writing schedule for long walks with her dog Kate, who is now fully recovered from dysplasia surgery. Her cat Mr. Jones "is now a country squire," Phyllis says. "He likes to spend time observing birds and mice and rabbits, but he's too much of a fat cat to chase them—which makes me very happy." Phyllis has also been learning more about conservation as she's joined the Perkiomen Valley Watershed Association, a local environmental group. She's gone on wildflower and bird walks and rock climbs with the association, which concentrates on both learning about the environment and learning how to protect it. Their latest success has been in persuading farmers to avoid using chemical weed killers and fertilizers on land adjoining the local reservoir. Phyllis says her life has been influenced by many people, but "the One Who really turned my life around was Jesus Christ. And He did it with love."

Bestselling inspirational writer MARJORIE HOLMES is not only busy writing and speaking these days, but has been taking time to enjoy life thoroughly. Her husband, Dr. George Schmieler, retired after 50 years of practice, is now more free to travel with her on speaking trips, which has taken the Schmielers as far afield of their MacMurray, Pennsylvania, home as California and North Carolina. They also spent more time at their Lake Erie cottage last year, where they did lots of swimming (George is a former champion). And last July they celebrated the 6th anniversary of their marriage. Marjorie says of her husband, "His patients describe him as 'the most wonderful person we have ever known.' I agree. Certainly he has been a tremendous influence in my life...I don't know how I ever wrote without him."

For MARILYN MOORE JENSEN, 1987 was a red-letter year. For one thing, she was promoted to publisher at the gift-and-greeting card company, C. R. Gibson, in Norwalk, Connecticut, where she was previously a vice president. Her family gave her lots of causes for celebration too—for one thing, her youngest daughter, Shawn, 24, got her BFA from the Minneapolis College of Art and Design and is now a professional photographer. Then, in

August, her paralegal-daughter Ann, 26, married Ken, apprentice to a contractor, in the Massachusetts Berkshires where they're building a log house. A month later, Marilyn flew to California to attend the wedding of her doctoral student-son Bill, 28, and his wife Beth, also a doctoral student. The two met while studying in Italy, and last spring Marilyn flew to Florence to spend Easter with them. "Our family scatters but keeps growing," she says. A philosophy professor, Dr. Van Tuinen, taught Marilyn "always to look at the other side of any issue."

As a retired reporter, SAM JUSTICE still enjoys researching free-lance articles. A Yonkers, New York, resident, he actively works for various religious organizations, and is just plain active: loving his golf and his gym. Sam's wife Ginny continues to be in charge of their church's nursery school, and their 19-year-old grandson Rocco still lives with them, working to earn money for college. Sam loves when his scattered family can get together. "It's touching to watch them because they really do care about one another," he says. They care about their parents, too. For a 43rd anniversary present, they sent Sam and Ginny on a Caribbean cruise. Sam's college professor, Dr. Hoyt Blackwell, impressed him deeply with his "high Christian values." Dr. Blackwell went on to become the president of North Carolina's Mars Hill College and continues to give Sam another reason to admire him—his longevity. Now in his 90s, Dr. Blackwell is still going strong.

Last year SUE MONK KIDD and her family—husband Sandy, Bob, 14, and Ann, 11—boarded a cruise ship for the Caribbean, where they each boasted of being "Captain Kidd" when the ship's captain allowed each of them a turn at the helm. They loved snorkeling in turquoise waters and lounging on a private island. Back home in Anderson, South Carolina, Sue's family did her proud as Bob made the All-Star Baseball team, Ann performed in several school plays and Sandy was presented the President's Award for outstanding service at Anderson College, where he's a campus minister and religion teacher. Sue continues to teach an adult Sunday school class, and began volunteer work with Habitat for Humanity. Last year Sue made a trip back to her little hometown of Sylvester, Georgia, to celebrate her grandmother Sue's 90th birthday. "It made me aware again of the thread of family which runs through life." The life and thought of the 20th-century monk and writer Thomas Merton "awakened me to the rich depth of prayer," Sue says of the person who has influenced her most.

Three years ago, CAROL KNAPP, her husband Terry and children Tamara, 13, Philip, 11, Kelly, 10, and Brenda, 9, piled into their station wagon and moved from Spokane, Washington, to a mobile home set in the woods of Big Lake, Alaska, 60 miles northwest of Anchorage. Carol enjoys living in Big Lake, which she says is "surprisingly up-to-date" with a country inn, small airport and shopping mall. Husband Terry is part owner of a recreation and marine business there. The Knapp children love Alaska too—except when they have to haul in wood for the woodstove in 30°-below weather. Carol, a winner in *Guideposts'* 1986 Writer's Workshop, says that now, "my craving for pen and paper (computers and I have a basic personality conflict) almost equals my craving for chocolate!" Her husband is the one she most admires: "He's the most unselfish person I know."

Now that CAROL KUYKENDALL's oldest son Derek is 16, she's reached a milestone in her life as a parent: teaching him to drive. "Learning when to speak, when to be silent and when to scream was a real challenge." Letting her two daughters pursue their favorite hobby is another challenge for Carol as she takes daughters Lindsey, 14, and Kendall, 10, to horse shows on summer weekends—with their horses. "They're born horse people—gentle, understanding, fearless—but horses scare me. Driving the horse trailer up mountain roads makes me nervous, so I have to pray my way through it." Carol and her husband Lynn, president of the Boulder, Colorado (where they live) Rotary, celebrated their 20th wedding anniversary with a trip to Munich, Germany, for his Rotary International convention. She is spending more time to write and speak on the subject, appropriately, of learning to let go. Carol thinks of the Apostle Peter—"impulsive, spontaneous, instinctively human Peter"—as a living example of how God changes lives.

ALETHA JANE LINDSTROM may live on a 90-acre wheat, soybean and corn farm in Battle Creek, Michigan, but that doesn't mean that she and her husband Carl (nickname: Andy), don't want to get away to the country. The Lindstroms also have a cottage on Lake Michigan, where Aletha goes for long rambles along the beach with her big farm dog, Collie, and

365

HOSPITALITY HOUSE

"beloved little beagle," Puppy. Along with the pleasures of nature, another blessing in Aletha's life is the marriage of her lawyer-son, Tim, to his teacher-wife, Jessica. "She's the daughter we've always wanted," Aletha says. Books are another source of pleasure to retired librarian Aletha. "I thank God for so many wonderful books, old and new, to read and reread. Because of them life can never be boring." In fact, it's a writer, the late E.B. White, whom she most admires. "Through his writings, I've learned that the loveliest things of all are the little, seemingly inconsequential, events of daily living."

For PATRICIA LORENZ, "single-parenting" three teen-agers and a second-grader means there's never a dull moment...although sometimes she wishes there were a few! After Pat's oldest, Jeanne, 18, graduated from high school, she left last fall to spend a year in Yugoslavia. Bubbly Julie, 16, is a varsity cheerleader and one of the most popular babysitters in the neighborhood. Sophomore Michael, 14, still takes drum lessons (seven years now!), plays basketball and stays on the honor roll. Andrew, 6, enjoys being part of a group for children of single parents in their parish church, St. Matthew's, in their hometown of Oak Creek, Wisconsin. Pat's mother Lucy showed Pat how to manage work, make time for herself and still "put her family's needs first." Pat says, "Like Mom, as long as my children are young, I'm determined to be there for them. So I work three days a week as copywriter for a radio station in Milwaukee and write at home the rest of the time. So far the system is working beautifully!"

Last year, DR. NORMAN VINCENT PEALE reached a milestone. His classic bestseller, *The Power of Positive Thinking*, reached its 35th anniversary. He and his wife Ruth Stafford Peale, weren't alone in the celebrations: Prentice-Hall did a special anniversary edition of the book, Simon and Schuster made an audio tape of it and Karl Lorimar released a 60 minute home video of Dr. Peale outlining the principles of the book. Dr. Peale, who has 33 other books to his credit (including his latest, *Power of the Plus Factor*, Fleming H. Revell, 1987), maintained a hectic schedule of lecturing all over the United States last year. *The Power of Positive Thinking*'s anniversary wasn't the only one the Peales celebrated in 1987—as of last June, they have been married 57 years.

RUTH STAFFORD PEALE is not only co-editor and co-publisher of *Guideposts*, she also became, in 1987, *Guideposts'* president. In addition, she is the chief executive officer of the Foundation for Christian Living, vice chairman of the American Bible Society, chairman of the Interchurch Center, vice president for the Americas of the United Bible Societies and on the boards of the Institutes of Religion and Health and the Laymen's National Bible Committee. In addition to her work as an executive and her writing, she is kept busy traveling on speaking engagements along with Dr. Peale. Mrs. Peale had reason to feel proud last spring as two of her grandchildren, Clifford Peale and Jennifer Everett, graduated from college.

ELAINE ST. JOHNS luxuriates in Arroyo Grande on California's Central Coast, close by Pismo Beach, Lake Lopez and the Hearst Castle. "I still write a lot, read a lot, pray a lot, and for excitement, I follow the thespian activities of my older grandchildren," she says. Last year, Jessica, 17, was in *Kiss Me Kate*, Bogart, 14, was in *Bye Bye Birdie*; and Robin, 6, played Tiny Tim in *A Christmas Carol*. In 1987, while her seven grandchildren, ages 2 through 18, all grew older, Elaine did not—her 93-year-old mother forbade it. "She was complaisant, even smug, about her own birthday, insisting on a full complement of candles, but when I remarked that I was about to turn 69 she said it made her feel old, and 'we'll have no more of THAT!' So, with apologies to Father Time, I shall remain 68 for the foreseeable future. It is obvious that my mother, known to reading and TV audiences as Adela Rogers St. Johns, remains a prime influence on my life."

A few years ago, ELEANOR SASS wrote a devotional about visiting the 1964 World's Fair with her then 5-year-old goddaughter Neva. Well, now Neva's all grown up, and in May of last year Ellie attended the wedding of Neva and Thomas Dula. When Neva walked down the aisle, her "something borrowed" was a small white Bible of Ellie's—the same Bible that Neva's mother, who'd roomed with Ellie in Manhattan for three years, had borrowed from Ellie at her own wedding 29 years earlier. "For me, everything that happened in '87 fell into one of two categories: 'before wedding' or 'after wedding.'" When not busy as an associate editor at

Guideposts, Ellie continues to play golf and to participate in programs offered by the New York Zoological Society. She especially enjoyed several viewings of Ling Ling and Yong Yong, the famous giant pandas of China at the Bronx Zoo. As to who has influenced Ellie's life, you can read about him in this year's Thanksgiving Day devotional selection. "Johnny Ray inspired me," Ellie says, "so whenever I meet someone who has the same problem, I try to inspire them by telling this story."

This year DANIEL SCHANTZ marks twenty years at the chalkboard, teaching audio-visuals at Central Christian College in Moberly, Missouri. His wife of twenty-five years, Sharon, also teaches writing at the college. Writing is a family affair for the Schantzes—both of Dan's daughters, Teresa, 22, and Natalie, 19, are majoring in magazine journalism at the University of Missouri (Teresa was a 1983 winner in *Guideposts'* Youth Writing Contest). Dan has written eight books for young people and often speaks to writers' workshops and groups of schoolchildren. Dan, who loves to garden, particularly admires the life of naturalist-teacher George Washington Carver, who "aimed higher than fame and fortune to a life of service to people."

Back in 1962, ELIZABETH SHERRILL, her husband John and their three children, then aged 6 through 11, took off on a year's adventure. Their destination was Africa, but unknown were the specifics: what countries they'd visit, what writing and teaching projects they'd undertake. Over the following twelve months they reported in *Guideposts* their mistakes and their discoveries: "above all, discoveries about the ways God leads us." In May 1987, they started another yearlong travel adventure: "Commitments in Yugoslavia and France—and twenty-five years experience in listening for God's voice—are our only fixed points," she says. According to Elizabeth, the person who influences her most is "the last person I am with." Because she's interviewed so many people in her writing career, she's like a human blotter and picks up that person's enthusiasm, concerns and moods. "Fortunately, I'm with John most of the time—and he's the best influence on me!" The Sherrills make their home in Chappaqua, New York.

A highlight of LINDA CHING SLEDGE's year was a spring trip to Honolulu, Hawaii, her birthplace. There she spent long afternoons reminiscing with her 92-year-old grandfather, walked on the most recent (and still hot!) lava flow at Volcano National Park on the Big Island and watched six-year-old Geoffrey splash in the surf. At home in Pleasantville, New York, Linda and her husband Gary took special pride in the teenage Sunday school class they taught together. Last June, the students formed their own Christian rock group, Joyful Noise, led by 14-year-old Tim Sledge, Linda and Gary's older son. She attributes her continuing delight in teaching young people (in addition to Sunday school, she's returned to college teaching) to her Chinese grandmother's influence. "My grandmother, Ching Yuk Wan, couldn't read or write, but she knew how to coax the best out of people. True wisdom like hers comes from instinct, not books."

HARRIETT AND FLOYD THATCHER, who celebrated their 49th wedding anniversary last August, have worked together as a team for many years, from the time they met as teenagers at the Ventura, California, church where Floyd's father was pastor. Both Harriett and Floyd were profoundly influenced by Mrs. Charles E. Cowman, a best-selling inspirational writer and missionary (she and her husband founded the Oriental Mission Society). Mrs. Cowman became the Thatchers' spiritual and professional mentor; in fact, Floyd was the president and Harriett the office manager of Cowman Publishing Company for 15 years. After that, Floyd served as a vice president for Zondervan and later as vice president/editorial director of Word Publishing in Waco, Texas, where the Thatchers live today. Since his retirement, Floyd acts as general editor of the Guideposts Home Bible study, and part-time as editor-in-chief of Word Publishing. The Thatchers are both active in St. Paul's Episcopal Church in Waco.

According to *Guideposts* magazine's editor, VAN VARNER, it's "quite possible" that University of California, Berkeley, history professor Dixon Wecter influenced his life more than any one person outside his family. When Dr. Wecter died at the age of 44, Van, then in graduate school at Berkeley, helped to prepare Dr. Wecter's unfinished biography of Mark

369

Twain, which drew him "away from the groves of academe and into the jungles of publishing." But Van says it's Dixon Wecter's intellect, his wide range of interests and his courtliness that he most remembers. "I feel his presence today because I still try, falteringly, to be the man I most want to be like." Van is still in publishing, at *Guideposts* after 34 years. "I find fresh excitement in the story of what the greatest Role Model of all can do in people's lives," Van says. In his free time, Van enjoys such traditions as joining in the Brooklyn Bridge's birthday celebrations with party hats and cake and his annual visits to Saratoga Springs, New York, one of America's great resorts.

SHIRLEY POPE WAITE writes her devotionals in beautiful Walla Walla, Washington, where she and her husband Kyle raised their six, now-grown children: Don, Sharon, Tim, Mark, Laurie and Steve. Shirley, who's lived in her state for 36 years, says, "Washington is a state of contrasts. Walla Walla is on the eastern side of the Cascades, where it's arid, so there's lots of dryland farming: wheat, peas and our famous Walla Walla sweet onions." There are three colleges in town, and Shirley, in addition to being a longtime free-lance writer and Christian retreat leader, teaches writing courses at one of them. Teaching is a family affair for the Waites. Kyle is a retired high school teacher, and three of their children either are or are preparing to be teachers. In fact, it was a teacher, the late Ellis Martin, who inspired Shirley's writing career back in high school as he challenged and encouraged her.

LEE WEBBER lives in lovely Santa Rosa, California, with his wife Margaret. But after two bouts with open-heart surgery, he was forced to give up the ministry in 1984. "I never expected to retire," Lee says. "I thoroughly enjoyed the responsibilities of being a pastor, and especially the involvement with people." But Lee has found plenty of things to keep him busy in his Santa Rosa home—restoring old cars, photography, gardening, making things with his hands, as well as keeping up with his four grown children, Peggy, David, Paul and Elaine, and five grandchildren. Lee learned from many people in his life, but one of the most influential was Dr. Dewitt W. Jayne, a college professor who was Lee's Sunday school teacher during his last year of high school in Wheaton, Illinois. He encouraged Lee to learn about philosophy. Lee did, and it became a passionate interest all his life.

MARION BOND WEST spent lots of time speaking and traveling last year. She was in time to see some Thanksgiving snow in Canada on one trip. Other treats last year included decorating Easter eggs with granddaughters Katie, 3, and Jamie, 7. "Katie stood on a chair watching the eggs boil and said, 'Oh, Nanny, don't let 'em drown,'" Marion reports. Marion and her family developed weekly rap sessions where her sons, Jon and Jeremy, 19, and daughters Julie, 27 and Jennifer, 25, sons-in-law Charlie and Ricky, meet for open discussions. "We are growing close as never before," Marion says. Congratulations are in order! As *Daily Guideposts* was going to press news reached us that on August 14, 1987 Marion was married to Dr. Gene Acuff, a professor of sociology at Oklahoma State University and a retired Christian Church minister of 25 years. The couple will reside temporarily in Stillwater, Oklahoma. We and all the *Daily Guideposts* readers wish them much happiness.

Fireside Friends...

These folks are a little shy. They've dropped in for a short visit; they've dropped in to say "hi." So you'll go out of your way to make them feel welcomed, won't you?

DON BELL is a retired cowboy as well as a very proud father. He and his wife Vera have three daughters, Donna, 28, Vickie, 26 and Bernadette, 23 (all of whom were high school homecoming queens in their hometown of Byron, Wyoming and college graduates) and one granddaughter, Sarah, 3. Recently Don had a chance to cheer two of his daughters as they ran in a marathon—"They finished in great time," he reports. They have a great reason to cheer their dad, too—last year he was a speaker at the Cowboy Poetry Gathering in Elko, Nevada.

GAIL BROOK BURKET started writing at age 8 and has been going steadily ever since; to date she's had eight books, a number of articles and several hundred poems published. When her husband William was alive, they'd write a new carol together every Christmas. Gail, who lives in Evanston, Illinois, has three grown daughters—Gail, Anne and Margaret, and three granddaughters.

Raised on a farm, MARY LOU CARNEY loves the "country" feel of her family's six acres near Chesterton, Indiana. As she takes walks along the shores of nearby Lake Michigan, she tries to enjoy winter's "bold, brittle beauty." She and construction-company-owner husband Gary have two children, Amy Jo, 15, and Brett, 12, to keep them busy.

JOHN COEN lives near Wellesville, Kansas, with his wife, Cherry, daughters Whitney, 3, and Jessica, 1—and 45 registered Holstein cows. John and Cherry farm 500 acres of corn, soybeans, milo and alfalfa in partnership with another couple. A *Daily Guideposts* reader, John was one of 200 who sent in a devotional in response to our March 11, 1987, invitation.

Though B. J. (BETTY JO) CONNOR now lives in Chattanooga, Tennessee, she and her family—husband Michael, daughter Nichole, 9 and son Sean, 5— have had the chance to discover a lot of America as they've moved nine times in the past 13 years! B. J. was a winner in Guideposts' 1986 Writers' Workshop. The "sunshine" of last year for the Connors was caring for their first foster child, a beautiful baby girl, named Stephanie.

DAVID CORNELIUS, a liberal arts major at Emory University in Atlanta, Georgia, likes to write, but this past year he found he liked news reporting, too, as he worked on Emory's student paper, *The Wheel.* When he graduates, he wants to work for a newspaper or magazine. David says his "incredible, independent mother" serves as inspiration for his "free spirit."

ROBERTA DONOVAN has lived almost all her life in small, friendly Lewistown, Montana, but small-town life hasn't impeded her free-lance writing career. Recently she went on a rattlesnake hunt and photographed longhorn cattle—close up. Roberta's also busy keeping close to her six grown children, her 11 grandchildren, two great-grandchildren and "more stepgrands than I can count."

FAYE FIELD continues to enjoy the beauty of flower-covered Longview in East Texas where she and her husband Tommy have lived for 41 years, and where they raised their son Mike. Mike, by the way, and his wife have just adopted a second child, a baby boy from Panama they named Tommy after his grandfather. Much-published Faye has found time to speak on inspirational writing this year.

DENISE GEORGE, her husband Timothy and their two children, Christian, 7 and Alyce, 5, savor life at home in Louisville, Kentucky. "I'm spending lots of time just enjoying my precious family and friends," she says. She's also become actively involved in her children's hobbies—Christian collects crosses and Alyce collects dolls.

At the age of 5, TERRY HELWIG collected butterfly wings to sew on her night-gown in the hope they'd help her fly. Last year, when she was 37, her wish finally came true when she went para-sailing for the first time. Though her feet are back on the ground with husband Jim and daughter Mandy, 5, in Louisville, Kentucky, "my head may be in the clouds for a long time!"

When MARY RUTH HOWES became a senior editor at *Guideposts*, she made the move north (to our New York offices, where she works, and Jersey City, New Jersey where she lives) from Nashville, Tennessee. But that's not the only move she's ever made: This missionaries' daughter has lived in Arizona, Pennsylvania, Illinois, Minnesota, Michigan, Texas and China, where she was born.

SYBIL LIGHT splits her secretarial career between New York City and Pawling, New York, but in spite of her substantial commute, she manages to make time for a number of activities. She's a church organist, Sunday school teacher and Christian school treasurer. She also quilts, paints, reads, cooks, gardens, and is a hands-on aunt for her brother's five children.

Although MARY JANE MEYER has always made time for reading, studying and walking, moving from full- to part-time work (she's now secretary at St. Luke's United Methodist) gave her more time to enjoy her family—her auto-body-shop owner husband, "Smokey" Meyer, four grown children, Don, Dean, Max and Linda, and six grandchildren; her amateur radio hobby; and simple pleasures like sitting in the sun or lunching with friends near her Enid, Oklahoma, home.

CORA JANE PETERS was born and raised in the foothills of the Smoky Mountains, but she and her doctor husband Bill moved 14 times before settling down in Hattiesburg, Mississippi. Cora is a volunteer, Sunday school teacher and homemaker—the Peters have two children, Eric, 17, and Anna, 13. Cora is a *Daily Guideposts* reader whose devotional was selected to appear this year. Cora is one of 200 readers who responded to a March 11, 1987 devotional.

Tennessee is home for VIRGINIA POEHLEIN, who lives with her husband, Denzil, on beautiful Kentucky Lake. Her sons, Rick, a Chattanooga doctor, and David, who has started a gospel-singing quartet with his family and who lives in nearby Camden, also love Tennessee. A retired secretary, Virginia teaches the elderly ladies in Sunday school at First Baptist Church, Camden. A *Daily Guideposts* reader, Virginia was one of 200 who sent in a devotional in response to our March 11, 1987, invitation.

TAMMY RIDER's full year included graduating summa cum laude from Minneapolis's Augsburg College (she was named by *Good Housekeeping* as one of 100 outstanding college graduates of 1987 and was in *Who's Who of American College Students*). She worked four part-time jobs, directed two plays, acted in one, wrote a 50-page term paper and was active in her church, Highland Park Presbyterian. Tammy's plans include becoming a minister.

VICKIE SCHAD, a winner in *Guideposts'* 1986 Writer's Workshop, lives in a little 18th-century home in the woods of Vassalboro, Maine (population 3,700), with her husband Jim, and sons Tim, 13, and Ben, 10. But though she lives in the country, she's not at all reclusive. She homeschools her sons, teaches piano and serves as the town clerk.

TONI SORTER and her husband Bill live in suburban Harrington Park, New Jersey, with their "very fluid" family: Laura, 22, Jim, 19 and Steve, 16. In addition to asking "How many for dinner tonight?" Bill and Toni busily work out of their home, he as a financial consultant, she as a full-time free-lance editor and writer. The Sorters have four computers now, but "I expect it'll be five-for-five by Christmas!"

ERIC THOMAS, an energy conservation program specialist for the U.S. Department of Energy in Washington, D.C., and his wife Gladys have two sons, Eric, 10, and Andrew, 8. On the event of their 14th wedding anniversary last year, Eric says, "God blessed our lives with an 8-pound, 12½ ounce girl, Kia Marie." An ordained Baptist clergyman, he's youth and children's minister at Wheaton Woods Baptist Church of Rockville, Maryland. A *Daily Guideposts* reader, Eric was one of 200 who sent in a devotional response to our March 11, 1987, invitation.

374

THE READER'S GUIDE

A helpful three-part index to all the selections
in DAILY GUIDEPOSTS, 1988

This comprehensive three-part index was created especially for *you*, to help you to make *Daily Guideposts* your very own. Now this book can be not only your daily spiritual companion, but, with the Reader's Guide, your special needs can be met regardless of the calendar day.

Perhaps you need to be comforted, challenged or inspired. Maybe you just want to nod, "Yes, I know what that's like," or find the Scripture that touched your heart but somehow missed your memory. With the Reader's Guide, you can find those special devotionals, like friends waiting to greet you with words of wisdom, comfort, assurance, love, support and care. You choose what you need, then let their faith and their humble lessons of living speak to you—whatever you're feeling, whatever you're needing—*now.*

Scripture Reference Index

An alphabetical index of Scripture references to verses appearing either at the tops of devotionals or, on occasion, within the text. Chapter and verse numbers are in bold type on the left. Numbers in regular type, on the right, refer to the Daily Guideposts page(s) on which the complete verse can be located.

SCRIPTURE REFERENCE INDEX

First Few Words Index

An alphabetical index to the first few words of Scripture verses appearing either at the *top* of the devotionals or as full verses *within* the text, as well as the first few words of poetry, prose and songs appearing within the text. Numbers given refer to the *Daily Guideposts* page(s) on which these can be located.

379

FIRST FEW WORDS INDEX

Be angry but do not sin..., 225
Be devoted to one another in brotherly
    love..., 275
Be of good courage..., 182
Be prepared..., 47
Be still, and know that I am God..., 288
Be ye doers of the word..., 130
Bear ye one another's burdens..., 15
Because there was no room for them in the
    inn..., 198
Behold, how good and how pleasant it is for
    brethren to dwell together..., 169, 218
Behold, I bring you good tidings of great
    joy..., 343
Behold, now is the day of salvation..., 151
Blessed are the peacemakers..., 225
Blessed are those servants whom the Lord
    when he cometh shall find watching...,
    338
Blessed be the God and Father of our Lord
    Jesus Christ..., 304
Blessed is he whose transgression is for-
    given..., 251
Blessed is the King Who comes..., 88
Blessed is the man that trusteth in the
    Lord..., 137
Blessed is the people that know the joyful
    sound..., 39
Boast not thyself of tomorrow..., 61
Break forth into joy, sing together..., 337
But be doers of the word..., 317
But encourage one another daily..., 307
But ever follow that which is good..., 144
But if we walk in the light..., 341
But Jesus said, "Let the children come to
    me"..., 143
But on the first day of the week, at early
    dawn, they went to the tomb..., 100
But the fruit of the Spirit is...faithfulness...,
    172
But the wisdom from above is first pure..., 139
But they that wait upon the Lord shall renew
    their strength..., 103
But thou, when thou prayest, enter into thy
    closet..., 72
But whosoever drinketh of the water that I
    shall give him..., 122
By day the Lord directs his love..., 288
By love serve one another..., 26, 232
By one Spirit are we all baptized into one
    body..., 22
By this shall all men know that ye are my
    disciples..., 277

Casting all your care upon him..., 52
[Charity] doth not behave itself unseemly...,
    87
Children are an heritage of the Lord..., 281
Choose this day whom you will serve..., 82

Come and dine..., 176
Come into his presence with singing!..., 10
Come to the Word unexpectantly..., 318
Come unto me, all ye that labor and are
    heavy laden..., 319
Comfort one another..., 134
Confess your faults one to another..., 263
Consider the lilies of the field..., 43, 273
Criticism of others nails them to the past...,
    228

Deal courageously..., 189
Do not judge by appearances..., 179
Do not return evil for evil..., 225
Do not withhold good from those to whom it
    is due..., 14
Don't you know that you yourselves are God's
    temple..., 142

Each of us should please his neighbor for his
    good..., 219
Evening, and morning, and at noon, will I
    pray..., 267
Every good gift...is from above..., 163
Every man according as he purposeth in his
    heart..., 317
Every one who is angry with his brother shall
    be liable to judgment..., 225

Faith is the substance of things hoped for..., 65
Fear not: for I have redeemed thee..., 28
Fear thou not; for I am with thee..., 235
Fear ye not, neither be afraid..., 289
First be reconciled to thy brother..., 278
Fix your thoughts on what is true..., 351
For a man's life consisteth not in the abun-
    dance of the things which he
    possesseth..., 268
For a thousand years in thy sight are but as
    yesterday when it is past..., 252
For as the body is one..., 308
For everything there is a season..., 316
For God is at work within you..., 188
For God, who commanded the light to shine
    out of darkness, hath shined in our
    hearts..., 39
For he loveth our nation..., 49
For he shall give his angels charge over
    thee..., 25
For I, the Lord your God...say to you, "Fear
    not..., 211
For if a man think himself to be something...,
    137
For in him we live, and move..., 246
For my thoughts are not your thoughts..., 309
For the Holy Spirit, God's gift, does not want
    you to be afraid of people..., 128
For the Lord thy God, he it is that doth go
    with thee..., 256

FIRST FEW WORDS INDEX

382

My heart is fixed, O God..., 276
My tears have been my food day and night...,
   288

No man, having put his hand to the plough...,
   231
None of us liveth to himself..., 173
Now the God of peace...make you perfect in
   every good work to do his will..., 294
Now therefore ye are no more strangers and
   foreigners, but fellow citizens..., 112

"O God my Rock," I cry..., 240
Oh that men would praise the Lord for his
   goodness..., 80
On the tenth day of this seventh month..., 263
Open thou my lips..., 119
Our Lord has written the promise of the
   Resurrection..., 87

Peace I leave with you..., 132
Practice hospitality..., 281
Praying always with all prayer and supplica-
   tion in the Spirit..., 159
Put new wine into new skins..., 111
Put off all of these; anger, wrath, malice..., 223

Rejoice always..., 27
Remembering without ceasing your work of
   faith..., 118
Return unto thy rest, O my soul..., 284

Say to them that are of a fearful heart..., 187
Search me, O God, and know my heart..., 241
Set a watch, O Lord..., 216
Show me your ways, O Lord, teach me your
   paths..., 287
[Sit] "while I go yonder and pray."..., 297
Smile and the world smiles with you..., 217
So be careful how you act; these are difficult
   days..., 28
So faith, hope, love abide, these three..., 48
So is it with the resurrection of the dead..., 102
Some trust in chariots, and some in horses...,
   251
Speak, Lord; for thy servant heareth..., 161
Sterling silver is beautiful..., 312
Strength and honor are her clothing..., 314
Success comes in cans..., 254
Surely he has borne our griefs..., 57
Surely I am coming soon..., 322
Surpasses human understanding..., 200

Take us the foxes, the little foxes..., 84
Tenderness and good will are potent factors...,
   135
That was the true Light..., 194
The dayspring from on high hath visited us...,
   344

The deepest word is Soul..., 130
The eternal God is thy refuge..., 19
The grass withereth, the flower fadeth..., 85
The grass withers, the flower fades..., 131
The heavens declare the glory of God..., 248
The Lord also will be a refuge for the
   oppressed..., 292
The Lord bless thee..., 170
The Lord came and stood there, calling as at
   the other times, "Samuel! Samuel!"..., 171
The Lord gave, and the Lord hath taken
   away..., 82
The Lord gave the word..., 278
The Lord God will wipe away tears from off all
   faces..., 32
The Lord is gracious and full of compassion...,
   215
The Lord is my shepherd..., 353
The Lord is my strength and my shield..., 230
The Lord is near to all who call upon him...,
   326
The Lord is...slow to anger..., 225
The Lord recompense you for what you have
   done..., 274
The Lord shall be thine everlasting light..., 68
The Lord thy God hath chosen thee to be a
   special people unto himself..., 219
The Lord upholdeth him with his hand..., 224
The Lord was with Samuel as he grew up...,
   172
The Lord will strengthen him upon...his
   bed..., 11
The patient in spirit is better than the proud in
   spirit..., 291
The purpose of tithing is to teach..., 55
The Spirit itself beareth witness with our
   spirit..., 324
The sun be warm and kind to you..., 354
The tender teens..., 283
The work of a man's hand comes back to
   him..., 249
Then he took the cup, gave thanks and offered
   it to them..., 92
Then Joshua built on Mount Ebal an altar to
   the Lord..., 205
Then let us no more pass judgment on one
   another..., 109
Then listen to me, Keep silence..., 254
Then Samuel took the horn of oil, and
   anointed him..., 312
Then the Lord said unto Moses, Behold, I will
   rain bread..., 135
Then thou shalt have good success..., 282
Then wrought...every wise hearted man...,
   264
There is a friend who sticks closer than a
   brother..., 149
There is...a time to cast away..., 116
There may be curves and turns..., 33

FIRST FEW WORDS INDEX

Authors, Titles
and Subjects Index

An alphabetical index to devotional authors; titles of special series, poems and songs; proper names of people, places and things; holidays and holy days; Biblical persons and events appearing in the text; and subjects with sub-heading breakdowns that will help you find a devotional to meet that special need. Numbers refer to the *Daily Guideposts* page(s) on which these can be located.

AUTHORS, TITLES, AND SUBJECT INDEX

AUTHORS, TITLES, AND SUBJECT INDEX

AUTHORS, TITLES, AND SUBJECT INDEX

Kuykendall, Carol
selections by, 42–43, 79, 202–03,
249–50, 267–68, 339–40
*Tandem Power for January, February,
etc.*, series by, 8–9, 38, 66–67, 101–
02, 128–29, 158–59, 188–89, 216,
246–47, 274–75, 302–03, 330–31

Labor Day, 249–50
Last Supper, 92–93
Laubach, Dr. Frank
quote by, 200
Spirit Lifter by, 228
Lawrence, Brother, *Spirit Lifter* by, 75
Leadership, taking turns leading, 120–21
Lehár, Franz, "The Merry Widow Waltz,"
by, 182
Leprosy *see* Hansen's disease
Letter writing, 28
to God, 52–53
Letting go
of beloved dog, 57–58
of children, 281–82, 321–22
of material blessings, 51–52, 268–69
of problems, 82, 224
of things one has outgrown, 116–17
Leutze, Emmanuel Gottlieb, painting by,
49
Liberty, 191
see also American way of life
Life after death, 309–10
God's Love and, 12
promise of, Easter and, 85–86
Light, Sybil, selection by, 142–43
Light therapy, for depression, 148
Lincoln, Abraham, quote by, 47
Lincoln's Birthday, 47
Lindstrom, Aletha Jane, selections by,
52–53, 119–20, 121, 145, 177–78,
224–25, 279–80, 292–93, 314–15
Listening, 37, 193
in the family, 171–72
to God, 8, 53–54, 140
Living in the present, 33–34
Loneliness, 147–53
at Christmas, 337–38, 347–48
God's Love and, 114–15
Lorenz, Patricia, selections by, 28, 49–
50, 55, 69–70, 86–87, 108, 140, 166,
191–92, 208–09, 240–41, 255, 283,
309
Louisiana Purchase Expo (1904), 208
Love, 87–88
see also God's Love; Husband and
wife; Marriage

as cure for after-Christmas letdown,
351–52
as the only reward, 277–78
cherishing loved ones, 163–64
communicating love to others,
239–40
coping with illness in a loved one, 32
earning one's neighbor's love, 105
enduring suffering for a loved one,
44–45
forming loving habits, 255
giving it away, 30
hearing it from loved ones, 247
"heart exercises," 129
in the family, 275
commitment and love, 227–28
expressing it, 199–200
loving as Jesus loved, 199–200
loving one another at Christmas, 331
loving the unlovable, 16
passing it on in little ways, 38
phrases for expressing it simply, 48
reaching out in love to others, 122
sharing it in unpleasant surroundings, 198
showing it through compliments, 309
"signing" love to others, 311
small gestures of, 281
Spirit Lifters about, 49, 75
telling God you love Him, 47–48
working together and, 118
Low, Juliette Gordon, 46
Luther, Martin, *Spirit Lifter* by, 87

McCormack, John 227
McHenry, Ft., 257
Magi, Three, story of, 12–13
Malawi (Africa), work of Scott Harrison
in, 232–39
Man O'War (horse), 13–14
Marriage
see also Husband and wife
encouragement in, 333–34
helping in, 291
working together in, 218
Martin Luther King Day, 23
Mary, mother of James, 100–01
Mary Magdalene, 100–01
Materialism and material possessions,
91–92
letting go of, 51–52, 268–69
Maundy Thursday, 92–93
May Day, celebrating, 121
Mealtime, grace before, 267–68
Meaning of Christmas, The, Advent
series by Elizabeth Sherrill

AUTHORS, TITLES, AND SUBJECT INDEX

395

AUTHORS, TITLES, AND SUBJECT INDEX

396

AUTHORS, TITLES, AND SUBJECT INDEX

A NOTE FROM THE EDITORS

This devotional book was created by the same staff that prepares *Guideposts*, a monthly magazine filled with true stories of people's adventures in faith.

If you have found enjoyment in DAILY GUIDEPOSTS, 1988 and would like to order additional copies for yourself, or as gifts, the cost is $8.95 for either the regular edition or Big Print edition. Orders should be sent to Guideposts Associates, Inc., Carmel, New York 10512.

We also think you'll find monthly enjoyment—and inspiration—in the exciting and faith-filled stories that appear in our magazine as well. *Guideposts* is not sold on the newsstand. It's available by subscription only. And subscribing is easy. All you have to do is write Guideposts Associates, Inc., Carmel, New York 10512. A year's subscription costs only $7.95 in the United States, and $9.95 in Canada and overseas. Our Big Print edition, for those with special reading needs, is only $7.95 in the United States, Canada and abroad.

When you subscribe, each month you can count on receiving exciting new evidence of God's presence, His guidance and His limitless love for all of us.